Illuminate
Publishing

WJEC
GCSE
Sociology

Janis Griffiths • Steve Tivey

Edite_____McIntosh

Published in 2013 by Illuminate Publishing Ltd, P.O. Box 1160, Cheltenham, Gloucestershire GL50 9RW

Orders: Please visit www.illuminatepublishing.com
or email sales@illuminatepublishing.com

British Library Cataloguing in Publication Data

A catalogue record for this book is available from the British Library

ISBN 978-1-908682-14-7

Printed by Cambrian Printers

06.15

The publisher's policy is to use papers that are natural, renewable and recyclable products made from wood grown in sustainable forests. The logging and manufacturing processes are expected to conform to the environmental regulations of the country of origin.

Every effort has been made to contact copyright holders of material produced in this book. If notified, the publisher will be pleased to rectify any errors or omissions at the earliest opportunity.

This material has been endorsed by WJEC and offers high quality support for the delivery of WJEC qualifications. While this material has been through a WJEC quality assurance process, all responsibility for the content remains with the publisher.

Editor: Geoff Tuttle
Design and layout: Nigel Harriss

Image Credits:

Cover image: © Shutterstock / Steve Mann

channel4learning, p119: Kate C, p24: Wikimedia Commons: p100; p104; p106; p115; p140; p142, p154; p185: www.whoneedsfeminism.com, p70
© Alamy: p113, Steve Vidler; p117, Matthew Chattle
© Fotolia: p133, Shariff Che'Lah; p163, David Freund
© Shutterstock: p8, nui7711; p10, Lucian Coman; p12, Patricia Hofmeester; p13, Olga Ekaterincheva; p16, marcovarro; p18, mrkornflakes; p21, Lyudmyla Kharlamova ; p25, Alexander Raths; p29, Kittisak; p31, Hal_P; p34, greenland; p37, Monkey Business Images; p40, Kzenon; p44, Pavel K; p46, oliveromg; p48, Mincemeat; p50, glenda; p52, smikesh; p56, Tsekhmister; p58, Featureflash; p60, Andre Blais; p62, Darren Baker; p66, T-Design; p72, Pressmaster; p74, schmetfad; p80, Paul Michael Hughes; p82, Pixel Memoirs; p84, Monkey Business Images; p86, Darrin Henry; p90, BLANKartist; p92, Janina Dierks; p94, Nayashkova Olga; p96, Fedor Selivanov; p98, Andresr; p100, EML; p103, Pedro Monteiro; p104, El Greco; p116, cozyta; p121, Donna Beeler; p123, s_bukley; p125, David Gilder; p131, Luis Louro; p141, Maksim Shmeljov; p146, StockLite; p149, Ivica Drusany; p149, Featureflash; p150, Hong Vo; p151, Anton Balazh; p152, Tonis Pan; p155, imageegami; p161, Alexander Raths; p161, Kati Neudert; p167, Zurijeta; p171, godrick; p172, zimmytws; p173, GSPhotography; p175, Ecelop; p179, Dariush M; p183, pogonici; p187, Corepics VOF; p189, ostill; p191, Sponner; p193, 1000 words; p197, ArTono; p199, Clive Chilvers; p200, Ensuper; p205, Helga Esteb; p214, Kamira; p216, Creativa; p218, Vladyslav Starozhylov; p220, Lisa S.

Dedication

Janis - For my family

Steve - For Mum, Dad, Ethan and Eloise

Acknowledgements

The authors and publisher would like to thank:

John McIntosh for the huge contribution he has made in putting this resource together, from helping to shape the original concept through to the finished article.

Nia Williams for her detailed review and expert insights and observations.

The authors would also like to thank the editorial team at Illuminate, Rick, Geoff and Nigel without whose patience, expertise and efficiency, this book would not have been produced.

Source articles for the 'Exam practice' feature:

The following are tinyurl weblinks or information regarding source articles for a number of the 'Exam practice' features appearing in the book.

p17: tinyurl.com/7zeyt; p51: www.fpsc.org.uk/family-values/; p61: Statistical Bulletin 2010, Office for National Statistics, Crown Copyright 2010; p69: tinyurl.com/d5gtgk4; p74: From the 'Interesting Facts' feature. tinyurl.com/mlaumb; p79: tinyurl.com/counwjr; p81: tinyurl.com/lnjo8u; p85: Source for image: www.guardian.co.uk; p97: tinyurl.com/yaxh6r8; p99: tinyurl.com/bptzvab; p101 tinyurl.com/c7bojf8; p103:tinyurl.com/c4thbwu; p107 tinyurl.com/cznc6ck; p109: tinyurl.com/chkbj2o; p110 tinyurl.com/qn8og; p111: tinyurl.com/d66yu77; p113: tinyurl.com/cjly9sj; p115: tinyurl.com/bvbhods; p116: 'Thinking point', www.prweek.com p117: tinyurl.com/3uw7td3; p119: tinyurl.com/cdcfs2l; p121: tinyurl.com/ chppkjh; p123: tinyurl.com/cmeg3kg; p125: tinyurl.com/cvruk69; p127: tinyurl.com/cxrktey; p129: tinyurl.com/d659qa2; p132: Prejudice, discrimination and disability: 'Public Perceptions of Disabled People 2009', Office for Disability Issues, Crown Copyright 2011; p133: tinyurl.com/cjqa6uw; p135: tinyurl.com/3tudtar; p137: tinyurl.com/d3zenh5; p139: tinyurl.com/3663au6; p141: tinyurl. com/24j65gl; p142: tinyurl.com/c4ykue6 p143: tinyurl.com/bqo8dpr; p145: tinyurl.com/cqmkxv; p147: tinyurl.com/ycnbxvl; p149: tinyurl.com/cxqussr; p153: tinyurl.com/d2jvwtp; p155: tinyurl.com/8j43t42; p157: tinyurl.com/cbhq7wo; p159: tinyurl.com/a467jmf; p161: tinyurl.com/dykwmxv; p163: tinyurl.com/c9zey7q; p165: tinyurl.com/bu54o85; p167: tinyurl.com/camvu4a; p169: tinyurl.com/cx5u8am; p171: tinyurl.com/czc296s; p173: tinyurl.com/d3sddpo; p175: tinyurl.com/cjwour7; p179: tinyurl.com/44n95pn; p181: tinyurl.com/c7fygu6; p183: tinyurl.com/bng75k5; p185: tinyurl.com/3g5kr48; p187: tinyurl.com/bru6p2z; p189: tinyurl.com/8962mnq; p191: tinyurl.com/7tc6qp9; p193: tinyurl.com/cfefarq; p195: tinyurl.com/btcq94s; P197: tinyurl.com/77wocfn; p199: tinyurl.com/bnfj m9u; p201: tinyurl.com/6pjh7us; p203: tinyurl.com/bt3y524; p205: 'At Christmas we celebrate the birth of our Lord Simon Cowell' 20/12/11, Daily Mirror; p213: tinyurl.com/ak7o9j2; p215: tinyurl.com/cr3agd6;

Contents

Unit 1: Understanding Social Processes

Unit 2: Understanding Social Structures

Contents

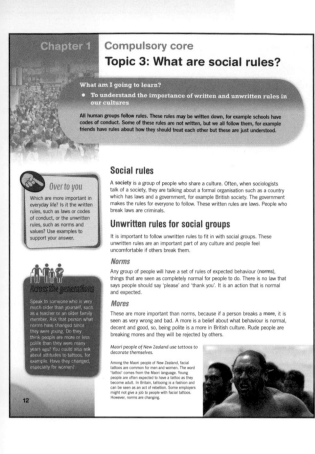

Chapter 1   Compulsory core

Topic 3: What are social rules?

How to use this book

The contents of this textbook are designed to guide you through to success in the WJEC Sociology GCSE level examination.

The book is organised in the same way as the examination, so the topics will match the sections on the examination paper. For each of the two units you will have a section on the compulsory core and notes on the two most popular options on that examination paper.

- Unit 1: Understanding Social Processes
  - Compulsory core
  - Option 1 Family
  - Option 2 Education
- Unit 2: Understanding Social Structures
  - Compulsory core
  - Option 1 Work
  - Option 2 Crime and Deviance

The section on research methods is important to you as it is tested on both examination papers. There is a separate chapter on Research Methods in the book. Where there is a key term from research methods this will be highlighted in <mark>yellow</mark>. This is a reminder that research methods questions will appear on both papers in Section A. Use these highlights as opportunities to revisit and learn these terms. In addition, there is a section on theory which can be used in all parts of the examination papers. There are a variety of features that will help you to think sociologically and to prepare you for the examination.

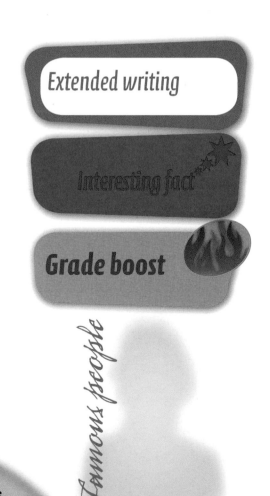

Special features to help you include:

- Extended writing
- Tips on how to answer the questions
- Help with the 'command words'
- Interesting facts
- Famous people
- Ideas for further study including websites, YouTube and the media
- Key terms

All these will make your study of sociology more interesting and boost your chances of success.

Extended writing questions will use the command words that are found on the paper and you will be given guidance on how to answer the question.

We have added a variety of other features to help you. These will be different in each topic, but include thinking questions to get you discussing ideas or suggestions for personal research. There are few simple answers in sociology, so we have tried to challenge you to think for yourself and to provide you with activities that will develop your understanding. Possibly the most important of the features is the key terms list for each topic. If you are to get into the top mark bands, you need to use the language of sociology.

Being a good student

A good sociologist is one who is interested in the social world and who wants to understand how it is organised and what effect it has on people. This means that good GCSE students will be taking a serious interest in what is happening around them. They should be watching how people behave and trying to understand what it is that affects how people act. They should be talking to adults to see how the world has changed and looking for new and interesting viewpoints.

Good students need to be able to see things from other people's points of view and have an interest in how other people see the world. They need to have opinions that they can back up with evidence and the willingness to share and discuss their ideas.

You will do better in Sociology if you read widely. Reading newspapers and looking at news websites will help you to get a bigger picture of the world. This has two effects:

- You will be able to read and write more quickly in the examination, and your language skills will improve.
- You will develop background knowledge and examples that you can refer to when you want to display your understanding of the world.

Most importantly, we think it is really important that you should take responsibility for your own learning and not rely on your teachers to give you notes or tell you how to gain the grades that you require. Look at the WJEC website www.wjec.co.uk. In particular, you need to be aware of the specification. The specimen examination papers, mark schemes and past papers are really useful when you are planning your revision and preparing for examinations.

Good luck with your course

Janis Griffiths

Steve Tivey

Key terms

Find out about

Stretch and challenge

Over to you

Personal research idea

Thinking skills

Across the generations

websites

Compulsory core

Topic 1: What do sociologists do?

What am I going to learn?

- **About the kind of work that sociologists do**

Many people study sociology as part of their job training. They also use the findings of sociologists who have carried out research to understand why people act as they do and how to plan for the future. Health care workers, market researchers and managers all use sociology as part of their jobs.

What do sociologists do?

Sociologists look at the behaviour of ordinary people in their daily lives to understand the things that they do: how they live together, how they make decisions about their lives and what factors affect them.

They do this in a careful and organised way so that other people can learn from their findings and understand how our social world works. This part of **sociology** is known as **research methods**. The results of sociological research are known as **research findings**.

Sociologists look at areas of ordinary social life such as families, work and education, to see how these systems work. They aim to understand how they affect the way that people think and behave. Sociologists know a lot about what is happening in the world about us now but they are also interested in how things change over time as well. This is so they can understand the reasons for social change.

Common sense and sociology

People often think that they understand how society works around them because it is just **common sense**. Sociologists say that common sense cannot be trusted because sometimes people believe very strange things about the world. To understand people, it is necessary to look deeper into what they believe and how they act. For example, in the past people believed women to be less intelligent than men, and so women were not allowed to take part in government.

Thinking skills

What problems might there be if we do not have sociologists telling us about how people think and behave?

Famous people

Talcott Parsons

Talcott Parsons is a very important figure in sociology because his ideas have influenced how sociologists have worked and what they have studied. He is associated with a sociological theory called functionalism and there is more in the book about this theory.

Sociologists at work

Sociologists are found in universities helping people in all kinds of subject areas: teaching, business and management, medicine, law, crime, government and politics. They also work for the government, gathering information about the effects of laws that are made. Many sociologists go on to social work careers to help solve the problems of society but sociology covers more than social problems.

Sociologists are interested in how we organise our society as well, so they may look at big issues such as:

- Inequality – for example, why do some people have more power to influence decisions about the world than others?

- Sexism – for example, why are men and women treated so differently in work or education?

- Racism – for example, why do some people mistrust or dislike people of different cultural backgrounds?

Check your understanding

Complete the following sentences:

a) The study of normal people in their daily lives is known as •••.

b) The process of studying people and how they behave is known as •••.

c) Subject areas in universities that might use sociology include •••.

d) Sociologists say that you cannot trust common sense because people often believe •••.

e) Sociologists are interested in change over time so they can understand •••.

f) Big issues that are studied by sociologists include •••.

g) The aim of sociology is to ••• people, what they do and how they think.

Exam practice

A famous sociologist, Talcott Parsons (1951), wanted to study the relationship between doctors and patients to understand the way that they treat each other. For example, we allow doctors to hurt us with injections or even to see parts of our bodies that are normally very private. He found that patients are expected to co-operate with doctors and do as they are told, but that doctors are expected to be scientific and unemotional with patients. Both patients and doctors have to follow strict social rules about how to behave.

a) Using the item, name one famous sociologist. (1)

b) Using the item, identify and explain one social rule that doctors must follow. (1)

c) Identify two areas of ordinary life that might be studied by a sociologist. (2)

d) Explain the meaning of the term sociological research, using an example. (2)

e) Describe two reasons why we need to have sociologists. (4)

Key terms

Sociology – the systematic study of society, how people think and behave.

Sociologist – someone who studies society.

Research methods – the methods that are used by sociologists to look at society.

Research findings – the results of study.

Common sense – everyday ideas about the world, these are not used by sociologists.

Stretch and challenge

Start your sociology research and learn how sociologists study the world by trying to think of ten rules for being a girl. When you have done that, think of ten rules for a boy. What differences do you notice in the rules that you have listed?

Develop your work by looking at the rules that other people have suggested.

Develop your thinking skills by asking yourself what you have learned about how people think about the roles of men and women in our society.

Compulsory core

Topic 2: What is culture?

What am I going to learn?

● **To understand what sociologists study**

Sociologists study people in groups. These can be small groups, such as families, or larger groups, such as people who live together in a country. Wherever people live together in groups, they develop a shared way of life with a set of rules for everyone to follow. This shared way of life is known as a culture.

What is culture?

A **culture** is a way of life that is shared by a group of people. It consists of the rules for expected behaviour and the knowledge that people need to feel part of the group.

Different cultures have different sets of rules, so people may find that even a small change, such as changing schools, means they need to learn a new set of rules. There will be a slightly different way of doing things in each place. This difference is known as **cultural diversity**.

Things that make a culture

Some of the things that go to make up a culture include: fashions and clothing, music, a sense of humour, rules, religion, history, music, art and language. When people learn a language, they often learn about the culture of the place where the language is spoken. When people go on holiday to different countries, they will see that the culture of the people may be different to their own culture.

Cultural relativity

Sometimes, things are acceptable to one group of people that would shock another group of people. For example, Japanese people eat raw fish, Welsh people may eat seaweed (laverbread) and many French people enjoy horsemeat.

Cultural relativity is the idea that what is normal in one culture may not be seen as normal in another. It all depends on what you have been taught by people around you.

Interesting fact

In many African cultures, fatter women are admired and considered extremely beautiful. Being fat is seen as a sign of health and wealth. Before girls are married, they will be kept in small rooms so they cannot move much. They are fed the best and most fattening foods such as butter and honey. They are massaged with oils and when they have become plump, then they are married. Look at this article on the BBC website: **tinyurl.com/bv7kw4u**.

Many African cultures view fat on a woman as a sign of beauty, health and happiness.

Cultural universals

There are some things that are found in all cultures. These are known as **cultural universals**. All cultures have some form of family life. People in all cultures have celebrations and festivals and most cultures have some form of religious belief, even if some people do not actually take the religion seriously. Cultures have special foods and ways of eating.

All cultures have sets of unwritten rules for how to behave and what to do. These rules are known as norms and values and they are very important in society.

Key terms

Culture – the way of life of a group of people.

Cultural diversity – the range of different ideas and cultures that exist.

Cultural relativity – the idea that what is normal in one culture would be strange in another.

Cultural universals – social behaviours that can be found in all cultures.

Check your understanding

Use the terms in the box below to answer the questions:

cultural diversity	cultural relativity
culture	cultural universal

a) What term refers to a way of life of a group of people?

b) What term refers to the fact that different groups of people may have different ways of living?

c) What term refers to the idea that what is normal in one culture would be strange in another?

d) What term refers to the idea that some social behaviours such as marriage can be found in all cultures?

Stretch and challenge

Using ideas from reading books, watching television and seeing films, suggest ten ways in which the culture of people in the USA (Americans) is different from the culture of people in Britain. Why do you think these differences have developed?

Develop your understanding by suggesting ten ways in which the culture of the USA and that of people in Britain are very similar. Why are there similarities?

Exam practice

People from different cultures may have different rules regarding touching. Many Arab men will hold hands when they walk as a sign of respect for each other. Arabs will also stand very close when talking as it is seen as polite. However, in Britain it is not usually acceptable for men to touch each other. An exception to this rule is on a football pitch when a goal has been scored. It is often seen as acceptable to pat a small child on the head in the UK, but in Thailand it is very rude. Thai parents would be upset if you touched their child's head as they think you would be touching the child's soul.

a) Using the item, describe how Arab men show respect for each other. (1)

b) Using the item, identify one social rule that British men should follow regarding touching each other. (1)

c) Identify and explain one difference between Thai culture and British culture. (2)

d) Explain the meaning of the term cultural relativity, using an example. (2)

e) Describe one cultural universal. (2)

f) Identify two elements of culture. (2)

Compulsory core
Topic 3: What are social rules?

What am I going to learn?

● **To understand the importance of written and unwritten rules in our cultures**

All human groups follow rules. These rules may be written down, for example schools have codes of conduct. Some of these rules are not written, but we all follow them, for example friends have rules about how they should treat each other but these are just understood.

Over to you

Which are more important in everyday life? Is it the written rules, such as laws or codes of conduct, or the unwritten rules, such as norms and values? Use examples to support your answer.

Across the generations

Speak to someone who is very much older than yourself, such as a teacher or an older family member. Ask that person what norms have changed since they were young. Do they think people are more or less polite than they were many years ago? You could also ask about attitudes to tattoos, for example. Have they changed, especially for women?

Social rules

A **society** is a group of people who share a culture. Often, when sociologists talk of a society, they are talking about a formal organisation such as a country which has laws and a government, for example British society. The government makes the rules for everyone to follow. These written rules are laws. People who break laws are criminals.

Unwritten rules for social groups

It is important to follow unwritten rules to fit in with social groups. These unwritten rules are an important part of any culture and people feel uncomfortable if others break them.

Norms

Any group of people will have a set of rules of expected behaviour (**norms**), things that are seen as completely normal for people to do. There is no law that says people should say 'please' and 'thank you'. It is an action that is normal and expected.

Mores

These are more important than norms, because if a person breaks a **more**, it is seen as very wrong and bad. A more is a belief about what behaviour is normal, decent and good, so, being polite is a more in British culture. Rude people are breaking mores and they will be rejected by others.

Maori people of New Zealand use tattoos to decorate themselves.

Among the Maori people of New Zealand, facial tattoos are common for men and women. The word 'tattoo' comes from the Maori language. Young people are often expected to have a tattoo as they become adult. In Britain, tattooing is a fashion and can be seen as an act of rebellion. Some employers might not give a job to people with facial tattoos. However, norms are changing.

Values

These are stronger again, because they are beliefs that most people share in a society. Breaking a **value** is seen as particularly bad. In British culture we see it is a value that we should care for other people. Disrespect, particularly of older people, is seen as bad. Therefore, our values say that we should respect others.

These unwritten rules are important because it is possible to break them without knowing it. However, people who do break these rules will be rejected by others. A person who breaks an unwritten rule is known as a **deviant**. However, all rules, even unwritten rules, may change over time. For example, eating food in a public place was once seen as deviant but is now normal.

Check your understanding

Match the word to the correct meaning:

a) Deviant – the unwritten rules of expected behaviour
b) Criminal – written rules for everyone in a country to follow
c) Norms – beliefs that people in a society share
d) Values – a group of people who share a way of life; a formal group such as people who live in a particular country
e) Mores – a person who breaks a law
f) Culture – a person who breaks a social rule
g) Society – a way of life of a group of people
h) Laws – beliefs about what is good or bad behaviour

Exam practice

What norms for girls in British culture is this Goth girl breaking?

People who do not behave in a normal and expected way are often seen as deviant. They may break social rules by dressing in an unusual way or enjoying activities that others see as unusual. Goths are a youth group who break social norms by wearing dramatic clothes and enjoying their own musical style. Paul Hodkinson, a sociologist who has studied Goths, said that many have to tone down their Goth style when they get jobs.

a) Using the item, name a sociologist who has studied Goths. (1)
b) Using the item, identify one social norm that many Goths break. (1)
c) Identify and explain one norm for teachers in your school. (2)
d) Explain the meaning of the term more, using an example. (2)
e) Using an example, explain the meaning of the term deviant. (2)
f) Explain the meaning of the term society. (2)

Key terms

Society – a group of people who share a way of life and a set of rules.

Norms – normal and expected behaviour.

Mores – ideas about what behaviour is right and wrong.

Values – shared beliefs about how to act.

Deviant – a person who breaks norms and values.

Stretch and challenge

Write a set of school rules for all children to follow. Make sure that they are clear and easy to apply. Rules such as 'Be kind' will not work, because how do you decide if someone is unkind? Think about how you would punish people who break your rules. How would you encourage people to follow the rules you made?

Compulsory core
Topic 4: What is social control?

What am I going to learn?

● **How cultures and societies control us even though we are not aware of it**

All cultures have a number of rules that people must obey. People learn the rules for their culture in each new situation. It is particularly important to teach the rules to children so they grow up knowing how to behave. People need to be encouraged to follow those rules and also to be punished if they break them.

Social control

If people break a law or a written rule then they know that they can be punished and that the punishments may be severe. Law courts can sentence people to prison, or even to death in some countries.

Deviance

If people break an unwritten rule, then they are seen as deviant. Deviant people may be punished. However, because norms and values change in different situations and at different times, the punishments are not always clear. These punishments for being deviant are known as sanctions.

● **Formal sanction** – this is a punishment that is official. Examples of such punishments include: prison, detention, fines.

● **Informal sanction** – this is a punishment that is unofficial. Examples include: nasty comments, jokes at your expense, rudeness, staring.

Formal sanctions are used when a person has broken a written rule and include prison (or detentions in a school). Informal sanctions are used in everyday life and form part of normal living. For example, if a friend borrows something and returns it broken then you may not talk to that person and you probably will not lend them other things again. That is an informal sanction for breaking a norm (return things you borrow) and a value (respect other people's property).

Grade boost

This is a popular topic in examinations so it is wise to make sure that you understand the agencies of social control and that you can explain at least one rule for each agency.

Extended writing

Describe five agencies of social control. (10)

Guidance: Make sure you have five agencies. For each agency, suggest a message that it might give you about how you should behave.

Over to you

You have a friend who is generally pleasant, kind and funny. This person has very poor personal hygiene and tends to be a bit smelly.

● What social rules are being broken?

● How would you deal with the problem without hurting your friend's feelings?

● How would you deal with the problem if the smelly person was someone that you disliked?

Agencies of social control

Agencies of social control (or agencies of socialisation) are groups in society that teach, enforce or encourage people to follow social rules. The first and most important is the family because it is in the family that children are first taught social rules. There are other important places where we are taught or forced to obey social rules: in schools, by the **mass media**, by our religion, by our friends and in work.

Agencies of social control influence people to follow rules by encouraging us to think in certain ways so that we are not always aware of their influence over us. For example, every time girls see magazine covers they are taught that it is a norm for girls to try to be thin.

Key terms

Formal sanction – a punishment for breaking a law or a written rule.

Informal sanction – a punishment for breaking an informal rule, imposed by people around you.

Agent of social control – a group in society that teaches us how to behave.

Mass media – a form of communication that reaches a lot of people at one time.

Stigma – something that marks a person out as very different from other people.

Check your understanding

a) What is social control?
b) What is deviance?
c) What is a formal sanction?
d) What is an informal sanction?
e) What is an agency of social control?
f) What is a stigma?

Stretch and challenge

In the past, smoking was believed to be good for people. Over the past fifty years, we have learned that tobacco smoke can lead to heart disease, lung cancers and other nasty illnesses. List different ways in which people are discouraged from smoking.

Exam practice

Most people accept a little difference and rule breaking in others. It can be seen as funny or clever if people break rules in some situations. For example, we often laugh at fancy dress when men dress as women. However, in some situations, obvious difference is seen as very wrong. A sociologist, Erving Goffman, pointed out that a person who is very different, perhaps because of a lifestyle, a different ethnicity or a disability, is marked out as wrong by others. This serious difference is known as a stigma. For example, a man who dresses as a woman all the time may expect to hear stupid comments from ignorant people.

a) Using the item, suggest one situation where it is seen as funny to break social rules. (1)
b) Which sociologist described the term stigma? (1)
c) Using the item, identify and explain the meaning of the term stigma. (2)
d) Identify and describe one agency of social control. (2)
e) Explain the meaning of the term formal sanction using an example. (2)
f) Explain the meaning of the term informal sanction using an example. (2)

Compulsory core
Topic 5: What is cultural diversity?

What am I going to learn?

- **That cultures and societies are all very different from each other**

All cultures have rules of expected behaviour; these rules are norms. Norms can vary from culture to culture, so things that we see as normal in the UK would be seen as strange, immoral or rude in other cultures. Through studying these differences between cultures, sociologists have come to learn that there are many different ways of looking at the world.

Famous people

Margaret Mead

Margaret Mead lived among a variety of different people around the world and described their way of life. She learned their languages and talked to them to learn about their cultures. She published her first book when she was just 26. Many of the people that Margaret Mead studied had not met people from other cultures before, and some of the tribes were head hunters and cannibals.

A New Guinea warrior who has decorated himself to look attractive to the women of his tribe. His people might have been studied by Margaret Mead.

Cultural diversity

Some people think that the way humans behave is natural to them because that is how they were born to act. However, sociologists say that it is more likely that people behave as they do because they belong to a culture and were taught expected rules by others around them. One piece of evidence that is used to support this idea is the way that human cultures tend to be very different from each other around the world. The term used to describe differences between human cultures is **cultural diversity**.

Anthropology

The study of different human cultures, especially tribal societies, is known as **anthropology**. Anthropologists show us that people from different cultures may have ideas that seem very strange to us. For example, we know that in the past, and in some remote tribes, it is seen as normal to eat other humans but most people in Britain would consider this idea completely disgusting.

Gender in different cultures

Some people tend to think that the differences between men and women are natural and to do with their biology. A famous anthropologist, Margaret Mead (1901–78), found that in the islands of New Guinea, certain tribes had very different ideas of what is natural to men and women. She discovered that among the Arapesh, for example, both men and women would seem to be feminine to Europeans. The Mundugumor were all very aggressive and masculine. Among the Tchambuli, traditional European male/female roles are reversed and men spend time making themselves attractive for women. This is evidence of cultural diversity.

Subcultures

Even within societies and cultures there are some groups who have slightly different ideas and beliefs from most others around them. For example, some youth groups may have slightly different views from **mainstream society**. In the past, hippies rejected society and more recently, there have been Emos and Goths. These groups, which are slightly different from most others in their culture, are **subcultures**.

Check your understanding

Complete the following sentences:

a) The rules of expected behaviour are known as •••.

b) The term used to describe differences between human cultures is known as •••.

c) The study of different human cultures is known as •••.

d) A famous anthropologist who studied cultural diversity and gender was •••.

e) Margaret Mead studied different tribes in •••.

f) One tribe where men and women both acted in a feminine way to European thinking was the •••.

g) There are some groups in cultures who have slightly different ideas and beliefs from most people around them. These groups are known as •••.

Exam practice

Kundol Lama lives in a remote area of Nepal, high in the mountains. She has three children and two husbands. Her husbands are brothers and they share their wife. The practice is known as **polyandry**. Polyandry is common in some villages, but the practice is dying out. Now fewer women have multiple husbands.

One reason for multiple marriage is because if one husband dies, the remaining brothers will take care of the wife and children. Another reason is because it limits the number of children born to a family.

Most people who believe in multiple husbands in Nepal are members of the Buddhist religion. Religious Hindus do not accept multiple marriages.

a) Using the item explain how many Buddhists in Nepal organise their families. (1)

b) What is the meaning of the term polyandry? (1)

c) Using the item, identify and explain one reason why some families in Nepal practice polyandry. (2)

d) Using an example, explain the meaning of the term cultural diversity. (2)

e) Identify and describe one culture where **gender roles** are different from the UK. (2)

f) Using an example, explain the meaning of the term subculture. (2)

Key terms

Cultural diversity – differences between human cultures around the world.

Anthropology – the study of different human cultures.

Mainstream society – the way of life of most people in a culture.

Subculture – a small group in society with different beliefs and norms from others around them.

Polyandry – one woman has many husbands.

Gender roles – social differences between the expected behaviour for men and for women.

Stretch and challenge

The British way of life is the best and only way to live. Make points for and against this idea.

Find out about

Find out about one culture that is very different from life in Britain. Describe ways in which the culture is different from our culture. You could create a poster or a PowerPoint and illustrate it with images. A culture you might find very interesting is Japanese culture and there is a lot for you to discover on the Internet.

Topic 6: What is the nature/nurture debate?

What am I going to learn?

● **To understand the nature/nurture debate in sociology**

There are many people who think that the way we behave is down to something that is born in us, the things we do are just human nature. Other people believe that we are the people we are because we have learned how to behave from others around us.

Grade boost

The nature/nurture debate is complex because there cannot be an answer either one way or the other. We will never know which side of the argument is correct, but in examinations it is sensible to remember that whatever your personal opinion may be, you are being asked about what sociologists say. Sociologists support nurture theories.

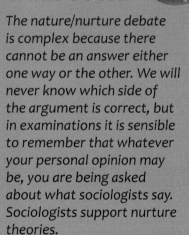

Over to you

Because people are human, they need to do certain things: walk, talk, eat, sleep and do more personal things. These needs are biological. However, in every culture, there are rules to tell you how to do these things and when you can do them. Suggest five cultural rules about eating that we could follow.

The nature/nurture debate

There is a **debate** (discussion) in sociology and psychology. The question is whether people are born to behave as they do because it comes naturally, or whether they learn to act as they do. Probably, there will never be an answer to that question but it is important to understand the points that are made on both sides.

Nature theories of behaviour

Nature theories of behaviour are ideas put forward by biologists and some **psychologists** to explain why people act the way that they do. Human behaviour is explained in terms of genetics or 'natural' differences. For example, they would say men are naturally more aggressive than women because that is how they are born.

Nurture theories of behaviour

Nurture theories of behaviour are preferred by sociologists who say that people are far more affected by how they are brought up than how they are born. They would say that if men are aggressive, it is because boys are brought up to play with guns and violent video games. It is seen as acceptable for boys to fight and they learn that they are expected to be violent.

If nature theories were correct, identical twins would have the same personality as each other because they have the same genes. However, many twins are very different from each other even if they look alike.

Why do sociologists prefer nurture theories?

There is **evidence** to support both nature and nurture theories of human behaviour. However, sociologists say that the evidence supports nurture theories more than nature theories. They use three types of evidence:

- Historical evidence shows that people's behaviour changes over time. This would not be true if people just did what came naturally to them.
- Anthropological evidence shows that people's behaviour varies from culture to culture. Which culture is most 'natural' to humans?
- Children who have not been brought up correctly behave in a way that is very different from most humans. This would not happen if we just acted on **instinct**.

Check your understanding

a) What is a debate?
b) What is nature theory?
c) What is nurture theory?
d) Give one example of a nature explanation for male violence.
e) Give one example of a nurture explanation for male violence.
f) What historical evidence is there for nurture theory?
g) What anthropological evidence is there for nurture theory?

Exam practice

Scientists know that children inherit physical characteristics from their parents so they may look like family members. However, most sociologists believe that the way that children are brought up affects them far more than inherited characteristics. Thus nurture is more important than nature. In 2003, a sociologist, Leon Feinstein, found that children who were born with equal intelligence did far worse in school if their families were poorer. They did better if their families were richer. Feinstein says that this difference is due to disadvantages that poorer children have in their homes and families. They do less well because of where and how they are brought up rather than their inborn ability.

a) Using the item, identify and explain one piece of evidence that shows that children inherit characteristics from their parents. (2)
b) Using the item, identify and explain one reason Feinstein thinks that poorer children do not achieve as well as richer children in school. (2)
c) Using an example, explain the meaning of the term nurture theory. (2)
d) Explain, with examples, two reasons why sociologists reject nature theories of human behaviour. (4)

Key terms

Debate – a formal argument between two different points of view.

Nature theory – the idea that we act as we do because we are born that way.

Psychologist – a person who studies the mind and behaviour.

Nurture theory – the idea that we act as we do because we are taught how to behave by others.

Evidence – something that can be used to support or challenge an argument.

Instinct – something that animals and people do without learning or being taught to do it.

Stretch and challenge

Adolf Hitler came to power in Germany in 1933. During his period of control, Germany invaded Czechoslovakia and Poland. Many people died in the resulting World War. In addition, Hitler oversaw the mass killings of Jewish people, disabled people, gay people and Gypsies from all over Europe.

Was Hitler born to be cruel or did something about the way he was brought up make him cruel? If Hitler had not been born, could the Second World War still have happened?

Compulsory core
Topic 7: What is socialisation?

What am I going to learn?

- **To understand the process of learning how to be a member of your culture**

The rules for any culture are very complicated. Each new situation we are in has a new set of rules, so people continually learn what is expected of them. The process of learning the rules for any situation is known as socialisation. Sociologists have identified a number of different forms of socialisation that take place.

Forms of socialisation

Socialisation is the process of learning the expected rules for your culture. This can happen to small babies who are taught good manners by their parents, but also to older people who may have to learn the rules for success in a new job. People need to learn new rules for any situation, so they will experience socialisation into very old age.

Primary socialisation

Primary socialisation is probably the most important form of socialisation. It usually takes place when we are young and learning the basic rules of society. We are socialised at first in our families and we develop our personalities. Families teach us norms, values, attitudes, behaviours and beliefs that we may have all through our lives.

Secondary socialisation

Secondary socialisation takes place when we begin to interact with the wider world. We learn what is acceptable and not acceptable to other people. There are many groups (or agencies) who are part of the process of teaching us the rules: schools, work, friends, people around us and the mass media such as television or films. We learn that the rules from our families may need to be adapted to new situations.

Informal socialisation

Most socialisation happens by chance. We live our normal lives and learn from people around us so we see things happen and we learn the rules from them. If people in your family are very tidy, you may not be tidy yourself, but you will still think that being tidy is a good thing.

Formal socialisation

This is when people or organisations set out to change us deliberately. For example, in schools, teachers deliberately try to teach children to be hard working. They train children to follow school rules and punish them if they misbehave. There are other groups who deliberately try and change how people act and how they think. Examples might be the Army or a religious group who will try and change people on purpose.

Over to you

What do you think are the most important things that your family have taught you about social life and how to get on with others?

Personal research idea

Get hold of a catalogue with toys, or look at websites. See what is presented as suitable for boys to play with and for girls to play with. What messages would the children get from the toys about how to behave as adults?

Check your understanding

Complete the following sentences:

a) The process of learning the expected behaviour for your culture is known as ●●●.

b) The term used to describe the socialisation that takes place in the home is known as ●●●.

c) The term used to describe socialisation that takes place in the wider world is known as ●●●.

d) Accidental socialisation is known as ●●●.

e) The deliberate attempt to change a person to fit into a new situation is known as ●●●.

f) Socialisation takes place in any ●●● social situation.

Key terms

Socialisation – the process of learning the rules of a culture.

Primary socialisation – being taught how to behave by your family.

Secondary socialisation – being taught how to behave by people in the wider world.

Informal socialisation – learning how to behave as you live your life.

Formal socialisation – when people deliberately set out to change how you act.

Exam practice

Children are given toys that teach them what is expected of them when they are grown up. The girls have tea sets and teddies and the boys have bricks and trucks. This is part of socialisation.

Children are taught to behave in a way that is normal for their sex when they are still very young. Parents may behave differently towards a child depending on its sex. Psychologists designed a social experiment to test this theory. They gave young mothers a very young child to play with. Sometimes it was dressed in pink and called 'Beth'. Sometimes the baby was dressed in blue and called 'Adam'. It was always the same child. When mothers thought it was a girl, they talked to the baby and played gentle games. They were rougher and more excitable with 'Adam'. This shows that socialisation takes place very early in life. Boys are taught to be rough and physical but girls are taught to talk more.

a) Using the item, identify one piece of evidence that shows that very young babies are socialised by their parents. (2)

b) Using the item, describe one difference in the way that parents may treat girls and boys. (2)

c) Using an example, explain the meaning of the term primary socialisation. (2)

d) Using an example, explain the meaning of the term secondary socialisation. (2)

e) Explain, with an example, how schools may deliberately try to change your behaviour. (2)

Stretch and challenge

What would the world be like if girls and boys were all brought up in exactly the same way?

Grade boost

Sometimes people use the word socialisation to mean something like 'getting along with others'. It is almost certain that in any GCSE examination paper in sociology, a question about socialisation will be asked. The everyday use of the word is not going to be given marks. Learn the sociological meaning and remember that it is the process of learning social rules.

Compulsory core

Topic 8: What are agencies of socialisation?

What am I going to learn?

● **To understand that there are a number of social groups involved in the socialisation process**

Socialisation takes place from birth until death. We are always in new situations and so we always have to learn new rules. We also have to learn new rules as society changes. Schools have had to change and develop rules as mobile phones have become more common. The most important social organisations that teach us the rules for our culture are: family, peer group, education, religion, work and the mass media.

Agencies of socialisation

Socialisation is the process of learning the expected rules for your culture. Certain social organisations teach us the rules for our culture. These are **agencies of socialisation**. To a small child the family is most important. As children get older, education, media and **peer groups** matter more.

● Family – This is an agency of primary socialisation and it will influence you all through your life. People learn the important rules such as norms and values (revise Topic 3 if you are unsure of these terms).

● Peer group – A peer group consists of people of a similar age and background. It is more than just friends, but includes them as well.

● Education – For very small children nursery school is probably the first time they meet people who do not love them. Children quickly learn the rules because if they do not they may be punished. Schools are agencies of formal socialisation.

● Religion – Religion is an important agency of secondary socialisation, even if people are not religious. Religion gives people the mores and values that they live by. Muslims may live by the Koran, but Christians and Jews follow the Ten Commandments.

● Work – Each workplace has a set of rules about what is expected. There may be a code of conduct that is expected. Some jobs may train people into what to say; for example, McDonald's employees tell you to 'Have a nice day'. There will be expected dress codes or a uniform.

Extended writing

Describe the meaning of the term agency of socialisation, using examples. (10)

Guidance: Explain the meaning of the term 'agency of socialisation'. You will then need to write about different agencies of socialisation and offer examples of the messages from each one. Write about 200 words.

Over to you

Create a mind map poster of agencies of socialisation. Link in some of the messages that they give us about society. Use the frame to the right as a starting point for your work.

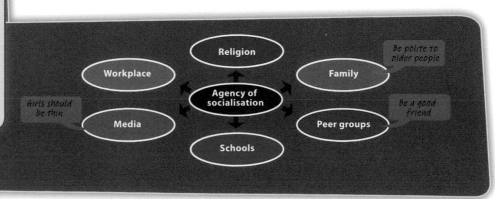

- **Mass media** – The mass media are a form of communication that reach large numbers of people at one time. They include television, films, games, the Internet or music. People may not be aware of the influence they have. The mass media try to make us to buy things through advertising. Importantly, the media may influence how we see the world. For example, girls are encouraged to be thin and boys are told to develop muscles.

Check your understanding

Use the terms in the box below to answer the questions:

Primary socialisation	Values	Agency of socialisation
Mass media	Socialisation	Norms

a) What term refers to an organisation that teaches us the rules for society?

b) What term refers to a form of communication that reaches large numbers of people at one time?

c) What term refers to normal and expected behaviour for any situation?

d) What term refers to the type of socialisation that you have in the family home?

e) What term refers to beliefs that most people share in a society?

f) What term refers to the process of learning the rules for your society?

Exam practice

Read this story from an unstructured interview with a lady aged 70.

Question: What did you learn in school?

Answer: In school, I was taught all the things that I needed to be a good wife and mother. I learned to cook and sew. I was taught knitting, but my brothers learned woodwork. Clever boys were taught Latin. The teachers said that it would lead to a good job for them. Teachers said that they wanted us girls to be ladies. We needed to find husbands who would be good to us. I would have liked to study science but the teachers told me that girls didn't need to do that kind of subject. We were told that we would give up work when we married.

a) Using the item, identify what subjects girls were expected to study in schools in the past. (1)

b) Using the item, describe one difference in the way that schools educated girls and boys. (2)

c) Using sociological knowledge, explain why girls and boys were taught different subjects in school. (4)

d) Using an example, explain the meaning of the term agency of socialisation. (2)

e) Name two agencies of secondary socialisation. (1)

Key terms

Agency of socialisation – a social organisation that teaches people how to behave in society.

Peer group – a group of people of the same age and similar interests.

Mass media – a form of communication that reaches a lot of people at one time.

Unstructured interview – an interview that takes the form of a conversation.

Stretch and challenge

Suggest five things that you learned in school that are not part of proper lessons (for example, you may have learned how to tell lies to teachers).

Find out about

Use the Internet to find out what happened in Fiji when television arrived in 1995. How did young women's attitudes to their body shapes change as a result of socialisation by the media? Put 'Fiji', 'anorexia' and 'Anne Becker' into a search engine. A starting point is an article on the BBC website: **tinyurl.com/5qyl7e**

Topic 9: What is social identity?

What am I going to learn?

- **To understand that we get a sense of who we are from the social groups to which we belong**

A person's identity is their sense of who they are. People gain a sense of identity from the social groups to which they belong. For example, people may feel that they belong to a family, a religion, a country, a town, a football team, a school or a gang. This makes them feel important, special and different from others who do not belong to those groups.

Over to you

Make a list of common stereotypes of young people in Britain today.

I'M PUNK SO I MUST DO DRUGS

I'M ASIAN SO I MUST LIKE MATHS

I DYE MY HAIR CRAZY COLOURS SO I MUST BE LOOKING FOR ATTENTION

I'M A PERSON SO I MUST BE STEREOTYPED

What is identity?

People like to feel that they are special. One way people feel special is to belong to a group of other similar people. This gives them a sense of pride in themselves and gives a sense of social **identity**.

Identity can be seen when people choose to wear clothes that are like a uniform, even when they don't have to. Muslim women choose to wear headscarves, and football supporters wear replica kit. This tells the rest of the world who they are and what matters to them. It is part of their identity.

Status

Some identities are respected. This respect is known as **status**. People who are given a lot of respect have high status. Police officers show their identity by wearing uniform. When they wear those clothes, they expect respect and have high status.

Stereotypes

People tend to see others who are members of a group without really thinking about who they are. The **stereotype** influences how people are treated. This makes daily life easier, because a stereotype is a simple way of thinking about others. A stereotype of doctors is that they are clever and care about people. That may be how doctors will think of themselves.

Labelling theory

People are sometimes given a **label** by others as bad or good. This affects how they are treated. For example, a rebel in school may always be treated harshly by teachers and see no point in being good. The rebel will then take pride in being naughty and mix with other rebels. Being a rebel can be an important part of their identity. If they are seen as bad, then it is difficult to change the label.

Roles

In every situation a person is in, there will be a set of expected ways of behaving. These expected behaviours are a person's **role**. People act according to those roles. A teacher is expected to tell people what to do and is bossy in school. At home, the same person will act differently because there is a different role for being a family member. Learning about the different roles we have is part of socialisation.

Check your understanding

Use the diagram to match the beginnings of the sentences to the ends of the sentences.

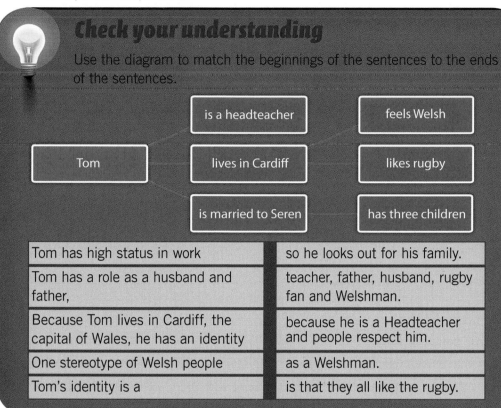

is a headteacher	feels Welsh
Tom	lives in Cardiff	likes rugby
is married to Seren	has three children

Tom has high status in work	so he looks out for his family.
Tom has a role as a husband and father,	teacher, father, husband, rugby fan and Welshman.
Because Tom lives in Cardiff, the capital of Wales, he has an identity	because he is a Headteacher and people respect him.
One stereotype of Welsh people	as a Welshman.
Tom's identity is a	is that they all like the rugby.

Exam practice

A doctor talks to her patient. She uses the stethoscope to show her identity.

a) Using the item, identify one identity for the person on the left of the image. (1)

b) Explain how you recognise the doctor in the picture. (2)

c) Suggest one reason why doctors have a high status in our society. (1)

d) Use the item to help explain the role of a patient. How is a patient expected to behave when with a doctor? (2)

e) Identify and explain one stereotype for criminals. (2)

f) Suggest one reason why people who are labelled as criminal often find it difficult to find jobs. (1)

Stretch and challenge

Write out the letters of your name down the page. Try and think of one word that describes who you are beginning with each of the letters of your name.

Grade boost

Write words and meanings on posters in bright colours. They are useful for putting up in your room so that you can revise without working hard at it.

Topic 10: What are the processes of socialisation?

What am I going to learn?

- **To understand how socialisation takes place in daily life**

Socialisation is very important in childhood because that is when we learn the norms and values of our culture. It is a complicated process and often we do not realise that it is happening. Ann Oakley described how we learn to behave as male or female. However, her ideas apply in all kinds of situations, not just for learning to be masculine or feminine.

Famous people

Ann Oakley

Ann Oakley (b. 1944) is a well-known sociologist, famous for being a feminist. She believed women should have more rights in society. She studied how children learned gender roles and looked at women's attitudes to housework among other things. She has also written novels and stories.

Interesting fact

Navajo Indians of the USA discouraged their children from crying or making noise. If a child cried, the parents would check the baby to see it was not in pain or hungry. Then they would take it to a safe place outside, well away from other people till the crying stopped. When the child stopped crying, it would be brought back into the home. Navajo children are remarkably quiet as a result because they learn that noise would result in lack of attention.

Processes of socialisation

We can be taught the **norms** and values for our society in a number of ways. Our families help us to develop our personalities and have a separate sense of **identity** through the following processes. It is through these processes that we learn our adult roles in society.

Manipulation

Parents encourage behaviour that they approve of and discourage bad behaviour through praise and punishment. Children may be rewarded by love and attention, or even through treats if they do as their parents want them to do.

Canalisation

Parents direct children's interests into things that they think are good for the children. They may read to them or take them to sporting activities. Children learn what is the norm for their family, some children may be taught to read at a young age to prepare them for school.

Language

Adults speak to girls and boys in different ways. Phrases such as 'Boys don't cry' are used. A child may be called a 'Little Princess' and this will teach her that she is precious and special. Boys are given tougher names. This teaches them their roles.

Social activities

Children might be taken to play groups before they are old enough to attend nursery. They will learn to play with other children, sharing toys and taking turns. Girls may be encouraged to do domestic tasks in the kitchen, whereas boys are often sent out to play. Boys are encouraged to participate in team games such as football, which emphasise competition, whereas girls tend to dance, which teaches grace and beauty.

Modelling

Children will **imitate** their parents and act as they do. Adults become **role models** for children who copy them. A psychologist, Albert Bandura, suggested that young children will copy what they see on television and believed that children learned violence from the media.

Toys and games

These are important part of the **socialisation** process. Children are given **gendered objects** to play with, and girls are offered pink toys. Girls may be allowed to do male things, but boys are not usually allowed to play with female objects.

Check your understanding

Complete the following sentences:

a) Socialisation is the ••• of learning the norms and values of your culture.
b) Children will ••• their parents and act as they do.
c) Bandura suggested that young children learn violence from the •••.
d) Children are ••• into certain activities that will teach them adult roles.
e) Ann Oakley was a famous •••.
f) Parents ••• certain behaviour through the process of manipulation.
g) Adults are ••• for children who will copy the adults they admire.
h) Parents use ••• such as pet names or phrases that teach children what is expected.
i) Girls are given toys in the colour ••• but boys have other colours.
j) Girls can play with boys ••• but boys are not usually allowed to play with girls' toys.

Exam practice

> Famous sporting personalities are often role models for young people. Personalities such as Tanni Grey-Thomson, who is one of the most famous Paralympians of all time, have inspired young people to copy them. Footballers are often admired by young boys, though not all footballers are good role models. Some footballers have been accused of racism and bad behaviour on and off the pitch.

a) Using the item, identify one positive role model for young people. (1)
b) Using an example, explain the meaning of the term role model. (2)
c) Identify and explain one reason why some footballers may not be good role models for young people. (2)
d) Using an example, explain the meaning of the term canalisation. (2)
e) Suggest one reason why parents would channel boys into sporting activities. (1)

Key terms

Norms – expected behaviour.

Identity – a sense of who we are in relation to others.

Manipulation – children are controlled into certain behaviour.

Canalisation – children are directed into certain interests.

Model – adults show children how to behave by what they do.

Imitate – copying.

Role model – people that children admire and copy.

Socialisation – the process of learning the norms and values of your culture.

Gendered objects – items that are intended for either boys or girls, but not both.

Stretch and challenge

Should all violence, including cartoon violence, be banned from any programme that could be seen by children? Make five points for and five against.

🔍 websites

tinyurl.com/d22ez3

You might find this short YouTube clip both interesting and shocking. It is called *Children see, Children do* and was made in Australia to promote good adult role models for children.

Compulsory core

Topic 11: How do children learn gender identity?

What am I going to learn?

- **To understand how children learn their adult gender roles**

For sociologists, sex refers to biological differences between males and females. These cannot be changed. Gender refers to the social differences between males and females or what is seen as masculine and feminine. These differences are learned and vary from culture to culture.

Grade boost

When you are studying a new topic, it helps to read around the subject in newspapers and on websites. It will help to develop your literacy skills and to widen your understanding of what the experts in the topic are saying as a result of recent research.

Personal research idea

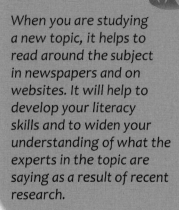

Collect catalogues from shops and mail order companies. Look at the pages of toys and children's items. Conduct a content analysis of the toys and clothes. Count how many pictures show traditional gender patterns. How many pictures show boys or girls doing non-gendered activities? Draw graphs of your findings. What do you learn from this research method?

How do we learn our gender?

Traditional gender roles in Britain saw women as **domestic** and men as working outside the home. Because attitudes are changing, the differences between the gender roles are not quite as strong as they once were for adults. Children are still taught that males and females have different gender roles through agencies of socialisation.

In the home

We learn gender roles in the home when we are still very young. The process of gender socialisation begins at birth when children are dressed in clothing and colours seen as appropriate for their **sex**. Male clothing tends to be more practical, whereas female clothing can restrict movement and is in colours that show dirt. If parents follow traditional gender patterns of the mother doing all the housework then children will see that as normal and do the same. Toys are often gendered.

At school

Reading books often show boys in active roles, whereas stories for girls are more concerned with emotions. Teachers may ask boys to move things around and girls to clear up. Some subjects are seen as more **feminine** than others, for example sciences are often seen as male and art subjects as female. Most teachers are female, especially in primary school, so it is said that boys do not have male role models to imitate.

Sport and leisure activities

Female sports people are paid less than males, and television coverage of top sports almost always focuses on men. There is much less female sport shown on television and often coverage focuses on how attractive the female athletes are rather than how good they are at sport. Children learn from this that sport is a **masculine** rather than a feminine activity.

The mass media

Most media products are gendered. Television programmes and films are targeted at males or females. Games for boys often involve violence whereas female magazines are concerned with beauty products. Children who see these images pick up messages about how they should behave and act when they are older.

Key terms

Traditional – something people have always done.

Gender – differences in social roles of males and females.

Domestic – to do with the home.

Sex – biological differences between men and women.

Feminine – seen as normal for females.

Masculine – seen as normal for males.

Mass media – forms of communication that reach a lot of people at a time.

Check your understanding

Use the terms in the box to help you answer the questions:

> Gender Domestic
> Mass media Imitation
> Sex Gender role socialisation

a) What term refers to a form of communication that reaches many people at a time?

b) What term refers to biological differences between men and women?

c) What term refers to social differences between men and women?

d) What term refers to the type of socialisation that teaches gender?

e) What term refers to things that are related to the home and family?

f) What term refers to the way that children may copy adult role models?

Exam practice

It is often difficult to tell the sex of a young child, so parents will dress their children in highly gendered colours and clothes. Girls are given toys that encourage caring, whereas boys are given toys that emphasise action and violence, such as guns, trains and cars. Girls are encouraged to have long hair, whereas boys have short styles. Studies have shown that many parents are negative towards boys who choose female gendered items, sometimes because they worry their boys will be gay.

a) What is the sociological meaning of the term sex? (1)

b) Using the item, identify and explain the meaning of the term gender. (2)

c) Using examples, explain two ways parents may teach gender to their children. (4)

d) Suggest one reason why some parents are unwilling to allow boys to play with feminine gendered items. (1)

e) Identify two toys that are seen as traditionally feminine. (1)

f) What may girls learn about gender from having long hair styles as children? (1)

Stretch and challenge

Can you identify gender stereotypes in this image of children playing football?

Activity: Suggest reasons why some parents encourage male children to play football.

Compulsory core

Topic 12: How do children learn their ethnic identity?

What am I going to learn?

● **To understand how children gain a sense of ethnic identity**

The country where we were born gives us nationality. Most people born in Britain can have a British passport and are British citizens. This is a legal matter and depends also on your parents' nationality. Ethnicity is a sense of belonging to a particular group or place. Many people who are legally British, for example, feel themselves to be Welsh, Scottish or perhaps British Asian. These are not legal identities but ethnic identities. Usually, but not always, the term ethnic is associated with minority groups. To complicate matters, in modern Britain, very many people have more than one ethnicity.

Grade boost

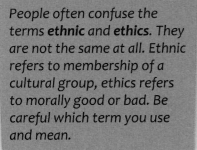

*People often confuse the terms **ethnic** and **ethics**. They are not the same at all. Ethnic refers to membership of a cultural group, ethics refers to morally good or bad. Be careful which term you use and mean.*

Extended writing

Explain how people learn their sense of their ethnicity. (10)

Guidance: Focus on how ethnicity is taught to children, think about the ways that they learn what their ethnicity is. Write about 200 words.

How do we learn our ethnicity?

Ethnic refers to membership of a cultural group. Children need to be taught that they belong to a particular social group and to take pride in their cultural background. They may be taught this in a number of ways.

In the home

Different ethnicities have festivals and traditions that they take part in. So families of Asian heritage will watch Bollywood films together. At this time children will learn the traditions of their own culture. Children from ethnic minorities often have the advantage of speaking a different language in the home from the one that is used in school. They may be encouraged to wear certain clothing such as salwar kameez.

At school

Schools can be important in teaching **cultural identity**. In Wales, all schools will teach some Welsh language and will teach about Welsh culture and society. There will be national festivals such as Eisteddfod. Many ethnic groups have their own schools where they will teach religion, language and cultural traditions, perhaps on a Saturday.

Sport and leisure activities

Sport is one of the most significant ways of teaching ethnicity. Some ethnicities are associated with particular sports, so in Wales, rugby is part of the tradition. People will watch the team play. The 2012 London Olympics was a major social event and gave people pride in being British.

Religion

Children may be taught a religion. For example, many sociologists have found that Muslim children feel that their religion is central to their sense of who they are, and Islam is a guide to how to live well. This will be part of home/family life and many children attend faith-based schools.

The mass media

The media show national sporting events on television so many people will make an effort to watch international matches or sporting fixtures. Sometimes television shows negative and stereotyped images of other ethnicities. For example, African-Caribbeans are often shown as criminals, whereas, of course, they could be or do anything.

Check your understanding

Use the terms in the box to help you answer the questions:

Negative image	Ethnicity	Eisteddfod
Nationality	Ethnic minority	

a) What term means the legal status of belonging to a country and having a right to a passport?

b) What term means a sense of belonging to a particular place or social group?

c) What term refers to a smaller group of people who have a different sense of ethnicity from most people around them?

d) What term refers to a group of people being shown in a way that makes them look bad?

e) What term refers to a festival held in Wales and celebrated by Welsh people?

Exam practice

Many people may feel their ethnic identity very strongly during competitions such as the Football World Cup. Tennis player Andy Murray, who is Scottish, was strongly criticised when he said he supported any team who played England during the Football World Cup in 2006. However, he was feeling his Scottish identity at the time. In football there are separate teams for each of the home nations, but not always in other sports. Fans travel abroad to follow their teams; others stay at home to watch matches on television. People will wear team jerseys. Children learn their ethnic identity as they watch sporting fixtures with their parents.

People often dress in national flags or national dress for important events or sporting fixtures.

a) Using an example, explain the meaning of the term nationality. (2)

b) Using an example, explain the meaning of the term ethnicity. (2)

c) Using examples, explain one way in which parents may teach ethnicity to their children. (3)

d) Outline and explain one way in which ethnic identity can be taught to children through secondary socialisation. (3)

Key terms

Nationality – legal citizenship of a country with the right to have a passport and vote.

Ethnic – refers to membership of a cultural group.

Cultural identity – sense of who you are and the culture you feel you belong to.

Stretch and challenge

What does it mean to be British? Consider what it might be that makes someone British. You may choose another ethnicity as well, to compare with Britishness.

Over to you

The UK Border Agency has a test for people who wish to become a British citizen or intend to settle in Britain long term. You can find out more at **tinyurl.com/czktpuy** or if you Google the term 'British Citizenship test'. Would you pass this test? Design ten questions that you would ask to find out if people are ready to be counted as British.

Compulsory core

Topic 13: How do the family act as an agency of primary socialisation?

What am I going to learn?

- **To understand the role of the family as an agency of socialisation**

The family are the first agency of socialisation for most people. Families remain significant to people all through their lives, so that people follow the patterns set by their parents. It is known, for example, that the children of smokers are more likely to smoke as well. Sadly, children who come from families where a parent is in prison are also more likely to grow up and have a criminal conviction themselves.

🔍 **websites**

You might find watching clips from the television series, *Supernanny* very interesting. It can be seen on YouTube. It shows problem families who are having difficulties socialising their children appropriately.

Extended writing

Discuss whether the family is the most important agency of socialisation of children. (20)

Guidance: You will need to consider both points of view in this writing. You will need to explain why the family is an important agency of socialisation, but then to consider other agencies of socialisation, too, and compare them with the family in importance. It is important to make a clear judgement and back it up with evidence.

How do families socialise children?

Humans are born with very little understanding of people around them, they do not understand their culture and this must be taught to them. **Families** are a major agency of primary informal socialisation. Parents begin the process of socialisation before birth, where children are bought toys, clothes, named and valued by their families. They are taught norms by their parents and learn social skills. They develop an identity so that they learn what appropriate behaviour for most situations is. They also learn their roles in the family, so daughters may be expected to do housework, whereas sons may expect to play or do hard work with their fathers. In some families, parents may spend a lot of time reading to children, whereas in other families watching television is the norm.

Sanctions

Sanctions can be either positive or negative. Positive sanctions or rewards follow on from behaviour that gains **approval**. Negative sanctions or punishments follow on from behaviour that others disapprove of.

Positive sanctions (rewards)

One method of socialising infants is through praise and pleasure. Children are encouraged to repeat behaviour through praise. They share activities with family members and enjoy social activities through conversation and play. They learn that certain activities should be repeated to gain parental approval. They may get smiles or praise. Parents may also reward children through buying them presents.

Negative sanctions (punishments)

If children behave in a way that is not considered acceptable, they may be punished. Some cultures rely on fear and physical punishment. For example, the Gusii of Kenya are very strict parents and beat their children with sticks. Japanese Taira people praise their children and punish by withholding praise. Sanctions may be physical so children can be smacked for example, or they may consist of not allowing children to play with their favourite items. Older children may be grounded.

Check your understanding

Use the terms in the box to help you answer the questions:

Canalisation	Approval	Gender
Family	Expectation	Sanction

a) What term means a group of people related by blood, marriage or adoption?

b) What term means a reward or punishment?

c) What term refers to the way that people reward other people through praise?

d) What term refers to behaviour that people think is normal and expect to see?

e) What term refers to the way that children are channelled into certain behaviours?

f) What term refers to the social behaviours that are expected of each sex?

Key terms

Family – a group of people related by blood, marriage or adoption.

Sanction – a reward or punishment used to make people act as you wish.

Approval – something that people think is good.

Expectation – a behaviour that people assume is normal.

Exam practice

Amy Chua, a Chinese-American mother, has written a book about Chinese parenting. It is called *Battle Hymn of The Tiger Mother*. In it she described how she was brought up by her family. They were very strict and controlling. They were also very supportive. Chua got into trouble for gaining marks as low as A⁻ in lessons. She had piano and mathematics practice every day and never had a boyfriend. Typical Chinese parents expect total respect, whereas in Britain, many parents allow children to express themselves more freely. Chua says she still loves her parents very much and feels that she owes all her success in life to their attitudes. She believes that Chinese parenting styles lead Chinese children to value education and success.

a) Using examples, explain the meaning of the term primary socialisation. (2)

b) Identify and explain one way in which parents may socialise children into their gender roles. (2)

c) With reference to the item, outline and explain one difference between Chinese parents and British parents. (2)

d) With reference to the item, explain one way in which Chinese parents encourage their children to do well in school. (1)

e) Outline and explain one way in which gender identity can be taught to children through primary socialisation. (3)

Stretch and challenge

Suggest ten rules that all families should have that will ensure the children have a good start in life.

Personal research idea

Conduct a small questionnaire-type survey on children in your class. Ask them what presents they were given by their parents when they were younger. How many of the children were given gender stereotypical toys from their parents? What do you learn from this?

Topic 14: How do the media act as an agency of socialisation?

What am I going to learn?

● **To consider how people may be influenced by the mass media**

The mass media are any forms of communication that reach a lot of people at one time. Examples include the Internet, television, computer games, films, newspapers and DVDs. The media are very influential in setting norms and values because it is difficult to avoid seeing media products. It is said that they have the strongest influence over children because young children find it difficult to tell the difference between fact and fantasy.

Extended writing

Explain why the media are an important part of the socialisation of children. (10)

Guidance: Consider two or three reasons why children are particularly likely to experience socialisation by the media. Think what is special about children and about the media aimed at children. If you look back throughout this book, you will see lots of references to the media and so this is a good revision question. Aim to write about 200 words.

What messages is this baby getting from watching television? How is it affected by what it sees?

The media are an agency of socialisation

The mass media are an important agency of informal secondary socialisation. This is because they are part of our everyday lives. They set norms and values but we are not always aware of how this happens. The media offer pictures and sounds so we concentrate on what we are seeing and hearing. This makes messages easy to pick up. When we use the media we pick up a variety of messages about the world.

The media are a huge business operation. The people who create the media know what will appeal to people. They sell media products (music and games) and they also advertise other products for us to buy (cars, phones, food, clothes, etc.). The media are therefore very powerful in their effects on people.

Stereotypes

A **stereotype** is a category into which we put other people according to some simple characteristics. The media often use stereotypes when telling stories because it makes stories easy for everyone to follow. Doctors are shown as brilliant, heroes are usually good-looking and baddies have a scar that makes them ugly, or a disability. Children learn to apply these stereotypes in real life and act as though they are real.

Representation

Representation is a similar idea to stereotyping. The media may show certain groups of people in a positive or negative way. Old people are often shown as helpless, or women are seen in the home looking after children. Older men are shown in positions of importance, but women tend to be excluded from programmes if they are older. The way that groups of people are shown may influence children to think that is how the world actually is.

If people in the media are always shown as remarkably good-looking, thin and attractive, children may believe that is how they should be. However, computer programs are used to alter photographs, spots are removed and bodies are improved. Some people believe that **anorexia** is encouraged by unnaturally thin images of women in the media.

Check your understanding

Complete the following sentences:

a) The media are an important agency of ••• socialisation.

b) Three important forms of media are •••.

c) Children are affected by the media because they spend a lot of ••• watching and using media products.

d) Children are also affected by the media because they find it difficult to tell the difference between ••• and fantasy.

e) The media are concerned with making money because they are a ••• operation.

f) Advertising is designed to make us ••• things.

g) A ••• is a category into which we put other people according to some simple characteristics.

h) ••• is when whole groups of people are seen in a positive or negative way.

Exam practice

In 2010, the Royal College of Psychiatrists called on the media to stop representing extreme thinness in women as beautiful. They said that it contributes to **eating disorders** such as anorexia. The doctors complain that the media use underweight models and then adjust the images to make them look even thinner. Magazines give out dietary advice to girls without warning of the dangers of anorexia so that it makes women unhappy with their more normal bodies. The argument is that the media is a powerful influence and the way young women are represented in the media causes people to feel that they are too fat, when in fact they are perfectly healthy.

a) Using examples, explain the meaning of the term mass media. (2)

b) Using an example, explain the meaning of the term representation in the media. (2)

c) Using an example, explain the meaning of the term stereotype in the media. (2)

d) Using examples, explain one way in which the mass media may influence people. (3)

e) Outline and explain one way in which ethnic identity can be taught to children through secondary socialisation. (3)

Key terms

Stereotype – a category into which we put other people according to some simple characteristics.

Representation – the way that certain groups are always portrayed in the mass media.

Anorexia – an eating disorder where people starve themselves and become very thin.

Eating disorder – people make themselves ill through under or over eating or only eating some foods.

Stretch and challenge

Should the mass media be forced by law to use models and images of people with a normal body mass index in advertising?

Grade boost

Be careful when addressing this topic and avoid saying that the media cause anorexia. This is difficult to prove, but many people think there is a link between eating disorders and media images.

Topic 15: How do schools act as an agency of socialisation?

What am I going to learn?

- **Schools and the education system are very important as a part of the socialisation process**

Schools are part of both the formal and the informal socialisation process. They deliberately set out to affect our personalities with codes of conduct and sanctions. They also teach us norms and values without intending to. They are therefore one of the most important agencies of secondary socialisation.

Over to you

In what ways do schools prepare students for future adult life? Think of a range of ideas from the subjects that you are taught to the ways that people speak to you.

Interesting fact

The first person to go to prison in Britain for not sending her daughter to school was Patricia Amos. She was jailed for two weeks in 2002 because her daughter, Emma, played truant. She served further time for the same problem with another daughter. Emma, however, gained qualifications and went on to gain a full-time job. Over 100 parents have been to prison because their children skipped school. Other parents have complained that the prison sentence made the situation worse for them and their children.

How do schools act as an agency of socialisation?

The stated aim of the education system is to train children to be the citizens of the future. Children are deliberately taught the things that the government and adults think will be important to them as adult members of society. This knowledge is known as the **formal curriculum** and consists of information and skills. It is written down and teachers must follow it. In England and Wales, it is known as the **National Curriculum**. If children do well, they are rewarded with good results in examinations.

Codes of conduct

Most schools have a formal set of rules and behaviours which are written down as a code of conduct. This offers a list of expected behaviours and there will be a discipline policy which will explain what happens when children break the codes of conduct. This is a gentler version of what happens in the wider world of work and is a preparation for adult life.

Agency of control

Schools are an **agency of control**, because people must follow the rules or they will be punished. For example, in Britain it is the law that all children should receive an education. If children do not attend school their parents can be sent to prison. Children can be punished by schools if they break rules; for example, exclusions or detentions.

Hidden curriculum

Schools often teach children things that they are not aware of. This is known as the **hidden curriculum**. In the past, early reading books in school often taught children gender roles, because Mummy would be shown in a kitchen and Daddy would be seen going out to work. This is a traditional gender role that would be taught by the school. Children may be prepared for working life through the hidden curriculum. They learn to obey teachers so that when they leave school, they will be good employees and do as they are told.

Check your understanding

Complete the following sentences:

a) Schools are an agency of ••• because they deliberately try to change us.

b) The subjects that the government requires children to study are known as •••.

c) Children are taught discipline through the school •••.

d) Children may gain messages without being aware of what they are being taught; this is known as the •••.

e) Sanctions used in school to control children's behaviour include •••.

f) The ••• consists of skills and knowledge that are taught in schools.

Exam practice

Children are often expected to wear school uniforms. What lessons do they learn about life from wearing uniforms?

Some sociologists have said that children learn gender roles in school. Girls are told to wear white shirts and ties, and this may teach them that education is associated with males, because adult females do not usually wear such clothing. Boys may learn that education is associated with females because there are few male teachers in primary schools. Boys and girls choose different subjects so that some subjects are seen as all male, and others as female.

a) Using an example, explain the meaning of the term gender roles. (2)

b) Using an example, explain the meaning of the term **formal socialisation**. (2)

c) Using an example, identify and explain one way in which children are prepared for work by schools. (3)

d) Using examples, explain the meaning of the term hidden curriculum. (3)

Key terms

Formal curriculum – things that are deliberately taught in school.

National Curriculum – a set of subjects that all children in England and Wales are expected to study.

Agency of control – group that makes people obey social rules.

Hidden curriculum – messages that are passed on to children unintentionally.

Formal socialisation – deliberate attempt to change your personality.

Truancy – taking time out of school without permission or reason.

Stretch and challenge

Suggest five ways in which schools could be bad for children and for society.

🔍 websites

www.education.gov.uk/

You can find out more about schools and the education system by looking at the Department for Education (DfE) website where there are lots of stories relevant to schools, how and what children are taught.

wales.gov.uk/topics/ educationandskills/

Compulsory core

Topic 16: How does sport act as an agency of socialisation?

What am I going to learn?

● **To understand some of the ways that sport can influence the way we see ourselves**

Sport is very important in many people's lives. They may be participants, because they play sport, or they could be supporters, because they watch sport. However they are involved, sport can be very important in influencing people and setting their norms and values. Sport is generally seen as a positive influence in people's lives but it can be negative as well.

Grade boost

Questions on the Unit 1 paper often ask you to describe two ways in which children may be influenced by an agency of socialisation. Usually there are three marks for each of those ways. Use the following plan to gain full marks. Describe how children are socialised, explain in a little more detail and offer an example. Use sociological language and terms to be certain of the mark.

Over to you

Why do so many people enjoy watching sporting events together?

Sport as an agency of socialisation

The term sport covers a very wide range of activities that are usually physical and which may involve competition between teams or individual people. Because high levels of skill are involved, people enjoy watching or participating in sporting activities. They often encourage their children to participate. Sport can be a very important part of a culture.

Sporting values and the socialisation of children

Sport is actively encouraged by parents and schools because it promotes many important **values** in our culture: teamwork, competition, health, fitness and personal development. People may feel more connected with each other if they share an interest. Thus, thousands of British children are involved in sporting activities of various kinds. Parents and teachers become involved in coaching, watching and taking children to matches and events.

Parents may buy children **replica** kit to show support for their favourite teams. If children have grown up **supporting** particular teams or sports, they will probably support the same teams all of their lives. As sporting events can be businesses, teams that build a large and loyal set of fans can make a lot of money.

Role models

Famous sportsmen and women become **role models** for children who are taught to respect and admire their success. They appear on television and can sometimes go on to become national figures; for example, Sebastian Coe was a famous middle-distance runner but has had a career as a politician and then as the organiser of the London Olympics in 2012. Thus, sports personalities can become positive role models for children to imitate.

Sport and identity

Sports activity can have a powerful influence on how people see themselves. For some boys, being sporty and fit is part of how they see themselves as masculine. In the past, girls were often discouraged from more physical sports such as rugby and boxing which were seen as masculine activities. Even today, female teams or players do not generally earn as much money or attention as males.

Check your understanding

Match the beginnings and ends of these sentences:

a) Sports are usually defined as activities that are   role models for children

b) People enjoy watching sport because of   to have careers in other areas

c) Parents often encourage children to   an important part of being masculine

d) Sports personalities can be positive   so football can be seen as masculine even though many girls enjoy the game

e) Many boys see sport as   the high levels of skill involved

f) Many sports personalities go on   competition, team work, and health and fitness

g) Some sports are gendered activities   participate in sporting activities

h) Sport actively encourages many positive values such as   physical, often involving competition and teams

Exam practice

From a forum site about netball:

'Why do I love netball? I started to play it in school. Girls could either play hockey or netball and I wasn't fast enough running to be good at hockey. I played netball with all of my friends twice a week. My Mum would come with me as she liked to watch the games. As I got better at it, I wanted to do well and win competitions. I think sport is good for children because it gives them important social values such as team spirit. The feeling of friendship between you and the rest of a team is brilliant. I've even toured in France and other countries with the Welsh team. It's a shame it is not shown on television more, but women's sports are rarely shown.'

a) Which sex is usually associated with playing netball? (1)

b) Using the item, outline and explain one social reason why the writer likes to play netball. (2)

c) Identify and explain one social value that the writer has learned from sport. (2)

d) Suggest and explain one reason why traditional female sport tends not to be seen on television as much as traditional masculine sport. (2)

e) Using the passage, identify and explain one way in which sport can socialise people into a sense of national or ethnic identity. (3)

Key terms

Values – beliefs that people in a culture share.

Replica – imitation of the real thing.

Supporter – someone who enjoys watching sport or following a team or sports personality.

Role model – people that children admire and copy.

Stretch and challenge

What would happen if football was banned in the UK?

Personal research idea

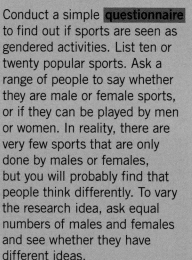

Conduct a simple questionnaire to find out if sports are seen as gendered activities. List ten or twenty popular sports. Ask a range of people to say whether they are male or female sports, or if they can be played by men or women. In reality, there are very few sports that are only done by males or females, but you will probably find that people think differently. To vary the research idea, ask equal numbers of males and females and see whether they have different ideas.

Compulsory core

Topic 17: How is work an agency of socialisation?

What am I going to learn?

- **One of the most important agencies of socialisation for adults is work**

Socialisation is not just a process that affects children. Everyone requires socialisation in any new situation they may find themselves in. One of the most important agencies of secondary formal socialisation for adults is work. They have to learn a completely new way of behaving to fit into the workplace.

How are adults socialised by work?

Most people have to learn an entirely new way of behaving at work. This does not just involve things such as good time-keeping or learning dress codes. It can involve learning workplace culture.

Employers want employees to behave in a certain way in work. They should work hard and be polite. Shop owners would go out of business if their staff were rude to customers. Some employers even give workers certain conversations to learn so that in a burger bar, you may be told to 'Have a nice day!'. Many adults are required to wear either a uniform or a special style of clothing to work. Teachers do not wear uniforms, but they usually dress smartly because that is part of their expected role.

Resocialisation

The process of being trained for an entirely new social situation is known as **resocialisation**. People may actually have to un-learn some ways of behaving and replace them with new ways of acting. For example, new teachers have to learn the rules of behaving as teachers, whereas before, they were students.

What sort of attitudes, personality and skills would an employer in a supermarket want the employees to have?

Personal research idea

Conduct some unstructured interviews. Talk to different people about their jobs and how they feel about their work. Ask them what things people need to learn to survive in their jobs. Ask open questions that cannot be answered with simple 'yes' or 'no' answers.

Across the generations

Talk to someone who is older than yourself about how work has changed over the past twenty years or so. Find out about whether jobs are easier or harder to find. Think about whether employers can be too controlling or not. You might want to think about reasons why people want to have jobs and how they have to behave when they are at work.

Professionalism

A **profession** is a job that requires special training. For example, nurses belong to a profession because they have to learn special skills for their work. They have to go on university courses and be trained by other nurses who show them how to behave and act as a good nurse should. They do not just learn about how to help sick people, they learn how to act in the role of a professional nurse.

Code of conduct

Many jobs have a **code of conduct**. This sets out the rules for how to act. If people have a code of conduct, they do not have to think about how to act or make decisions. They know what to do and behave correctly.

Key terms

Resocialisation – when people have to learn a new set of rules for a new situation and change their normal way of behaving.

Profession – a job that requires special training.

Code of conduct – formal set of rules for how to behave in a particular situation.

Check your understanding

Complete the following sentences:

a) Work is an important secondary agency of ••• for adults.
b) People need to learn ••• to fit in with other workers.
c) Many employers insist on ••• so that employees will look smart and promote the company.
d) Some employers give employees set things to say, such as •••.
e) A set of rules for how to act in a formal situation is known as a •••.
f) A ••• is a job that requires skills and training to do.
g) The process of being trained for an entirely new situation is •••.

Stretch and challenge

Design a job advertisement for someone to be your new Headteacher. Be clear what kind of person you would like in the post and how you would like that person to act when she or he is in the job.

If you were part of the interview panel, what kinds of questions would you ask to make sure that you got the best person for the job of being your Headteacher?

Exam practice

When you start a new job as a waiter or waitress, you will need to learn some basic rules. You need to know how to do the job, what tables you look after and where things are. You may be told what to say to customers. You may need to look smart and wear certain clothing or a uniform. You may even be told to smile and act happy even when you are tired or cross and people are grumpy and rude to you. You will have to work hard and your feet will hurt but, if you like people, it is a good job to do.

a) What do waiters and waitresses need to know to do their jobs? (1)
b) Using the item, identify and explain one reason why employers want people to wear a uniform to work. (2)
c) Identify and explain one norm for waiters and waitresses in work. (2)
d) Suggest and explain one way in which people learn the rules for their workplace. (2)
e) Outline and fully explain the meaning of the term resocialisation. (3)

Over to you

What kind of work do you want when you are older? How might you have to change your appearance, behaviour and personality to fit into that kind of job?

Compulsory core

Topic 18: How do your peer group work as an agency of socialisation?

What am I going to learn?

- **We are highly influenced by people around us who are of the same age and a similar background**

A peer group refers to people who are like ourselves in terms of culture, age and background. We do not have to like them and they do not need to be our friends, though we tend to choose friends who are like ourselves. The peer group are people like us and they can be a big influence in our lives.

Over to you

Write an advice letter or web page article for a parent who is worried that her teenage child is getting into trouble with a bad lot of friends.

Across the generations

Talk to someone who is older than yourself about how life as a teenager may have changed over the past twenty years or so. Find out about fashions, music, style and social attitudes. Is it more or less fun to be a teenager now than in the past?

How are we affected by our peer group?

When children are very small, the most influential people in their lives are probably the people who bring them up. Their first teachers will also be influential. People do not remain children forever and they have to leave their family homes and survive on their own as adults in their own right. Part of the process of learning how to do this is by learning how to get along with people of their own age, these are their **peer groups**.

Peer groups and young children

Many people first meet others of the same age in nurseries and playgroups. Psychologists have learned that very small children do not naturally play with each other. They have to learn this skill. Many children are often quite selfish till the age of about eight, and they have to learn to consider the feelings of others. They have to learn to play in groups. Parents may encourage children to learn this skill by taking them to activities such as theatre or sports groups.

Peer groups and older children

Many older children seem to have a strong need to be accepted by their peer group. They will do this by imitating the fashions and sharing ideas. Groups often feel closer if they keep other people out, so **adolescent** peer groups adopt norms, language and fashions that older people cannot join in. Sometimes the effect of this is that they reject or even bully people who are different in some way.

The process of peer pressure
How does being part of a group improve our self-confidence and self-esteem?

People want approval from those around them	People copy friends and peers to feel part of the group	They may behave in a particular way to fit in with peers	People who do not behave like others feel left out

Peer group pressure

Peer group pressure can be positive and help people do well but sometimes young people are so anxious to feel part of the group that they will do things that are unhealthy or which could cause them harm. They feel pressured by others of the same age to fit in and so do things such as taking drugs or smoking so they feel part of the group. They may misbehave in school so others will admire them.

Check your understanding

Match the beginnings and ends of these sentences:

a) A peer group is a group of helps people to do well and makes people feel very good

b) Peer groups are an important part of feel a need to fit in with others like themselves

c) Small children are taught to fit in with their peer groups encourage people to do risky or dangerous things

d) Peer pressure is when people secondary socialisation

e) Positive peer pressure as a normal part of growing up and away from their families

f) Negative peer pressure can group of people with similar attitudes and ideas that are different from most people in society

g) A subculture is a people of similar age and culture to us

h) People turn to peer groups by being taken to playgroups and schools

Exam practice

Positive peer group pressure will consist of being supportive and helpful to others. People have fun with friends and may make relationships that last their entire lives. However, **negative peer group pressure** may happen when young people put each other down. Examples of this in school may be when they discourage others from learning, disrupt lessons and perhaps form anti-school attitudes. Negative peer group pressure is when people do not consider the effects of what they are doing and saying. This means that people feel pressured to do things by the group that they would not do on their own.

a) What is a peer group ? (1)

b) Suggest one place where people learn to get on with their peer groups. (1)

c) Identify and explain one reason why peer groups are an important part of socialisation. (2)

d) Using the passage, identify and explain the meaning of the term negative peer group pressure. (2)

e) What is an **anti-school subculture**? (1)

f) Outline and fully explain one reason why young people are more likely to experience negative peer group pressure than are older people. (3)

Key terms

Peer group – people of similar age and background.

Adolescent – teenager, stage between childhood and adulthood.

Positive peer group pressure – people support each other through encouragement and kindness.

Negative peer group pressure – people encourage each other to do dangerous or silly things.

Anti-school subculture – peer group that discourages learning and disrupts education for others.

Stretch and challenge

List ten ways in which peer group pressure can be a positive influence in the lives of young people.

websites

tinyurl.com/cvbzfmq

Look at the story of Sophie Lancaster who experienced extreme violence from her peer group for being a Goth.

Compulsory core

Topic 19: What happens to unsocialised children?

What am I going to learn?

- **To understand that if children are not socialised, they can never behave as fully normal human beings**

Sometimes, for one reason or another, children are not properly socialised. Some have been reared with animals such as dogs. Others have been completely neglected by their parents. Such children are known as feral children, or wild children. They rarely grow up behaving as normal human beings and cannot fit properly into society.

Personal research idea

Conduct some secondary research by looking at what other people have found out about feral children. Google the term, or use YouTube to find out more. Write out the story of one such child, but do not copy and paste, use your own words and ideas to develop the point. What does the study of these children tell you about the importance of early socialisation of children?

Interesting fact

There is a legend (story) that the city of Rome, capital of Italy, was built by twin brothers, Romulus and Remus. They had been abandoned as babies and grew on the milk of a wolf. This was said to make them powerful and aggressive. Romulus killed his brother, Remus, and went on to name the new city after himself. The image of the wolf feeding the babies milk is found all over Rome today and many statues of it are very ancient.

What are feral children?

Something that is feral is **wild** or untamed. A **feral child** is a human being who has never been **socialised** properly. Scientists are very interested in feral children because they help us to understand the **nature/nurture debate**. If nature was the most important influence on behaviour, then these children would be quite normal. However, feral children do not behave like normal children. Fortunately, these cases are quite rare, but there are examples of such children.

Genie

One of the most famous feral children was Genie. Genie lived in California, and was found in the 1970s. She was severely neglected by her father and mother. They tied her to a potty chair by day and in a caged cot at night. She never saw anyone, never played and hardly saw daylight. No one spoke to her. She was a teenager when she was found. Physically, she grew well, but although she learned to say words, she was not able to put them together to make sense or talk.

Oxana Malaya

Oxana Malaya is a more recent case who was found in Russia. Her parents ignored her and left her with the family dogs in a kennel. Oxana learned from the dogs and when she was found was more like a dog than a human child. Oxana still finds human contact difficult and will behave in a dog-like fashion, barking and growling. She can be seen on YouTube clips.

Could the twins, Romulus and Remus, who were said to have been brought up by a wolf, really have grown up to be normal people in your view? How likely is the story of Romulus and Remus to be true?

The wolf girls of Midnapore

These two girls were found in a wolf's den in India in 1920. They were aged about 1 and 8. They were found by a Reverend Joseph Singh who named them Amala and Kamala. When they were found they would not wear clothes, and would only eat raw meat. They slept in the day but woke at night and howled like wolves. They never really recovered from their upbringing, and sadly they both died.

Check your understanding

Use the terms in the box to help you answer the questions:

> Nature
> Nurture
> Feral child
> Socialisation
> Genie
> Speech

a) What term refers to the process of learning how to behave in the expected way for your culture?

b) What term refers to a child who has not experienced socialisation?

c) Which word is the name of a child who experienced neglect in California in the late 1960s?

d) What important language skill do feral children rarely develop?

e) What term refers to the theory that children act as they do naturally?

f) What term refers to the theory that says children have to learn social roles?

Exam practice

Isabel Quaresma, also known as the chicken girl of Portugal, was found living with the family chickens in 1980. She was aged about 9, but had been brought up with the chickens all her life. Her mother had left her with the birds and fed her on scraps of bread and food rubbish. Neighbours knew about the child, but in Portugal it is considered bad to report on people and so this had been the child's life for eight years. Isabel was undersized and could not walk when she was found. She flapped her arms to communicate. Now, in her early forties, she can walk and understand simple requests. She cannot speak at all.

a) Where was Isabel found? (1)

b) Using the passage, identify one way Isabel was different from normal nine-year-olds. (1)

c) Using an example, explain the term feral child. (2)

d) Suggest and explain one reason why Isabel cannot talk to people. (2)

e) What does the case of Isabel teach us about the nature/nurture debate? (4)

Key terms

Feral child – wild or unsocialised child.

Wild child – feral or unsocialised child.

Socialisation – the process of learning the rules of a culture.

Nature theory – the idea that we act as we do because we are born that way.

Nurture theory – the idea that we act as we do because we are taught how to behave by others.

Stretch and challenge

If you discovered a feral child, how would you try and make the child more human-like? How successful do you think you would be?

Over to you

Look up the story of Genie, there is a lot about her on the Internet. Find out about her life; it is very sad. There are lots of video clips on the Internet of her as a child and stories from scientists who studied her development.

Families

Topic 1: What is a family?

What am I going to learn?

- **All cultures have some form of family, so families are a cultural universal**

Human beings seem to be group animals. They like to be with other people. The most basic unit of human group is the family and all cultures seem to have some form of family unit. Not all cultures or experiences of family are the same, however.

Over to you

How would you define a family for a dictionary? Think carefully about this as it is not as easy as you may think. If your favourite brother went to live in Australia, would you still be family? If you have never met your grandparents, are you family? Are your parents' best friends whom you see most days, family?

Personal research idea

Interview people in your class who are willing to share information about their families. What do they like about being part of their families? What do they find difficult about their families? As this is a sensitive topic, you should make sure that your questions are ethical. People should be asked if they are willing to take part and information should be kept anonymous. What do you learn from your questions?

Families often get together to mark special occasions such as religious festivals or family celebrations such as weddings or birthdays. Why do they do this?

Families

Families are groups of people who are related to each other through blood ties, adoption, choice or marriage. People may feel very strong ties to families, even if they do not always like all of their family members. When studying families in sociology, we look at how families organise themselves, that is known as **family structure**. We look at how people feel about belonging to a family, that is known as **kinship**. We also look at how many people feel about the idea of families and that is known as **family ideology**.

Socialisation

Families are very important to the study of sociology because families are an agency of socialisation of children. They are also part of the socialisation of adults, too. Adults in families are expected to behave in certain ways and have special roles so they, too, are being socialised. Children may even affect their parents' behaviour, so parents have to be careful how they act in front of their children. For example, they may choose not to smoke in the same room in order to protect their children's health. Families are a huge influence on each other, possibly more than we realise.

Kinship

How we feel about families is personal. Some people may like their families, but other families may actually be bad for their members. Despite that, we feel responsible for our family and have a sense of duty to these people. That feeling is known as kinship. In some families, there are just a few people with whom a person may have a sense of kinship. People may have family members they do not speak to. In many cultures, kinship is so important that family pride is seen as more important than individual feelings. Anyone who is a relation can claim kinship and it is family duty to look after them.

Cultural universal

Family is a **cultural universal**. This means that some form of family structure is found in all societies, though who is considered family may vary considerably.

Check your understanding

Match the words to their meanings:

a) Cultural universals	the way of life of a group of people
b) Family structure	ideas of what a 'proper' family should be like
c) Kinship	a group of people related by blood, marriage or adoption
d) Family ideology	social behaviours that can be found in all cultures
e) Norm	how people organise themselves as family
f) Socialisation	normal and expected way to behave
g) Primary socialisation	sense of duty and feelings to family members
h) Canalisation	the process of learning the rules of a culture
i) Family	children are channelled into certain behaviours and activities by parents and other adults
j) Culture	being taught how to behave by your family

Exam practice

When Emily's grandmother died, large numbers of people came to the funeral service. Emily met relations that she had not seen for many years, since she was a small child, in fact. One of her uncles travelled from Australia, bringing his wife and children, her cousins, whom she met for the first time. She was very surprised to see that one of her cousins looked just like her youngest brother, though he sounded different. She spent a lot of time talking about family history with her uncle and found out a lot about her own parents that she did not know before.

a) Using the item, name one family occasion when families may get together. (1)
b) Suggest two ways in which you can become a member of a family. (2)
c) Using examples, explain the meaning of the term family. (2)
d) Explain the meaning of the term kinship, using an example. (2)
e) Outline and briefly explain one reason why most societies have some form of family structure. (3)

Key terms

Family – a group of people related by blood, marriage or adoption.

Family structure – how people organise themselves as family.

Kinship – sense of duty and feelings to family members.

Family ideology – ideas of what a 'proper' family should be like.

Cultural universals – social behaviours that can be found in all cultures.

Stretch and challenge

What would the world be like if there were no families and all children were brought up in special groups by trained nurses and teachers?

Interesting fact

In the early days of the Israeli state, many people joined communities known as kibbutz. These were farming communities, but believed in community values. Children were looked after by the community and not by their parents. This freed mothers for work on the land. Often children would sleep away from their parents in special dormitories. As children got older, they would see less of their parents.

Topic 2: What cultural variations exist in families?

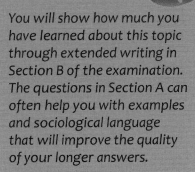

What am I going to learn?

- **All cultures have family structures and traditions but these vary significantly from society to society**

Many people tend to assume, quite wrongly, that what is normal for their culture is normal for all cultures. However, study shows that cultures vary considerably in how they organise families into structures, who they consider to be family and how important family is in their lives.

Grade boost

You will show how much you have learned about this topic through extended writing in Section B of the examination. The questions in Section A can often help you with examples and sociological language that will improve the quality of your longer answers.

Jacob Zuma

Famous people

In 2010, Jacob Zuma, then president of South Africa and a powerful man, got married for the fifth time to Thobeka Madiba. He already had two other wives with him. One wife had previously died and another had divorced him. Zuma is a member of the Zulu tribe and multiple marriage is common among Zulu people. Zuma had nineteen children at the time and was also engaged to another woman when he got married to Madiba.

Variations in family around the world

Families are very different all around the world. Some cultures practise **polygamy**, which is marriage to more than one partner at a time. Attitudes to **divorce** differ as well, with some cultures seeing it as normal, whereas others insist on marriage for life. Which member of the family makes the important decisions can vary, as in lots of cultures, men control family life (**patriarchy**) whereas in others, mothers are in control (**matriarchy**).

Attitudes towards family life

In **collectivist cultures**, which see communities as more important that individuals, family life is a serious matter. Many British Asian families, for example, believe in **izzat**, which is a form of family honour and reputation that must be protected. Members of families will put family needs before their own and marriage is seen as uniting two families. Some collectivist cultures practise **arranged marriage**, and it is a very common practice around the world.

In **individualist cultures** such as Britain, individual needs are seen as important so wider family is less important. Kinship is not so strong. People usually choose their own marriage partners. They even choose which family members they will keep in contact with.

Polygamy

Polygamous marriages involve a number of people; there may be a number of husbands or wives. In Britain, polygamy is illegal and people can go to prison. We practise **monogamy** and only marry one person at a time. In some African cultures, men

Is the traditional British pattern of one partner at a time, chosen by the couple themselves actually the best way of organising a family? Why do other cultures sometimes have different ideas of a perfect family?

may have many wives. The practice probably originated in the man taking a second wife to help his first wife. It sometimes developed as a way of ensuring all women were cared for and to increase the number of children a man could have.

The roles of men and women

In many cultures, men dominate women in the home. Looking after the home and children is seen as a female task. For example, traditionally in Korean culture, men never set foot in the kitchen. However, in Western cultures, men and women are usually expected to have more equal roles in the home.

Check your understanding

Use the words in the box to answer the questions:

Patriarchy	Arranged marriage	Polygamy
	Collectivist cultures	Monogamy

a) What term means marriage to more than one partner?

b) What term means marriage to only one partner at a time?

c) What term means that males control family life?

d) What term refers to a culture where people believe community life is more important than individual wants and needs?

e) What term refers to a situation where marriage partners are selected by someone who is trusted, such as a parent or a matchmaker?

Exam practice

Many cultures practise arranged marriage, including Indians, Pakistanis, Japanese and Jewish people. Until recently, royal families in Europe arranged marriage for their children. Introductions in arranged marriage can be via families, matchmakers or even Internet agencies. Robert Epstein, an American researcher, has interviewed couples in arranged marriage to assess their feelings towards each other. He says that people in arranged marriages are more likely to commit to each other for life, whereas people in Europe and the USA have relationships that are much less strong. He claims people in the USA base marriage on feelings of physical attraction, but arranged marriages are more careful, with people thinking about whether they are mentally and socially matched for each other.

a) Using the item, which researcher studied arranged marriages? (1)

b) Explain the meaning of the term arranged marriage. (2)

c) Name two cultures which practise arranged marriage. (1)

d) Fully explain reasons why arranged marriages are said to be successful. (2)

e) Explain the meaning of the term polygamy, using an example. (2)

f) Explain the meaning of the term monogamy, using an example. (2)

Key terms

Polygamy – marriage to more than one partner at a time.

Divorce – legal ending of a marriage.

Patriarohy – males control family life.

Matriarchy – females control family life.

Collectivist cultures – people believe community life is more important than individual wants and needs.

Izzat – Asian term meaning family pride.

Arranged marriage – marriage partners are selected by someone who is trusted, such as a parent or a matchmaker.

Individualist cultures – people expect to put their own needs before those of others around them.

Monogamy – marriage to only one partner at a time.

Stretch and challenge

Make five arguments for more than one marriage partner at one time and five arguments against more than one marriage partner at one time.

Topic 3: What is a nuclear family?

What am I going to learn?

● **The most common kind of family is the nuclear family; many people also believe it is the best kind of family**

A nuclear family is a term for a family structure that consists of a man, a woman and their children. This type of family is also sometimes known as a cereal packet family because it is used in advertising images. It is the most common family type in much of Europe and the USA, but some sociologists and politicians have also said it is the best family type.

Over to you

Find examples and images of nuclear families in television programmes, magazines and books.

Interesting fact

Richard Berthoud, a university professor, has found out that nuclear families are more common among people from Asian backgrounds. Asian men and women are more likely to be married with children and the divorce rate is very low compared with White and African-Caribbean families. Women from Asian families are more likely to stay at home to look after children than women from other backgrounds, though this pattern is changing as women get qualifications and take on work.

Nuclear families

The **nuclear family** consists of a **heterosexual** couple and their children. This family structure is seen by some sociologists as better for society and for individuals than any other family type. However, not every sociologist agrees on this point.

In the 1940s, George Murdock said that all societies have nuclear families, even if there are other relatives in families. In the 1950s, Talcott Parsons said that a nuclear family is essential for the proper socialisation of children and of parents.

Is the traditional nuclear family the best way for parents to bring up their children?

However, this has been questioned by other writers who say that many different types of families exist and are normal. **Feminists**, who are writers who support women's rights, say that the basic family is actually a mother and a child. They say that other types of family are perfectly good if everyone is supported. They also say that families can be very dangerous places for some people, especially if they have an abusive partner or parent.

Nuclear family and modern politics in Britain

Conservatives generally support what they call family values. These usually consist of the following ideas:

● A nuclear family is best for everyone.

● A working father should support his children economically.

● The mother should look after and care for children, old people and those who are ill.

● Other forms of family are not as good as a nuclear family.

David Cameron, a **Conservative** who became Prime Minister in 2010, has said that he wanted to encourage people to marry because it was good for children. He views family breakdown as a problem for society. Other Conservatives have said that it is important for children to be brought up by both a mother and a father.

Extended families

In some parts of Britain, extended families are common. The extended family may consist of wider family who have close or daily family contact with the nuclear family. Grandparents or brothers and sisters may live close and share family life.

Check your understanding

Match the beginnings and ends of these sentences:

a) A nuclear family consists of a married couple and   nuclear families

b) An extended family consists of a nuclear family   it doesn't matter about family structure if there is love and care for children

c) George Murdock said that all   because it is better for children

d) Some people believe nuclear families are the best kind of family   and other relatives who live close by or with the nuclear family

e) Talcott Parsons said that a nuclear family is   societies have nuclear families

f) Feminists and other sociologists say   essential for the proper socialisation of children and of parents

g) Many politicians such as David Cameron support   their children

Exam practice

Traditional family values often refer to morality, religion and a way of life that recognises right from wrong. Children who are not in nuclear families are more likely to be linked to crime, violent and anti-social behaviour, and addictions to drugs, smoking and alcohol; children and young adults from broken families are also more likely to have sex at an early age, drop out of full-time education and receive prison sentences.

a) Explain the meaning of the term nuclear family. (1)

b) Use the item to describe one traditional family value. (2)

c) Identify two problems that the writer thinks have been caused by children who are not part of nuclear families. (2)

d) Using sociological knowledge, name one political party that supports the nuclear family. (1)

e) Explain one situation in which a nuclear family can be a dangerous place for people, especially women or children. (2)

f) Outline and explain the meaning of the term extended family. (2)

Key terms

Cereal packet family – another term for a nuclear family.

Nuclear family – a family consisting of a man, a woman and their children.

Heterosexual – sexually attracted to people of the opposite sex.

Feminists – people who think that men and women should be equal in society.

Conservative Party – a political party that has traditional values.

Stretch and challenge

Watch soap operas and comedies on television. Identify what kinds of family types are portrayed.

Extended writing

Discuss whether nuclear families are the best kind of families for children to live in. (20)

Over to you

Think of five advantages and five disadvantages of living in a traditional nuclear family.

Topic 4: How have families changed since the 1950s?

What am I going to learn?

● **To describe how families have changed over the years**

Families, like society itself, change with every new generation of people who are born. Norms and values do not remain the same. Recent changes in family structure seem to have happened very quickly and this has had an effect on society, just as changes in society have had an effect on families.

Across the generations

Talk to someone who is much older than yourself about changes to family structure and family life since they were young. Ask if they feel all of the changes that have taken place are a good thing for society and for individuals.

What makes a good family in your view?

Extended writing

Describe how family structures have changed in Britain since the 1950s. (10)

Guidance: List things that have changed; for example, you could say that in 1950s Britain, people had larger families but now fewer children are born. Do not give reasons for change, the question is asking you to list changes so you need to say what Britain was once like and what it is like now.

Describing family change

Not all families would fit the patterns described but many would have done.

1950s families

A **household** is a group of people who share a house. In the 1950s, most households would have been a family. Most families would have been nuclear families or extended families. Poorer people usually started married life living with their parents. Women married earlier than they do now, and tended to have more children. They started their families at a younger age. Women did not generally have good jobs outside the home, though they may have been in low-paid jobs. Divorce, sex or children outside marriage would have been seen as very shocking. **Contraception** was not easily available to women.

1970s families

Ideas about family life were changing very rapidly. Divorce, sex and children outside marriage were still not generally acceptable but more common. More women were taking jobs outside the home so they began to delay having children or went to work when the children were grown up. Men and women were experimenting with new ways of living in families.

Modern families

There is probably no such thing as a 'typical family' any more. There are many ways of living. People have freedom in how to organise their lives so we now have people who live together without marriage (or **cohabit**). Others choose to remain single or take partners of the same sex. It is acceptable to have children without a partner. Contraception is in the hands of women and the numbers of children being born are falling. Fewer people marry even though they have children together. There is little shame in having children out of marriage, except perhaps for very young mothers. People can choose not to stay in unhappy relationships if they wish. Divorce is common and large numbers of children are being brought up in single parent families. Nevertheless, many people still live in nuclear families even if there are children from more than one relationship.

Key terms

Household – group of people who live in one house.

Contraception – birth control methods to prevent unwanted children.

Cohabitation – living together without marrying.

Beanpole family – people have more contact with grandparents and great grandparents, but fewer brothers, sisters and cousins.

Check your understanding

Fill in the missing words from the sentences:

a) There is probably no such thing as a ••• in modern Britain.

b) It is now seen as more acceptable for people to ••• without marrying.

c) A gay marriage or Civil Partnership is when two people of the ••• live together and form a couple.

d) The number of children being born is •••.

e) The legal ending of a marriage in a ••• is more common.

f) People have ••• in what sort of family life or structure they wish to live in.

Stretch and challenge

What would Britain be like if divorce were made illegal and people had to stay together in marriages?

Exam practice

Julia Brannen is a sociologist who has studied family structures in modern Britain. She says that although family structures have changed, people still feel a sense of kinship with relatives, so grandparents may support a lone mother with child care. She says that people have fewer contacts with cousins, but because people live longer, they are more likely to have grandparents and great-grandparents still alive and healthy. She describes this as a **beanpole family**.

a) Who conducted the research into changing family structure described in the item? (1)

b) Explain the meaning of the term household. (1)

c) Use the item to explain the meaning of beanpole family. (2)

d) Fully explain the meaning of kinship. (2)

e) Identify and describe two changes that have taken place in families since the 1950s. (4)

Grade boost

When you are asked a question about changes since a certain date, be careful not to write about things that happened before that date because you cannot have marks for those points. In the WJEC examination, you are not expected to write about things that happened before World War Two ended in 1945. Generally it is better to know about recent things.

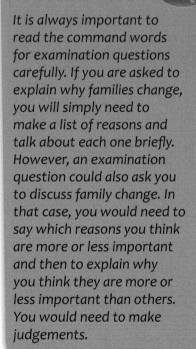

Topic 5: Why have families changed since the 1950s?

What am I going to learn?

● **To understand why family structures have changed since the 1950s**

What is seen as a normal family now may be different from the 1950s. There has been a shift from nuclear families to a wider variety of family types. There are many reasons to explain this social change, these have all acted together to make what we see as normal family life different from 60 years ago.

Grade boost

It is always important to read the command words for examination questions carefully. If you are asked to explain why families change, you will simply need to make a list of reasons and talk about each one briefly. However, an examination question could also ask you to discuss family change. In that case, you would need to say which reasons you think are more or less important and then to explain why you think they are more or less important than others. You would need to make judgements.

Over to you

What do you think a typical family in Britain will be like in 50 years' time? What is the future of family life?

Reasons for family change

There are many reasons why families have changed over the years. It is possible that some reasons are more important than others.

Changing norms and values

Over the years, people have developed different ideas about families. It is not seen as unusual for people to live together before marriage, or even to have children outside marriage. **Homosexuality** is more accepted, so same sex couples can form relationships and even have children together. In the past women were expected to get married. On marriage, they were expected to give up work and stay at home to be looked after by a husband. Now men and women expect to be more equal.

Technological change

Until the 1960s, couples generally only used contraception if the man was willing. The first contraception that women controlled was the pill. This meant women had the freedom to choose when to have children. Families became smaller and women could have sex outside marriage if they chose to. Medical technology also means that more people live into extreme old age.

Secularisation

For many people, if not everyone, religious ideas are less important. The Christian religion teaches people that marriage is sacred and that divorce is a bad thing. If people are not religious, then they are less likely to marry before having sex and also more likely to have a divorce.

Gender attitudes

Feminism is the belief that men and women should be equal partners in society. In the 1970s, more women became feminist and began to challenge traditional ideas that they stay in the home or that men were in charge of society. More of them got jobs for themselves and no longer had to rely on their husbands to give them money. It also meant that they could divorce if they were unhappy, because they could afford to live on their own. They no longer had to tolerate **domestic abuse** if they chose not to.

Check your understanding

Match the beginnings and ends of these sentences:

a) There are many reasons for changes that have which is where organised religion is less important in people's lives

b) One reason for family change is secularisation have sexual relationships before marriage

c) In the 1970s, many feminists began to challenge and women expect to be more equal in families

d) As contraception became easier for women to use, so the idea that men should be in control of society

e) One norm that has changed in British society is the idea that people should not taken place in family structure

f) In modern society, men family size began to fall

Key terms

Homosexual – sexually attracted to people of the same sex.

Secularisation – religion is less important in people's lives than it once was.

Domestic abuse – controlling or violent behaviour in the home.

Illegal – against the law.

Stretch and challenge

Create a mind map to explain reasons for family change. Add ideas of your own. Use images and pictures to help you understand the key points.

Exam practice

As social norms and values have changed over time, so have laws. Many laws affecting family life have changed over the past 60 years. For example, divorce is now much easier to arrange than it was in the 1950s. Another law that has changed family life is the abortion law. Before 1967, if women wanted to end a pregnancy, they would have to break the law. Many women died from unsafe **illegal** abortions. Now, women can choose whether to continue with a pregnancy. Men who are not married have more rights over their children than they once did; however, they do not have the same rights as married fathers.

a) Using the item, explain why laws governing family life have changed. (2)

b) Describe one change to family law since the 1950s and explain how it has affected family structure. (2)

c) With an example drawn from family life, explain the meaning of the term norm. (2)

d) Fully explain the reason for one change that has taken place in family structure since the 1950s. (4)

Interesting facts

Family-related laws change frequently. For example, in 1886, homosexuality between men was made illegal in Britain. Many men were sent to prison, including the famous writer, Oscar Wilde. It was not till 1967 that the law was changed to allow gay men some freedom to express themselves.

In 2002, homosexual couples were given the right to adopt children. In 2004, homosexual couples were given the right to have civil partnerships, which are similar to, but not actually, marriage.

Topic 6: What types of family and household structure are developing in modern Britain?

What am I going to learn?

● As people have more choice in how to organise their family lives, fewer people are choosing to live in traditional nuclear families

Family structures are changing as fewer people are choosing to form nuclear families, or if they do, to stay in them for life. There are still many nuclear families, but new household and family forms are developing.

Famous people

Often celebrities set a trend that other people follow. Elton John is a well-known musician. He is in a civil partnership with David Furnish and they have a son Zachary who was born to a surrogate mother in 2010. The identity of the mother has not been revealed, but she has been paid for becoming pregnant with the child and she is a friend of their family. Sperm from both men was mixed to fertilise the egg; this process is not legal in the UK, but Zachary was born in the USA. It is thought that the surrogate mother did not provide the egg.

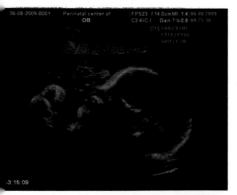

Does it matter if a child does not know who its biological parents are?

Newer family and household forms

Cohabitation

People are choosing to live together before marriage. Some couples never marry at all, but live together with their children. Partly this is due to changing social norms, but weddings are expensive.

Singlehood

More people are choosing to live alone. Many are old people living alone after a partner has died, but relationship breakdown and **divorce** leaves people choosing to remain single.

Couples and the childfree

People may live together in empty nest families where children have grown and left home. Increasingly, couples are actively choosing not to have children but to live freer, wealthier lives.

Gay families

Homosexual couples of both genders are forming and many choose to bring up children. This is happening more openly now that laws on gay adoption and civil partnerships have been changed.

Reconstituted families

These families appear to be nuclear families but there are children from more than one relationship. People who have been through previous broken relationships form new families with another partner. This is a very common family type.

Lone (or single) parenthood

This can be the result of divorce, separation, choice or death of a partner. The majority of single parents are women in their thirties as a result of relationship breakdown, and many go on to form new relationships, so single parenthood is a phase in their lives.

Apart/together

Some parents may be in a relationship, or have had children without being in a relationship but they remain in friendly contact. They choose to live in different homes and allow the children to move between their homes at various times.

Multiple parenting

The most basic principle of multiple parenting is adoption, where a child has birth parents, and social parents are those who bring the child up. However, technology allows **IVF**, sperm donation, surrogacy and egg donation so the birth parents and social parents are no longer so clearly understood.

Key terms

Cohabitation – sharing a home.

Singlehood – living alone.

Divorce – legal end of a marriage.

Gay family – both parents are of the same sex.

Reconstituted family – parents and children from more than one relationship form a family (sometimes known as blended family).

IVF – in vitro fertilisation – the child is conceived outside a human body.

Check your understanding

Match the word to the meaning:

a) Cohabitation
b) Apart/together
c) Singlehood
d) Lone parenthood
e) Blended family
f) Gay family

people bring up children alone
both parents are of the same biological sex
people live in separate homes and children move between them
people choose to remain without a partner
people live together
there are two parents but children from more than one relationship

Stretch and challenge

How would the world be different if both men and women could choose and were able to give birth to children?

Exam practice

In 1985, 11% of women over the age of 45 had not had children. By 2005, 18% of women reached 45 without having given birth. Researchers McAllister and Clarke have looked at why increasing numbers of women choose to be childfree. They said that many women felt single parenthood was not a good option, especially if they had a career. Children are expensive and demanding of time. People choose not to take on the financial risks of children. The main reason was that they took the decision to have children seriously and felt they did not want the responsibility for a child's life and getting parenthood wrong.

a) Using the item, what percentage of women over the age of 45 remained childless in 2005? (1)
b) What trend can be seen in women's behaviour with regard to parenthood? (1)
c) Explain the meaning of the term childfree. (1)
d) With an example drawn from family life, explain one financial reason why women choose not to have children. (2)
e) Fully explain the reason why many women prefer not to be single parents. (3)
f) In your own words, explain one reason why women in the past were not able to choose to be childfree. (2)

Over to you

Many people live in more than one family or household type as they go through their lives. Discuss how many family or household types your parents or carers have lived in throughout their lives.

Topic 7: Is single parenthood a problem for society?

What am I going to learn?

- **To understand social debates surrounding the rise in single parenthood**

There has been a rise in the number of children being raised in families with only one parent. A hundred years ago, the main cause of single parenthood was the early death of one parent. Now, there are many causes of single parenthood. There is also public debate because some people think that bringing children up with only one parent can cause problems for society.

Personal research idea

Interview people who are part of a lone parent family. For ethical reasons, you must ask if they are willing to be interviewed and tell them that they do not need to answer questions that make them feel uncomfortable. Ask them what problems lone parents experience.

Famous people

The author of Harry Potter, JK Rowling, became a single parent when her marriage broke down at about the time her daughter was born. She wrote Harry Potter in her spare time, for her own pleasure. She says that there is prejudice in society against single parents. Now she is rich, she donates money to single parent charities. She says single parents do not want to live on benefits, but want a chance to support their children properly. She says being a single parent is better than living in an unhappy relationship.

Do you agree with JK Rowling when she says that single parenthood is better than a bad relationship?

Lone parenthood

There are many ways that **lone parent** families can be formed: death of a partner, divorce, separation and choice.

Who are single parents?

There are around 2 million **single parents** in the UK. **Government statistics** show that about a quarter of families with dependent children have only one parent. Most of these people are women, and their average age is in their late 30s. Most of these parents were in settled relationships which broke down. Fewer than 2% of lone parents are under the age of 20. Approximately 6% of births are registered in the mother's name alone, and a further 10% are registered to parents who do not share an address.

Single parents and poverty

Children in single parent households are more likely to be poor than other children. About a quarter of children in lone parent households are in low income families. Even if the parent has a job, it is often part time or low paid so the families remain poor. Many single parents do not get money from their former partners. The average paid to single parents from former partners is below £40 per week.

Why do some people see lone parenthood as a problem?

Reports published for the government in 2008 showed that children of lone parents were more likely to experience behavioural problems. Rodgers and Pryor found that children from broken families did less well in school and were more likely to be ill. It is said by other studies that children from single parent families are more likely to use drugs and become criminals.

What is the debate?

Some people say that the problems faced by the children of lone parents are caused by the family background. They claim that children need to be in a nuclear family. An opposing view is that the problems are caused by children being poor, or parental conflict. A different point is that single parents often rely on benefits, so they cost the country a lot of money from taxpayers.

Key terms

Lone parent – single parent, family with only one adult.

Single parent – lone parent, family with only one adult.

Government statistics – information in the form of numbers, gathered by officials. Usually fairly accurate.

Check your understanding

Are the following statements true or false?

a) Most single parents are teenagers.

b) Single parents are caused by people not marrying.

c) The children of single parents will turn to crime.

d) Most single parents have jobs to support their families.

e) Unmarried parents are single parents.

Stretch and challenge

Should parents stay together in a bad relationship for the sake of the children? Make five points for and five against the question.

Exam practice

There are about 200,000 single fathers in the UK. A charity for single parents, Gingerbread, studied 115 single fathers. A quarter of the fathers questioned said that they had given up their jobs. Of those fathers in jobs, a quarter said that being a single parent had affected their careers negatively. Men were expected to work long hours or work away from home. The charity argued that people were not supportive of men who wanted to spend time with their children because being a single father is not seen as a norm. They called for family-friendly workplaces to help both men and women.

a) Name a charity for single parents. (1)

b) What is the meaning of the term single parent? (1)

c) How many single fathers are there in Britain? (1)

d) Which gender is more likely to be a single parent? (1)

e) Explain one way in which a man can become a single father. (2)

f) With an example drawn from family life, explain one reason men had to give up work if they became single fathers. (2)

g) Fully explain one reason why single parents often have less money to spend than two parent families. (3)

Over to you

Think about the following statement: the government should not give benefits to single parents. They should be encouraged to work for a living. What arguments can you make for and against this idea?

🔍 websites

tinyurl.com/d9ubt47

Look at the website of Gingerbread, a support and campaign group for single parents. They have a page which looks at negative stereotyping of single parents and tries to offer a more honest picture of what life is like for lone parents in the UK.

Topic 8: Why are there changing attitudes towards divorce?

What am I going to learn?

● **Over the years, there have been changes in divorce rates. Does this mean that marriage is less successful than it once was?**

Divorce is the legal end of a marriage. In the past, in Britain it was seen as a matter of deep shame to a family if someone had a divorce. The Christian religion believes that people should marry for life, so laws against divorce were very strict. However, divorce is more acceptable nowadays and more marriages end in divorce.

Over to you

Suggest reasons why it would be **unethical** for you to ask people about their experience of divorce.

Extended writing

Explain reasons why divorce rates have changed over the years. (10)

Guidance: You will need to write about social reasons for divorce and explain them. For example, if you write about the law, say that it has changed and then explain what impact the change has had on divorce rates. Write about 200 words.

Changes in divorce

Patterns of divorce

In 1970, just over a quarter of all marriages ended in divorce; however, divorce rates rose rapidly until 1994 when over 150,000 couples ended their marriages. This was a failure rate of 33% of marriages. The numbers of divorces have been getting lower since 1994, but probably not because fewer relationships are ending; it is because fewer people are getting married. Some people believe that high divorce rates mean that marriages are less happy now. We do not really know because people in the past may have been unhappy, but they could not divorce easily and so had to stay together.

Some people have parties and cakes to celebrate their divorces from their partners. What does this tell us about modern attitudes to divorce?

Legal changes to divorce

One reason why fewer couples divorced before the 1970s was that divorce was seen as shameful. It was expensive and difficult to obtain, so many people lived together in '**empty shell marriages**'. The law changed to make divorce easier in 1969, and more people divorced after that date. Other changes to the law since then have made it still easier.

Secularisation

Fewer people are religious, so they do not feel that they have to follow religious rules against divorce.

Changes to women's lives

In the past, women were expected to get married and have children. There were few options. Now women have jobs and careers. They do not have to be married if they do not want to be. They do not depend on their husbands for money. They are less likely to put up with a bad marriage. In most cases where the divorce was asked for by the wife, the reason was her husband's behaviour.

Changing norms and values

It is no longer seen as a matter of shame to be divorced. As more people experience divorce, perhaps as children, they are likely to have a divorce themselves if they are not happy. This has given rise to a pattern known as **serial monogamy**. People marry, divorce and remarry, sometimes many times.

Check your understanding

Match the beginnings and ends of these sentences:

a) Divorce is more common now than   been relaxed to make it easier

b) The laws controlling divorce have   it was in the 1950s

c) Divorce is   among people aged 40 and over

d) Attitudes towards divorce have changed as it is no longer   a distressing and stressful experience for most people

e) The divorce rate is highest   fewer people are getting married

f) Divorce rates appear to be falling because   seen as a matter of family shame

Exam practice

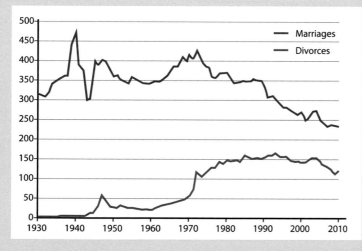

a) In what year was the number of marriages at its highest? (1)

b) What is the overall trend for the number of marriages since 1970? (1)

c) Approximately, how many divorces were there in 2005? (1)

d) Using your own knowledge and the graph, suggest one reason why divorce rate seems to be dropping in the late 2000s. (1)

e) Fully explain one reason why divorce rates are higher than they were in the 1950s. (3)

f) Fully explain one reason why marriage rates are lower than they were in the 1950s. (3)

Key terms

Empty shell marriages – people live together as a married couple but do not love each other.

Secularisation – religion is less important in people's lives than it once was.

Serial monogamy – marriage to more than one person, but only one at a time.

Stretch and challenge

What do you think are the effects of the increasing numbers of divorces on British society?

Grade boost

When talking about divorce under examination conditions, avoid giving personal reasons why people may choose to have a divorce, or making general claims about people having affairs. Concentrate on social reasons why divorce is more common now than in the past. The main point is that it is easier for unhappy people to separate now than it would have been in the past.

Families

Topic 9: Is the family under threat from social change?

What am I going to learn?

- **There is a debate in society about families: some people think that families are under threat and traditional nuclear families are dying out**

Those people who think that family structure is important are very worried because traditional nuclear families are not as common as they once were. On the other hand, people who think that family feeling is important say it does not matter who is in a family so long as the family relationships are good.

Over to you

Make a list of five suggestions to back up whether you think family life is dying out, and then make a list of five suggestions to back up the idea it is just change. What do you think about the topic, based on the evidence and ideas that you have collected together?

Across the generations

Ask people who are older than yourself if they think family life is better or worse than in the past. Ask them for the reasons that they have for their opinions. Make this an unstructured interview, and aim for a deep understanding of their viewpoint.

Changing families

Throughout the world, people are concerned that there is a movement away from traditional family forms, towards newer patterns of fewer children, more singlehood and a greater variety of family structures. This has been given the name of **post-familial** society. Some people say that families are dying out and it is a bad thing, others claim that families are changing and adapting to a new world and people have more choice.

Arguments used to say families are dying out

Some politicians from the **Conservative Party** say that the high divorce rate and the fact that fewer people are marrying is evidence that family life is not as good as in the past. They claim that people lack family values and are selfish. They say that children brought up in families with only one parent have worse lives and develop social problems. In the UK, nearly half of all children will have seen their parents' relationship come to an end. Unmarried couples are more likely to separate. In the USA, it is considered such a problem that Congress spends $150,000,000 a year promoting marriage and fatherhood. Church leaders such as the Pope and the Archbishop of Canterbury have both spoken out against gay marriage in 2012.

Are lone parents really a threat to society and to children brought up by them? What is your view?

Arguments used to say families are just changing

Anthony Giddens, a famous British sociologist, said that in the past, romantic love meant that once people had married, they were stuck with each other. Now, people choose to marry or cohabit and remain together. People can talk to each other about what makes them happy, so they put more work into relationships. Divorce and family relationship breakdown rates may be high, but most people form new relationships. Now, people are in **families of choice**, for example it is now possible for gay people to celebrate their relationships openly and to have children. **Feminist sociologists** say that traditional marriages are not good places for women or children who are often controlled by men.

Key terms

Post-familial – worldwide change from traditional family structures to new family forms.

Conservative Party – political party that supports traditional values and limited government control on people.

Families of choice – people may choose to have their deepest relationships with friends rather than family.

Feminist sociologists – believe that women and men should be equal in society.

Check your understanding

Match the words and meanings:

a) Gay marriage
b) Families of choice
c) Feminist sociologists
d) Singlehood
e) Fatherhood
f) Post-familial society

people choose to remain unmarried
worldwide trend where people are choosing not to form traditional family structures
men take an active role in the lives of their children
same sex couples live together as partners and have gone through a civil partnership ceremony
argue that women and men should be more equal in society
people choose who they consider as family

Stretch and challenge

Suggest ways that the government could encourage and support people to stay together. When you have made your list of ideas, go back again and look at them and see whether you think they would work.

Exam practice

David Cameron, the Conservative Prime Minister in 2012, said family breakdown is the chief problem in modern Britain. He said, 'children do better on the whole when mum and dad are there to bring them up'. However, Karen Woodall of the Centre of Separated Families said that family separation affects everyone, but if it is handled well, then the outcome for children does not need to be an issue.

a) What did David Cameron think is the chief problem in modern Britain? (1)
b) Suggest and explain one reason why David Cameron's opinion is very important to us. (2)
c) What does David Cameron feel is the best form of family? (1)
d) Identify and describe one new form of family. (2)
e) Explain the meaning of the term 'families of choice'. (2)
f) Suggest and explain one reason why feminists often reject traditional nuclear families. (2)

Grade boost

There is no one correct answer to this discussion in public life. The task for the sociologist is to examine the evidence carefully and then to put forward a point of view based on that. Are the arguments made on both sides of the discussion based on facts about society or opinions?

Topic 10: How are the roles of children in the family changing?

What am I going to learn?

- **To understand that the role and status of children in the family has changed**

Many years ago, there were far more children in families on average. Women had more babies. In addition, homes were different. Changes in society, family and in women's lives have meant that the experience of childhood has changed, too.

Over to you

Suggest one law that the government could make that would make childhood better for all children. Explain why you think your law is a good idea.

Extended writing

Describe two changes to childhood since the 1950s. (10)

Guidance: You will need to choose two particular changes. Focus on each one separately. Write about what things were like in the 1950s and then explain how they have changed nowadays. You do not need to say why they changed, but to write about how things are different. Add detail and sociological language. Write about 200 words.

Childhood

Childhood is that period in your life when you are dependent on your parents. In the 1950s, childhood lasted a much shorter time than now. Most children left school at 15 and were expected to start work and help support the family immediately. Now, people can depend on their parents beyond the time when they are legally **adults**.

Childhood in the 1950s

The average number of children in a family in the 1950s was 2.4. Mothers were generally younger when they started to have children and had more of them. Mothers would generally not have worked outside the home, except doing work such as cleaning or cooking. Homes were less well heated, they had fewer televisions, and no computers. Children often had fewer toys and spent more time outside playing with their friends as there was no room inside the home. Family discipline was often very harsh.

Childhood now

Sue Palmer, a writer, claims that modern children have a higher risk of mental health problems, obesity, limited opportunity for play and limited freedom. She calls this a **toxic childhood**. Parents control children excessively because of fears of **paedophiles** and stranger danger, but child **abduction** or murder is remarkably rare. This focus on the safety and care of children is known as being **child-centred**. As a result, children are required to stay in and play computer games rather than going to parks and playing ball games. They eat **processed foods** in the home as parents have limited time to cook. Children do not talk to adults as much as they should. They are pushed into an awareness of fashion and style and even sex well before the age at which they are ready to understand these things, and partly as a result of media pressure on them to buy things. The exam system is another form of pressure and it results in parents and schools pressurising children to do well rather than relax and enjoy learning for its own sake. However, this is seen as negative because children have more rights and more material goods than in the past.

Check your understanding

Complete the table by matching the following statements and putting them into the correct boxes:

Typical 1950s childhood	Modern childhood
Children lived in large families and had many brothers and sisters	Children tend to stay indoors and play computer games or they go to organised activities and clubs
Children left school at 15 and began work to support the family	Children live in a variety of family arrangements and may have parents who live separately
Children played outside in the street with each other because there were few cars	Children stay on in school and college for much longer as there is little work for young people
Children usually had two parents, a working father and a housewife mother	Children are protected by law from violence in the home and many parents disagree with smacking children
Children would experience harsh discipline in the home and hitting was very common	Children often live in small families with few brothers and sisters

Exam practice

Laws governing children in the family change regularly; the first such law was in 1889 to prevent children being beaten. By 1989, the Children Act gave every child protection from abuse, and took the view that children are usually best looked after in their own families. In 1999, the Protection of Children Act made strict laws ensuring that anyone with a history of harming children could not work in child care. In 2003, the first government minister for children was appointed.

a) When was the first law protecting children passed? (1)
b) Suggest and explain one reason why we need laws to protect children in the home. (2)
c) What does the Children Act consider to be the best place to bring up children? (1)
d) Identify and describe one change the lives of children since the 1950s. (2)
e) Explain the meaning of the term toxic childhood. (2)
f) Suggest one way in which the lives of children in the family have improved since the 1950s. (2)

Key terms

Child – legal term describing person under age of 18.

Childhood – period of dependency on parents.

Adult – legal term describing people over the age of 18.

Toxic childhood – toxic means poisonous, so toxic childhood means harmful or unpleasant childhood.

Paedophiles – have an inappropriate sexual interest in children.

Abduction – stealing a person and removing them from their families.

Child-centred – children are the focus of family life and concerns.

Processed foods – food that has been prepared in a factory, for example chicken nuggets, rather than made from fresh ingredients (cooked dinner).

Stretch and challenge

Compare childhood in the 21st century with childhood in the 1950s. You should use YouTube, the Internet, information from people older than you and books to gather information.

Topic 11: How have the lives of old people in families changed?

What am I going to learn?

- **To understand the role of older people in family life**

More people are living longer and healthier lives than ever before. In the 1970s, life expectancy was around 72 years, now it is closer to 80. As these are average figures, it means that many more people are living longer than that. This is having an impact on family life.

Interesting fact

Britain has an ageing population. Over 10 million people are over the age of 65 and by 2050, the number will probably be around 19 million people. By 2050, a quarter of the population will be over 65. The government is so worried about the cost of providing these people with pensions that the age for receiving the old age pension has risen and it may yet rise again!

Extended writing

Explain how increasing life expectancy of older people has affected families in Britain. (10)

Guidance: Make a list of four or five effects of increasing numbers of old people on families, for example: caring for children, supporting grandchildren, needing care and support. This will form your basic plan. You can then explain each one and offer examples, sociological language and facts.

Older people in families

Life expectancy

People are living longer for a variety of social reasons. Changes in people's lifestyles mean that they stay healthier into old age. Many single person households are elderly people who have lost a partner, or who have chosen not to remarry after divorce.

Positive effects of older people in families

Older people, particularly those still in their 60s or 70s, often provide care for grandchildren to allow their own children to go to work. When families break down, grandchildren often become the responsibility of grandparents. Increasing numbers of children are brought up by grandparents.

Often adult children in their 20s and 30s will return to the family home. This may happen if they have financial problems or a relationship breakdown. This situation is described as '**boomerang**'. Increasing numbers of adult children are part of the boomerang generation.

Grandparents are a source of family history and can pass on traditions as they may have more time than parents, particularly if they have retired. Grandparents are often a financial support for their families, they can provide money for education of grandchildren or to buy luxuries for the family.

Older people are living longer than ever before and in greater numbers. This is partly because they take more care of their health and fitness, and they eat more healthy foods.

Negative effects of older people in families

Approximately one in three people require support over the age of 80. This is for reasons of health, such as **dementia** or a physical illness. Care is usually provided by a family member such as a child, usually a daughter who is in her 50s or 60s. Sometimes these women also care for children or grandchildren. The term that is used for these women is the **sandwich generation** – they look after their children and grandchildren as well as their elderly parents.

Increasing numbers of older people are demanding divorce when they retire and find out that they have little in common with their partners and do not want to spend time with them.

Check your understanding

Fill in the missing words from the sentences:

a) Life expectancy for most people is around ••• years.

b) People who live over the age of 80 require ••• because they experience ill health and dementia.

c) People who look after their children and their parents are known as the ••• generation.

d) Adults over the age of 20 who live in the family home are known as the •••.

e) Grandparents are an important part of the lives of grandchildren and often provide child care if the mother has a •••.

f) Many single person ••• are elderly people who have lost a partner.

Exam practice

According to a variety of research studies on families in England, when mothers are studying or in work, then in most families grandparents provide the child care. Over 25% of families use grandparents as child carers, particularly in school holidays. Grandparents also step in for emergencies such as hospital visits or sick care. They are particularly important for support if the grandchild is disabled. In the USA, it has been shown that children with good relationships with grandparents are less likely to experience depression, particularly if the child is in a single parent family.

a) Explain one reason why people live longer now than in the past. (2)

b) What percentage of families uses grandparents for child care? (1)

c) Suggest and explain one reason why parents would like grandparents to be involved in child care. (2)

d) State one positive benefit for teenage children of having a good relationship with their grandparents. (1)

e) Explain the meaning of the term 'sandwich generation'. (2)

f) Explain the meaning of the term 'boomerang generation'. (2)

Key terms

Life expectancy – how long you can reasonably expect to live.

Boomerang – adult children return to the family home for financial or relationship reasons.

Dementia – range of diseases that affect the brain, particularly the ability to remember things in the short term.

Sandwich generation – people who care for their children, grandchildren and their parents at the same time.

Stretch and challenge

When you are 90, what do you think will be important to you in life?

Personal research idea

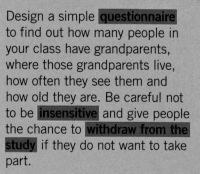

Design a simple questionnaire to find out how many people in your class have grandparents, where those grandparents live, how often they see them and how old they are. Be careful not to be insensitive and give people the chance to withdraw from the study if they do not want to take part.

Topic 12: What is the role of men in the family?

What am I going to learn?

- **Traditionally men were in control of families, but the role of men in the family has changed**

Families have been changing in structure; this has affected the roles of people in families. Men's roles in families now are generally different from how they would have been in the past. Many modern families do not even have an adult male living in the family home.

websites

www.wikihow.com/Be-a-Good-Father

This is a list of suggestions for how to be a good father.

Extended writing

Discuss how the roles of men in the family have changed since the 1950s. (20)

Guidance: Make a list of four or five changes in the role of men in the family. You can then explain each one and offer examples, sociological language and facts to show how the roles of men in the family have changed. However, a discussion question requires you to put an opposite point of view, so you might also want to consider if all men have changed. Perhaps men have not changed that much really.

The roles of men in families

In the 1950s, men and women had different roles in the family: these were known as **segregated conjugal roles**. Men were traditionally seen as the head of the household. The father would control the money because he earned it. He was the **breadwinner** for the family. He would discipline the children. Women would look after the men, cooking and cleaning for them. Men would not be expected to do housework; it was seen as a matter of shame.

Why have men's roles in families changed?

A number of things have affected the role of men in the family. Women now go to work and so men must help in the home. Women may earn more than men. There are fewer traditional male jobs in the workplace so some men stay at home. Changing norms and values mean it is seen as acceptable and positive for men to be caring and involved in bringing up children. Men can be involved in their children's lives as people generally do not work as long hours as they once did. Fathers are even encouraged to be at the birth of their babies.

The new man

This term is used to describe men who are not afraid to be in touch with their feminine side. New men help in the home and take on traditional female roles. They were first described by th sociologists Young and Wilmott in the 1960s.

House husbands

This term is used to describe men who stay at home to look after the family while women work outside the home.

Non-resident fathers

Fathers may be involved in their children's lives even if they do not live with the mother. They may still expect or wish to provide money, care and emotional support for their children.

Gay fathers

Gay fathers who share children often divide domestic work, and research shows that they can be effective parents.

Check your understanding

Complete the table by matching the following statements and putting them into the correct boxes:

Typical 1950s family role for men	Modern men in families
Most men did not do housework or cook as these were seen as women's roles	Men are more caring fathers and involved in their children's lives
Men disciplined children and some would hit them if they were naughty	Men and women do not necessarily live with each other but share responsibility for parenting
Men worked long hours outside the home and went to pubs in their leisure time	Men are willing to help in the home and many enjoy cooking
Men lived in family homes with their wives and children	Gay men can set up civil partnerships with other men and bring up children together without it seeming unusual or wrong to most people children
Men would hide the fact they were gay because it was against the law; they would often marry women and hide their sexuality	Men are happier to stay at home with their families and share in family life

Exam practice

The modern-day father comes in many forms. Today's father is not always the traditional married breadwinner who is responsible for discipline in the family. He can be single or married; employed or stay-at-home; gay or straight; an adoptive or step-parent. He can be a capable caregiver to children with special needs. Research across families from all backgrounds suggests that fathers' affection and increased family involvement help to support children's social and emotional development. Fathers can provide important role models for their sons to show them how to behave as good men.

a) Using the item, describe and explain one role of fathers in the past. (2)
b) Suggest and explain one reason why the role of fathers in the family has changed. (2)
c) Suggest one reason why many families do not have an adult man in the family. (1)
d) State one positive benefit for children of having a good relationship with their father. (1)
e) Explain the meaning of the term new man. (2)
f) Explain the meaning of the term house husband. (2)

Key terms

Segregated conjugal roles – men and women are expected to do different jobs in the home.

Conjugal – marriage or married.

Breadwinner – earns the family money.

New man – man who is willing to help in the home.

House husband – looks after the family home while women work.

Stretch and challenge

What do you think are the characteristics of a good father and an ideal man? Write a job description and an advert for the role of a father in a family.

Over to you

If boys do not have fathers as role models, where can they learn what it is to be a man?

Across the generations

Ask someone who is older than you about how fathers behaved in families in the past. Ask them if things have changed and if they feel it is for the better.

Topic 13: What is the role of women in the family?

What am I going to learn?

- **To understand that the lives and expectations of women have changed dramatically, both inside the home and family and in the outside world**

The possibilities for women have grown since the invention of contraception that women can control. Attitudes to women's roles have changed. They no longer expect to live their lives only as wives and mothers. They can take on good jobs and, if they choose, can live without husbands to provide them with money. This has given them confidence and choice.

Personal research idea

Create a simple **quantitative questionnaire**. Make a list of jobs around the home, include things like painting, decorating, cleaning, washing and ironing. Find out from as many people as possible who does which of those jobs in the home most, males or females. How much have things changed since the 1950s in reality? What does your research tell you?

Grade boost

In a question on this topic, you may be tempted to write about women in the world of work. Avoid doing that and focus on the family or you will not be answering the question.

Do women still need feminism in your view? List a number of different reasons why feminism may still be relevant to women today.

Changes in the lives of women in the home

1950s women

Women have always worked outside the home; the nature of that work has changed. In the 1950s, women would have taken on low-paid jobs in factories or as cleaners to help support the family. This would not have been their major role, however, the main role for women was to be in the home cooking, shopping and cleaning for the family. For poorer women this was hard labour, as there were few **domestic appliances** such as washing machines and no central heating. Homes were heated by coal fires. Women made much of the family clothing by sewing and knitting.

Modern women

Women have the choice of not having a family at all, being part of a family structure of their choice, or bringing up children on their own. The fact that so many work means that they do not have to rely on marriage or men to live.

The impact of Feminism

In the 1960s, the Women's Movement became influential. Feminists claimed that society was dominated by and for men. The name given to this **dominance** was **patriarchy**. Writers challenged the view that women should be in the home because they said it meant that they had no power and left them in the control of men. Many women began to take on careers instead of just jobs. They wanted more from their lives. Other women began to point out that the **family** has a **dark side** of domestic abuse, so they brought that to the attention of the public. Women are much less likely to put up with violence now and will be supported if they challenge abusive men. Norms and values regarding women's roles have changed dramatically.

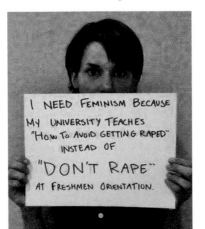

I NEED FEMINISM BECAUSE MY UNIVERSITY TEACHES "HOW TO AVOID GETTING RAPED" INSTEAD OF "DON'T RAPE" AT FRESHMEN ORIENTATION.

Contraception

The arrival of the **contraceptive pill** meant that women could control the number of children they had. This gave them more time for careers. In addition, it removed the link between sex and marriage.

Check your understanding

Complete the table by matching the following statements and putting them into the correct boxes:

Typical 1950s family role for women	Modern women in families
Women worked in the home, cooking, cleaning and shopping	Women expect men to help, and have appliances to make life easier
Women had larger families, so they were unable to work because of regular pregnancy and childbirth	Women have careers and can support the family on their own without a man if they need to
Women might have had jobs, but the husband might not like it, because it would seem he could not earn enough to support a family	If both men and women earn pay, they can choose how to spend their money together. Women have more power to make decisions
If husbands were abusive and dominant, women had to put up with it. It was seen as her problem for provoking him	Women have access to contraception, so they have smaller families and more time to do other things
Women were not often in charge of the family money. Husbands would give women housekeeping money and spend the rest on themselves	Women have the option of leaving a violent partner if they can. It is seen as a failure of a man if he hits his wife.

Key terms

Domestic appliances – technology such as vacuum cleaners and fridges which make domestic life easier.

Dominance – power to control others.

Patriarchy – dominance of society by men.

Dark side of family – family abuse and violence that is hidden behind closed doors.

Contraceptive pill – first form of birth control that women could take charge of.

Triple shift – women now have jobs, do the housework and the caring side of family life.

Stretch and challenge

Do women and girls still need feminism or are they completely equal with men and boys in families?

Exam practice

It is claimed by many writers and journalists that women in modern society are expected to 'have-it-all'. They are under pressure to have families, to work in good jobs and to stay beautiful as well. Instead of being made free by feminism, they are under more pressure than ever. Sociologists Duncombe and Marsden described this as the '**triple shift**'. Women are expected to take responsibility for the family, do a full-time job and also to worry about the emotions and well-being of family members.

a) Describe and explain one change in the role of women in the family. (2)

b) Suggest and explain one reason why the role of women in the family has changed. (2)

c) Using the item, explain the meaning of the term 'have-it-all'. (1)

d) Who suggested the idea of the triple shift for women? (1)

e) Explain the meaning of the term triple shift. (2)

f) Explain the meaning of the term feminism. (2)

🔍 websites

For more about feminism and why lots of people (not just women) support feminist viewpoints, have a look at the Fawcett Society website: **www.fawcettsociety.org.uk**

For reasons why many men and women feel they need feminism, look at: **www.whoneedsfeminism.com**

Education

Topic: 1 What is the purpose of education?

What am I going to learn?

● **To understand that all cultures recognise that children need to be taught the social and technical skills to fit in with their cultures, but that there are different ways of teaching children**

Children are taught how to fit in with their cultures. In some cultures, this process takes place in the family. For example, fathers may teach sons skills to earn money or provide food while mothers will train girls in domestic duties. In most societies, there are systems which have developed to teach children the skills that they cannot acquire from the home. This is the education system.

Extended writing

Explain the meaning of the term education. (10)

Guidance: Education is a '**contested concept**'. This means that not everyone agrees on exactly what the term means. There are various ways of understanding it. You need to show that you understand this point, that you know about formal and informal education and that you understand that education differs from place to place in the world.

Are schools bad for children?

About education

People do not all agree when it comes to the purpose of education: some people think it is about teaching people to earn a living, whereas other people feel that education is a good thing in its own right. It is said that people should be taught to explore new ideas and to think for themselves.

Informal education

Children learn the skills they require to become adults from adults around them. Some parents may teach children skills such as cooking, gardening, swimming or even reading and writing. This process is part of growing up and often children learn those things because they want to and they enjoy learning.

Formal education

Children are taken away from their parents to special places known as schools where trained staff known as teachers will deliberately teach them things that adults or the government think that they need to know. The children are then tested on that knowledge and, if they do well, they progress to do more study until they have passed a lot of tests and examinations. At some point, they leave education and try to get work. Generally, in our society, people who pass a lot of tests and examinations will earn more and live longer lives than those who do not. In British law, all children must have a **formal education**, even if they are taught at home.

Over to you

What would Britain be like if children did not have to attend school but could choose whether to go or not? Think around the subject, for example what would happen to teachers?

Education in other cultures

What and how children are taught is very different around the world. For example, in Norway, children do not start school till they are six and then spend a year learning how to get on with each other. In Japan, children attend school and then go to private after-school classes. Japanese children are trained to be obedient and follow group rules in school. French and American children do not usually wear uniforms; however, French schools focus on knowledge and good marks.

Check your understanding

Match the beginnings and the ends of the following sentences:

a) Formal education consists of   tested by assessments and examinations

b) Informal education is when people   being taught skills by teachers who are paid to teach children

c) Formal education is usually   system is different for each country

d) In Britain all children must receive a   earn more than people who do not have qualifications

e) People who have a good education tend to   formal education whether at school or in the home

f) Wherever you go in the world, the school   learn things they need to know for their own pleasure or needs

Exam practice

Education in Nigeria is similar in many ways to education in Britain. The best schools are very good indeed. However, in some schools, the school buildings are not in good condition, and there are few facilities. The floors may be of dirt and there may be no doors or windows. Teachers may be unqualified to teach the lessons. Children are expected to pay money for their education. Children value education and are anxious to do well, because it can be a way for them to get a good job. Many people in Nigeria are very poor, so education is a way to escape having a very hard life.

a) Using the item, describe one way in which Nigerian schools are different from British schools. (2)

b) Explain why Nigerian children are anxious to succeed in school. (2)

c) Using examples, explain the meaning of the term formal education. (2)

d) Explain the meaning of the term informal education, using an example. (2)

e) Briefly explain one reason why most societies have some form of education system. (2)

Key terms

Domestic duties – jobs in the house, housework.

Skills – abilities that are learned and help one to solve problems.

Informal education – learning new skills from people around you.

Formal education – training in a school or college from someone who deliberately teaches things that are needed for adult life or work.

Contested concept – there is a debate about what a term means.

Stretch and challenge

Design the perfect school for you and your friends. Think about the school day, the subjects, the rules and the equipment. Think about what you need to know for adult life and whether you would get it in your school. Show your ideas to someone else and see if they like what you suggest.

Education

Topic 2: Why do we have an education system?

What am I going to learn?

● **To understand why the education system developed in Britain**

The education system that we have in Britain developed for a number of reasons and there are different ideas about why it developed, too. Partly, the system developed because it served the needs of society for soldiers and workers. Some sociologists think that it exists to sort out the best people to take on important jobs. Others think it developed to control people's minds so that they will do as they are told by governments and other powerful people.

Interesting facts

Government statistics show that in the UK, the average person spends 13 years in school, though compulsory education lasts for 12 years. Around 28% of British children say they dislike school, which means that 72% like school. Slightly more than half of British adults do not read or write as well as they would like. Britain ranks about 7th in the world in terms of mathematical ability for adults. Britain has fewer problems of bad behaviour than Australia, New Zealand and The United States of America.

🔍 websites

http://tinyurl.com/cc6zxwn

A video programme for History lessons describing life in Victorian Britain, before compulsory education was introduced can be seen on the BBC website in their Learning Zone section called 'Child labour in Victorian times'.

Why do we have an education system?

The system that we have of making sure all children have an education dates back to 1880. Partly, the idea of **compulsory education** was introduced to stop parents sending children to work in factories. Other historical reasons for having an education system in Britain are to do with preparing children for the world of work and reducing the number of young people who are unemployed or on the streets. Employers need people with skills to work for them, and the government tries to improve the education of children so that they will produce people who can work well in various industries.

There are other benefits of having an education system. It means parents can work knowing their children are safe. In addition, education is a way of controlling children. It is known, for example, that crime rates tend to go up in school holidays.

Sociologists are not completely agreed about the main reasons for having education systems. There are two different points of view about schools.

Socialisation

One of the most important reasons for having an education system, according to Emile Durkheim and Talcott Parsons, is to socialise children into the norms and values of wider society. They say that school is a way of supporting children while they learn the wider social skills needed for adult life. Thus, the children who pass examinations are the best students and they will get the good jobs and lead society when they are adult.

Is this child experiencing socialisation that will be good for her personal development or being controlled so that she will obey authority?

Social control

Sociologists who believe that the purpose of education is to control people say that the way the system works is to make sure that the children of rich people do well in school so that they can continue to run society for their own benefit. The rules are there to teach children to be obedient and not to think for themselves so they will be good workers and do what the bosses tell them.

Key terms

Compulsory education – children must have a proper education by law.

Respondent – someone who participates in sociology research.

Open question – cannot be answered with 'yes' or 'no'.

Check your understanding

Match the words to their meanings:

a) Norm
b) Socialisation
c) Secondary socialisation
d) Informal socialisation
e) Formal socialisation
f) Agencies of socialisation
g) Social control
h) Compulsory education

being taught how to behave by people in the wider world
groups in society that teach or encourage people to follow social rules.
learning how to behave as you live your life
a system of making people follow social rules
the process of learning the rules of a culture
the law states that children must have an education
normal and expected way to behave
when people deliberately set out to change how you act

Stretch and challenge

What is more important, educating children for work, or teaching them to form good relationships and become confident people?

Exam practice

Taken from an **unstructured interview** with a 40-year-old **respondent** with two children who was asked the **open question**, 'What do you think about school?'

'I hated school when I was younger because I was bored and had to study subjects that I did not think I would need. I was forced to go, but thought that school ruins learning because the focus was all on examinations and jobs. It was all about training people to obey rules. Now I am adult and a teacher, I insist my children go to school because I can see the importance of earning a living. I can see that I learned to get on with other people and learned good values even if I did not see it at the time.'

a) Using the item, identify and explain one reason why the respondent hated school. (2)

b) Explain why the respondent expects his children to go to school. (2)

c) Using examples, explain two ways in which schools may socialise children. (6)

Extended writing

Explain reasons why we have schools in our society. (10)

Guidance: You can either write about practical reasons for educating children in school, such as preventing them being exploited in work, or you can write about socialisation and social control. It might be that you want to do both. Make sure that you make a point and then say why we have schools as a result of that point.

Topic 3: What is the education system of England and Wales?

What am I going to learn?

- **To understand that we have a variety of schools in England and Wales and that differences are developing between the English and Welsh education systems**

In the past, the education system was tightly controlled by the government and by Local Education Authorities. Schools did not have much control over their own money or the way they were run. Since the 1960s, there have been a lot of changes, so that there are many different types of school that children can attend. It depends on where they live.

The variety of schools in England and Wales

In the 1970s, there was quite a narrow range of schools available to children. State schools were run by local authorities such as councils. In some areas children attended either **grammar schools** or **secondary modern** schools, depending on how well they did in an examination called the 11+. This system ran from the late 1940s but was being replaced by comprehensive schools. Most children went to **comprehensive** schools which accepted children of all abilities. During the 1980s and 1990s, the effect of **Margaret Thatcher**'s governments was to encourage a greater range of schools and funding systems, and this trend has been carried on by all governments since then.

Academies

These are schools set up by sponsors such as religious or business groups. They get money from the sponsors and from the government directly. They were often set up in areas where schools were not achieving well as a way of trying to improve results.

City Technology Colleges

These were schools set up in towns and cities and they teach science, technology and world of work.

Faith schools

These are schools that are funded by religious groups and by local authorities and government. They tend to take children from one religious group.

Specialist schools

These are state schools that specialise in one or two areas such as arts, business, science or performing arts.

Extended writing

Describe how schools have changed in Britain since the 1970s. (10)

Guidance: List things that have changed; for example, you could say that in 1970s Britain, most children went to local authority comprehensive schools. Do not give reasons for change, the question is asking you to list changes, so you need to say what education in Britain was once like and what it is like now. Be careful and look at the date with questions like this. Do not write about systems that existed before the 1970s or you will not get marks.

Free schools

These are schools that are set up by any group with an interest in education and as a result of parental demand. They are funded by the group and by government. They can choose what to pay teachers and do not have to follow the **National Curriculum**.

The difference between England and Wales

Scotland and Northern Ireland have always had their own education system and exams. Since Wales gained its Assembly as result of laws passed in 1999, it has had control over its own education system, so most of the new school types described are only found in England.

Check your understanding

Match the school with the description:

a) Comprehensive school	specialise in a particular part of the curriculum such as art or sports
b) Grammar school	are owned and funded by businesses and focus on sciences
c) Faith schools	all children can attend regardless of ability
d) Specialist schools	teach about their own religion as well as normal subjects
e) Academies	teaches traditional academic subjects
f) City Technology Colleges	set up in areas where schools need to improve and are funded by business or faith groups; they can select their pupils

Exam practice

Academies are schools that are owned and run by private groups but paid for from government money. They do not need to follow the National Curriculum and they can pay teachers differently from other schools. Some have increased teaching hours. In May 2012, there were 1807 Academies in England and more are converting to Academy status all the time. Many teachers are against the Academies because their pay and conditions can get worse and they argue that they are not good for education. Some Academies refuse to take children with Special Educational Needs or behaviour issues. Welsh Assembly government is against the system and points out that some teachers in Academies in England are not qualified.

a) Using the item, identify and explain what an Academy school is. (2)
b) Suggest one reason why the government is in favour of Academies. (2)
c) Identify one difference between an Academy school and a state school. (2)
d) Suggest one reason why the Welsh Assembly government rejects the Academy system. (2)
e) Explain the meaning of the term Faith school. (2)

Key terms

Grammar school – teaches traditional academic subjects in a traditional way.

Secondary modern – taught practical subjects.

Comprehensive – all children can attend regardless of ability.

National Curriculum – the subjects that must be taught in most state schools by law.

Ideology – belief system about how the world should be run.

New Right (Thatcherism) – a belief that society will get better if there is more competition and a return to traditional values.

Stretch and challenge

Should rich people be allowed to opt out of the state education system and attend their own special private schools where only other rich children or very clever children are educated?

Over to you

Create a poster or revision cards to describe the different types of schools that are found in England and Wales.

Education

Topic 4: What changes have taken place within schools since the 1970s?

What am I going to learn?

- To understand that it is not just the way that schools are run that has changed since the 1970s, there have been cultural and legal changes in schools since that time

In the 1970s, schools were often brutal places, especially for boys. Teachers could use corporal punishment, so children could be hit by teachers. In addition, not all children sat public examinations. Teachers often decided what children studied and whether they sat examinations. While some gained an excellent education, others did not gain qualifications for work.

Extended writing

Discuss how schools have changed in Britain since the 1970s. (20)

Guidance: You will need to develop your writing. In terms of discussion – there are structural changes to schools in that we have new forms of school such as Academies and City Technology Colleges and there are cultural changes so that children all study the same subjects as a result of National Curriculum. You might want to explain the effect of the changes on society and on children's experiences of school to make up your discussion.

Over to you

If you were in charge of schools, what would you put into the National Curriculum to teach to all children? Why would you make any changes that you did?

Changes in schools

The culture of schools in the 1970s

In the 1970s, it was legal to punish a child through the use of physical punishment. Many teachers would use a cane to hit children. Physical punishment was outlawed finally in 1987, though many schools had stopped using it before that.

Teaching tended to be very formal, with teachers writing on boards and children copying down what was written. Teachers could decide what was taught and how to teach it. Many secondary school teachers were not trained to teach, they were just trained in a subject and expected to teach with little or no experience of children. Children were expected to **learn things by rote**.

Boys and girls were often taught different subjects. Boys were given metalwork lessons and girls learned domestic science subjects ready for the expected roles in adult life.

What has changed?

The National Curriculum was introduced in 1988, so all children studied the same subjects. This meant that children were tested and assessed on their progress more frequently, so schools have a lot of information on the progress of children. Teachers and schools can be assessed on the performance of their pupils in these tests. Schools are much more target-led and there is an emphasis on improving pupil standards. Schools are inspected regularly to see that they are meeting the new standards.

Teachers are now more concerned with pupil welfare, so most schools have a pastoral system which looks after children. Teachers can lose their jobs if they touch a pupil inappropriately. **Pupil voice** is now part of schools, so teachers may ask for feedback on lessons to see how to improve their own teaching. Most teachers are now highly qualified in a subject and in teaching as well, though not necessarily in Academies or private schools.

There is far more teaching technology such as computers and projectors in schools, and more concern with **ICT** skills. Children spend more time talking or thinking and less time writing.

Check your understanding

Complete the table by matching the following statements and putting them into the correct boxes:

Typical 1970s education	Modern education
Violence in schools was common and many children were hit or caned	Most children sit examinations all through their school experience
Teachers used chalkboards and chalk	Teachers must follow the National Curriculum
Lessons often involved copying from a blackboard or a textbook	Teachers may not touch children
Girls and boys had different lessons and boys were believed to be more clever	There is computer technology in schools, and teachers use PowerPoint and produce workbooks on computers
Few children sat examinations	Pupils learn through group work, discussion and games
Teachers taught what they wanted	Girls and boys study the same lessons and girls tend to do better

Exam practice

'When I was in school in the 1970s, a kid was cheeky to the teacher. The teacher hurled the heavy wooden block board rubber at him. It missed the kid by inches and was thrown with such force that it took a chunk of plaster out of the wall. The kid ran out of the class. Half an hour later, another teacher arrived and called our teacher out of the lesson. The cheeky kid had got his revenge. He had gone across the road to a shop; he had bought a tin of cigarette lighter fuel and set fire to our teacher's car in the car park. He then said that if our teacher bought a new car, he would do it again and again. Our teacher left within a month and found another job.'

a) Using the item, identify and explain one way that teachers in the 1970s might discipline children. (2)

b) Fully explain one thing that this story may tell you sociologically about the relationship between students and teachers in the 1970s. (2)

c) Give one reason why this story may not be a valid piece of evidence regarding school life in the 1970s. (2)

d) Identify and fully explain one change that has taken place in schools since the 1970s. (4)

Key terms

Corporal punishment – punishment by hurting someone.

Rote learning – memorising facts or poetry word for word.

Pupil voice – children are consulted on their education and give feedback to schools.

ICT – computers (information and communication technology).

Stretch and challenge

Speak to some of your older teachers and find out what changes they have experienced in education during their careers. Do they prefer teaching now or in the past?

Across the generations

Talk to someone who went to school in England or Wales in the 1970s or before. This time, focus on what was taught, how it was taught, the relationships between teachers and students and how learning was tested. Make a clear list of differences between their experiences and yours.

Topic 5: Is the education system meritocratic?

What am I going to learn?

- To understand that some people believe that educational success is simply based on ability and hard work, while others think that the education system works to the advantage of some children more than others

We are taught in schools that if people are clever and work hard, they will do well. They will pass their examinations and be rewarded with good jobs. However, when sociologists look carefully at who succeeds and who fails, it is clear that something far more complicated is happening and it seems that some groups in society are more likely to achieve than others.

Are girls really more intelligent than boys? What social factors might make girls more likely to have done well in schools in recent years compared with boys?

Who succeeds in school?

Some sociologists believe that schools are **meritocratic**. They think that the people who succeed in school are the cleverest and hardest workers. They pass examinations because they deserve to. **Functionalists** believe that the job of schools is to sort out the good students from the weaker ones. To succeed in school, it is important to be clever and hard-working.

However, there are plenty of clever students who do not pass examinations. This suggests that schools may not be working as well as they should for all students. Students who tend to do less well than others are: male, from poorer working-class backgrounds or from some ethnic minorities. It is unlikely that one gender, race or social background is cleverer than any other, so sociologists want to know what causes these patterns.

Boys and girls

In the 1960s, boys did twice as well as girls in examinations. Examination results for boys and girls are rising, but much faster for girls than boys. Therefore girls are doing better than boys in examinations and more are going to university.

Poorer working-class children

The term **working class** is used to describe people who take jobs that do not require academic skills, but practical skills. The pattern is clear; if your parents have been to university, then you are likely to do twice as well in school as someone whose parents are not well educated, regardless of how clever you are. All the government statistics show that a person's background gives the best clue to their future chances of educational success.

Ethnic minorities

African-Caribbean children are ahead of most British children when they start school. This is supported by school tests. However, by the time they get to GCSE, they are doing far less well than others. The question is why this happens. The situation is not clear, because some White minorities also do badly, whereas Indian and Chinese children seem to do better than most.

Extended writing

Describe patterns of achievement in British schools. (10)

Guidance: You will need to identify the groups of pupils who do well in school and pupils who do not do so well in school (poorer, working class, boys). Recognise that some children belong to more than one group, so rich girls do better than rich boys, but rich children do better overall than poor children. Point out that ethnicity is an issue. Chinese children tend to do better overall, but African-Caribbean and Bangladeshi do worse.

Check your understanding

Fill in the missing words to these sentences:

a) The belief that the best people will do well in education is known as •••.

b) Girls tend to do better than ••• in public examinations.

c) Indian and ••• pupils tend to do better than most in examinations.

d) Children who receive ••• school meals tend to come from homes that have a lower income.

e) Children whose parents went to ••• are more likely to go to university themselves.

f) Working-class people are people who take jobs based on ••• and work with their hands.

Exam practice

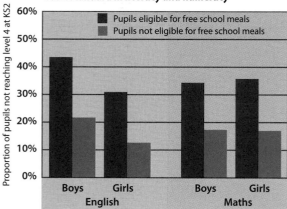

Percentage of 11-year-old pupils not achieving basic standard in literacy and numeracy

- Pupils eligible for free school meals
- Pupils not eligible for free school meals

(y-axis: Proportion of pupils not reaching level 4 at KS2, 0%–60%)

English: Boys, Girls — Maths: Boys, Girls

Eligibility for free school meals is used to show the children who come from homes where money is tight. They may be in families who live on benefits, or whose parents earn low wages.

a) Using the item, what percentage of boys who are eligible for free school meals did not achieve basic standards in English? (1)

b) Using the item, what percentage of boys who are not eligible for free school meals did not attain basic standards in English? (1)

c) Using the item, what differences can you see between those children who are eligible to have free school meals and those who are not eligible to have free school meals and their ability to achieve basic standards in English and Maths? (4)

d) Using the item, what differences can you see between the failure of boys to achieve basic standards in English and Maths and girls who do not achieve basic standards in English and Maths? (4)

Key terms

Meritocracy – the best people will do well in society and success is based on ability.

Functionalists – sociologists who look at how society works as a system.

Working class – people who have not been to Higher Education and who would take jobs with practical skills.

Stretch and challenge

If you were a teacher, what would you look for in a good pupil? What social characteristics do 'good pupils' share?

Grade boost

*Look very closely at graphs. The writing around the image often tells you a lot. The graph in this question shows children who **do not** achieve basic standards.*

Over to you

Suggest what things a child needs to succeed in school. Think about facilities at home, social attitudes, help from parents and any other ideas.

Education

Topic 6: What is the cause of some children doing less well than they should?

What am I going to learn?

● **To recognise that there are a number of possible causes of school failure and that the experts are not agreed on which is the most likely cause**

Since the 1940s, there has been a massive amount of legal and administrative change, all with the intention of improving education. However, whatever politicians decide, or teachers do, large numbers of very intelligent people fail to do as well as they should. This is a waste of government money, as the education system is a big investment for a country. It is a waste of individual potential as people are not able to have the chances or lives that they are capable of.

Extended writing

Discuss reasons why children in some social groups achieve better in education than others. (20)

Guidance: Show that you know which children appear to be disadvantaged in school. Make a list of four or five reasons why some children are disadvantaged. You can then explain each one and offer examples, sociological language and facts to show why those social groups are disadvantaged. A discussion question requires that you show that you know there are opposing points of view; are schools to blame for the disadvantage or are parents responsible? It could be a mixture of things causing the problems – the choice is yours as long as you have good evidence.

Theories to explain school underachievement

Children who do less well in school tend to come from certain social groups. They are likely to be male, from poorer backgrounds and possibly from certain ethnic groups. This is not to say that that everyone in these groups will all fail, but that some children have to work harder to achieve what comes fairly easily to others. Intelligence is spread evenly throughout the population; school success is not. This is widely known and understood by everyone. What are the possible reasons for this unevenness of success? Sociologists have put forward a number of ideas.

Factors in schools that may cause children to fail

Economic factors: To lack the things that others in a society have is known as **deprivation**. Poorer children tend to go to schools in poorer areas and such schools may lack resources and equipment. Teachers may not want to work in such schools because they are seen as 'challenging'.

Social and cultural factors: Teachers may assume that children from poorer families do not want to learn or expect that they will not do as well, so they do not encourage them to do well. They may be racist or sexist without realising it, so children **underachieve**.

Suggest and mind map reasons why children from poorer homes may do less well in education than they should regardless of the ability they were born with.

Factors at home that may cause children to fail

Economic factors: Children who live in poor homes may lack support to buy books and computers. This difference in access to computers is known as the **digital divide**. They may not have a warm room in which to work.

Cultural and social factors: Parents in poor homes may not have the time or ability to help their children. They may not expect children to do well and do not encourage them properly. They may have done badly in school themselves and do not know how to support their children. They cannot arrange for work experience in good jobs or do not know how the education system works so they can benefit their children.

Check your understanding

Are these statements true or false?

a) All children have an exactly equal chance to do well in school.

b) Poor parents do not care about their children's success in school.

c) Richer parents are sometimes more likely to read to their children when they are small.

d) Children from poorer families are more likely to develop problems in school.

e) Intelligence and potential for success is probably spread equally throughout the population.

Key terms

Economic – things that are concerned with money in particular.

Deprivation – not having the things that others in society have, being poor or lacking things.

Underachieve – to do less well than you should in life or in examinations.

Digital divide – the difference in access to knowledge between those with and those without access to the Internet.

Stretch and challenge

Use the BBC news website and newspapers to find as many stories as possible about why some children are not doing as well as they might in the education system. Make a collage of the most interesting. Now you have considered the news stories, think, are schools or parents to blame in your view?

Exam practice

David Egan, a Professor of Education in Wales, has said that reading to children when they are still very young will help to prevent social and emotional problems in later life. He says that the most important influence on children and success in education is their parents or other adults. Some children are more than two years ahead when they get to school aged 5, because they have been read to and talked to by adults. Children in the poorest families were eight times more likely to develop problems in school. He says that the way to close the education gap between boys and girls is for fathers to read to their children more often.

a) Using the item, what does David Egan believe will prevent children from developing social and emotional problems? (1)

b) Using the item, how far ahead are children who have been read to by adults? (1)

c) Using the item, which children are more likely to develop problems in school? (1)

d) Suggest and explain sociologically, one way in which all children could be helped to do better in school. (2)

e) Explain the meaning of the term deprivation with examples from education. (2)

f) Outline and fully explain one way in which schools may affect children's ability to do well. (3)

Over to you

Write an article for a parenting magazine explaining how children can be encouraged to do well in school.

Education

Topic 7: What are the reasons for gender inequality in education?

What am I going to learn?

- **To understand the possible explanation for the failure of boys to improve as much as girls in terms of examination success**

You are probably part of the first generation of people where girls achieve better examination results than boys in education. Boys' examination results are improving far more slowly than girls, so now girls are doing better in school, even in subjects that are traditionally male. More girls are applying to university than boys.

Extended writing

Explain why girls appear to be achieving better results in school than boys. (10)

Guidance: Briefly mention patterns of attainment in school, but do not spend much time on it. Identify three or four reasons to explain why girls seem to do better overall. Follow the basic pattern, when explaining each reason, of making a statement, developing the point to show you understand and then offering an example or saying why that means girls do better in school.

Over to you

Do you think boys and girls should be educated in single-sex schools, with boys being taught by men and girls being taught by women? Make points for and against the idea.

Why are girls the gender of school success?

In the 1960s and 1970s, boys achieved far better results in schools than girls. This was usually explained in terms of boys having greater intelligence and ability. Feminist sociologists disagreed with that explanation at the time. Now girls are achieving better examination results, boys' results are seen as a problem. Teachers are being told to ensure that boys improve their results. Sociologists offer different explanations for why boys are not achieving their full potential in schools.

Crisis of masculinity

A number of writers have suggested that males are no longer certain of what it is to be a man in our society. Girls have challenged male roles so they can do all the things men can do, and it has left boys being uncertain of their role in life. They respond by acting in a masculine fashion and rejecting school.

Lads and laddishness

Boys adopt 'laddish' attitudes. They gain peer group status from messing around and rejecting the pressure of constant testing. Clever boys pretend not to work in school but work at home instead; but white working-class and African-Caribbean boys fall behind. Girls, however, often work hard because they expect careers and families.

Feminisation of education

When women started to challenge male superiority in schools, schools became more feminine places. Fewer male teachers in schools meant boys did not have male role models and subjects were taught in a fashion that appealed to girls.

What strategies would you suggest to the government to encourage more men to go into teaching as a career?

Primary socialisation

Parents spend less time reading to their sons. In addition, reading is taught by mothers and grandmothers, so it is seen as a feminine activity. Females in the home are organised and sensible, but male role models, especially in the media, reject authority. Some boys are more likely to develop behavioural problems, so they are disruptive in class and **excluded**.

Patriarchal society

Men are used to being dominant in society. Feminists say that this makes them over-confident so that boys think that they do not have to work.

Check your understanding

Match the beginnings and the ends of the sentences:

a) Girls tend to outperform boys   say that men do not spend enough time reading to male children

b) Feminists suggest that boys are over-confident because   influence as boys adopt laddish behaviour to gain respect from their mates

c) The crisis of masculinity suggests that boys   no longer know what it is to be a man and lack confidence as a result

d) Home-based theories of male failure   we live in a patriarchal society

e) School-based theories of male failure suggest that schools   at all levels of the education system

f) Some sociologists say that peer groups are an   are feminised places as there are too many female teachers

Exam practice

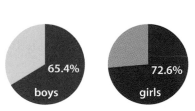

Proportion of pupils obtaining A*–C

65.4% boys

72.6% girls

The 2010 GCSE examination result figures showed that more girls attained pass grades at GCSE than boys. The pass rate for all pupils was 69.1%, but for boys it was lower and for girls it was higher. More girls than boys attained A and A* grades. In 2012, the majority of children leaving school with no qualifications were boys.

a) Using the item, what percentage of boys attained A*–C grades at GCSE in 2010? (1)

b) Using the item, what percentage of children attained A*–C grades at GCSE in 2010? (1)

c) Suggest and explain sociologically, one school-based reason why girls are outperforming boys at GCSE. (4)

d) Suggest and explain sociologically, one home- or culture-based reason why girls are outperforming boys at GCSE. (4)

Key terms

Crisis of masculinity – males are no longer certain what it is to be a man.

Laddish behaviour – showing off and silliness in school to impress peer group.

Feminisation of schools – schools are more girl-friendly places and teachers are female.

Excluded from school – formal sanction where children are told not to attend school for a period of time.

Stretch and challenge

Create a magazine cover for a teachers' magazine with the cover story that boys are not performing to their best ability in school. Think about some questions or titles for articles that people would want to read and offer suggestions as to why boys fail. Make it interesting and write trailers for stories that others would find challenging.

Grade boost

If you are asked about boys or girls specifically, then write about boys or girls only. However, if you are asked about gender, then you must write about both sexes equally or you will not have answered the question.

Topic 8: What are the reasons for ethnic inequality in educational attainment?

What am I going to learn?

● **To understand some of the reasons why children from some ethnic minorities appear to do very poorly in school while children from other minorities do well**

Children from certain ethnic groups seem to do less well than other children. Many writers have claimed, with good evidence, that the problem is to do with racism in the British education system. However, children from other ethnic minorities do very well, so it is possible the problem is to do with the home cultures.

Extended writing

Explain why children from some ethnic minorities appear to be underachieving in school. (10)

Guidance: Briefly mention patterns of attainment in school, but do not spend much time on it. Identify three or four reasons to explain why some ethnic minorities may fail in school. Follow the basic pattern, when explaining each reason, of making a statement, developing the point to show you understand and then offering an example or saying why that means some children fail despite having high levels of ability.

What causes ethnic minority underattainment, something in schools or something in society?

Ethnic minorities and school attainment

The pattern of attainment of GCSE results in British schools suggests that some **ethnic minorities** achieve very well. This is true of pupils of Indian and Chinese origin. However, groups with lower attainment overall tend to be African-Caribbean, Bangladeshi and Traveller children. There is disagreement over the cause of these patterns of attainment between the various ethnic groups.

Inside schools

Children from African-Caribbean backgrounds are far more likely to be excluded than White children. Very many studies have suggested that teachers are racist, or that schools are racist, often unintentionally. There are fewer teachers from ethnic minority backgrounds to act as role models and the curriculum tends to overlook other cultures. While this may have been true in the past, schools are working hard at creating a **multi-cultural environment** and it may not be so true of modern schools. Some sociologists have found that children from ethnic minority backgrounds have rejected racism by achieving well despite their teachers' attitudes.

Poverty and deprivation

The ethnicities that do less well in school are those which tend to be less well-off than others. The problem may be nothing to do with ethnicity, and everything to do with having very little money and no work. Chinese children are often from business-owning families and many British doctors have an Indian background. The pattern may be due to the effects of social background.

Cultural explanations

Some sociologists have argued that the problem is to do with the culture of the home. Chinese families often have very high expectations of their children. They claim that African-Caribbean and Bangladeshi parents are not involved in their children's education. Others have said that this is not true, often ethnic minority groups set up their own weekend schools. Some writers have claimed that children from ethnic minority backgrounds struggle with English, but again the evidence seems to suggest that people who speak two languages or more develop high-level thinking skills.

Check your understanding

Fill in the missing words:

a) Ethnicity refers to membership of a ••• group.

b) Ethnic minorities which do well in school include ••• and ••• groups.

c) Ethnic minorities which underachieve include ••• and Bangladeshi children.

d) African-Caribbean children are more often ••• from school than White children.

e) It is claimed that some staff in British schools are ••• and prejudiced against children from ethnic minority backgrounds.

f) Schools are fighting racism through developing ••• education.

Key terms

Ethnic – refers to membership of a cultural group.

Ethnic minority – people who belong to a smaller cultural group than the dominant culture, for example British Asians.

Multi-cultural environment – a school which values all cultures and backgrounds and acknowledges cultural differences between students.

Poverty – lacking the money for essentials in life.

Deprivation – living a life where you do not have things that you need.

Stretch and challenge

Suggest reasons why children from some ethnic minorities do much better in school than the average White British child.

Exam practice

a) Using the item, what percentage of African-Caribbeans attained 5 A*–C passes at GCSE in 2000? (1)

b) Using the item, what percentage of White children attained 5 A*–C passes at GCSE in 2000? (1)

c) Suggest and explain sociologically, one school-based reason why children from some ethnic minorities appear to do less well in school. (4)

d) Suggest and explain sociologically, one home or culture-based reason why children from some ethnic minorities appear to do less well in school. (4)

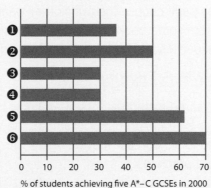

Cultural background and exam success

❶
❷
❸
❹
❺
❻

0 10 20 30 40 50 60 70

% of students achieving five A*–C GCSEs in 2000

❶ African-Caribbean
❷ White
❸ Pakistani
❹ Bangladeshi
❺ Indian
❻ Other Asian (including Chinese)

Grade boost

Remember that most children from ethnic minorities are British and were born in the UK. Also, be sure to use both words, not just 'ethnic'; we all have ethnicity; only some of us are members of a minority ethnicity!

Education

Topic 9: What are the reasons for social class inequality in schools?

What am I going to learn?

- **To understand that the most significant inequality in British schools is related to social class and the reasons for this are not fully understood**

While ethnicity and gender are very important causes of school failure in British society, the most significant cause of underperformance is social class. Children whose parents are highly educated and high earning are far more likely to do well in school and get high-earning jobs themselves than children from families whose parents did not do well in school. This is so well understood by everyone that government policies target the failure of the working class to do well.

Why do working-class children underachieve in schools?

Extended writing

Discuss reasons why children from working-class backgrounds appear to be underachieving in school. (20)

Guidance: Briefly mention patterns of attainment in school, but do not spend much time on it. Identify three or four reasons to explain why working-class children may fail in school. To gain evaluation and discussion points, you need to consider which reasons you think are the most important. Is it to do with schools, money, culture or society? Use evidence to back up your view.

The government of the UK has been trying to improve the attainment of working-class children in schools since the 1940s, but with little success. Currently, about 15% of working-class boys gain five A*–C grades at GCSE – which means that 85% of poorer boys have low levels of educational qualifications and may find getting a job difficult.

Schools

Rich middle-class children often go to schools which get good examination results. These may be popular state schools or private schools. Some schools can still choose the pupils they want to teach (**selection**) so they reject children from some backgrounds. Poorer parents may not be able to afford fees or other expenses like uniforms, so richer children get a better experience of education.

Cultural capital

Well-educated parents often know how to 'work the system' to get advantages for their children. For example, they ensure their children can read before they go to school and they can help with schoolwork or get special support if there are problems.

Material disadvantage

Poorer children do not have as much money or as many possessions to help them do well in school. For example, in some areas, children go to school without food in the morning. They are too hungry to concentrate and some schools provide breakfasts. The **digital divide** is important as some children cannot afford computers.

Cultural deprivation

Some sociologists say that poorer children do not have the same cultural background as richer students. For example, richer parents may speak in a different way to their children and their children have more developed language skills. The children may be encouraged and develop the confidence to do well.

Multi-factor explanations

Some of these problems may work together, so a parent who struggles for money may be stressed or ill, so the child does not have money, but also the parent may not be able to support the child emotionally either.

Check your understanding

Match the words and their meanings:

a) Cultural capital
b) Selection
c) Multi-factor
d) Cultural disadvantage
e) Digital divide
f) Material disadvantage
g) Working class
h) Deprivation

more than one reason acting together
knowledge of how the education system works
the difference in access to the Internet between rich and poor
being without things that are essential for living in your culture
schools choose the pupils that they want and reject ones that are difficult
having a job which depends on skill with your hands
the idea that some cultures are not as 'good' as others
people do not have the things they need for success

Key terms

Selection – schools teach the pupils that they want and reject those who are not able.

Cultural capital – knowledge of how the education system works so you can use it to benefit your family.

Material – things that are concerned with money or possessions.

Digital divide – the difference in access to knowledge between those with and those without access to the Internet.

Cultural deprivation – the idea that some cultures are not as 'good' as others.

Multi-factor – more than one reason acting together.

Exam practice

A teaching organisation, the ATL, conducted a survey of 627 teachers in 2011. They found that more than 85% of those teachers said that being poor had a bad effect on children's education. They claimed that many came to school hungry, and that poorer children lacked confidence. The worst stories came from teachers in inner city schools. One reported that a sixth former had gone without food for three days, waiting for his mother's pay day. Another claimed that a child wearing too small shoes had infected feet. One child had been severely bullied as he had no underwear. The government responded by saying that changes to the benefit system and the increasing numbers of Academies would target poor pupils.

a) Using the item, what do teachers from the ATL believe is the cause of poorer children failing to do well in school? (1)

b) How valid do you think the opinion of the teachers is? Give a sociological reason for your point of view. (3)

c) Suggest and explain sociologically, one material reason why children from poorer working-class homes appear to do less well in school. (4)

d) Identify and briefly explain one government policy that has been designed to tackle the problem of working-class underachievement in schools. (2)

Stretch and challenge

List reasons why it is a problem for a society if clever working-class children are not achieving well in education.

Find out about

Many sociologists have said that teachers are middle class and do not understand working-class culture. They claim that children from poorer homes are labelled by teachers. Find out more about labelling theory using books or Google.

Education

Topic 10: What processes in schools may cause some children to fail?

What am I going to learn?

- **You will learn that what goes on in schools can affect the learning of some children without people being aware of what is happening**

In school, children and teachers spend a lot of time together. Teachers can have a huge influence on children without realising what they are doing. Mostly teachers are anxious for their pupils to do well, and choose to teach for good motives, but nevertheless they may unintentionally cause children to fail.

Extended writing

Explain reasons why school processes are sometimes thought to cause underachievement in some social groups. (10)

Guidance: Focus on a range of different reasons why schools may cause children to fail. Try to think about children's attitudes and how they respond to teachers.

Grade boost

It may be tempting to tell personal stories about your experience in school; this can be accepted as evidence. However, avoid being rude about anyone because examiners must refer any personal information in examination scripts back to the school and you may find your paper cancelled.

Teachers and pupils

Labelling theory

Most people develop stereotypes to deal with the social world. Teachers are no different from other people and they will have a stereotype of an ideal pupil. If children do not fit the teacher's stereotype, then the teacher may have a low opinion of them. They will treat them differently from their ideal pupils and praise them less or behave as though they were naughty or less able. Children pick up on the messages that teachers give, and come to believe the labels.

Banding or streaming

In many schools, children are placed in bands or streams depending on their ability in the subject. The problem is that sometimes children who are clever are put in low bands because they are naughty, and disrupt the lessons for the ones who could do well. They are put in lower bands or streams where they disrupt the lessons of the less able, and they become bored.

Self-fulfilling prophecy

The real danger of these two social processes is that children may come to believe the labels and act as though they were true. The children teachers like do well and gain confidence, but other children come to believe they are not able, and this can lead to failure. The label becomes true.

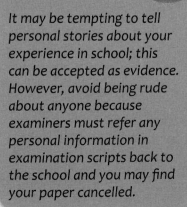

In the past, children were made to wear dunce caps and stand in a corner if the teacher felt they had done or said something foolish. What effect might this have on the child if it happened?

Hidden curriculum

Schools may give messages through socialisation that they do not intend to give. They pass on messages about life unintentionally. For example, if children tell lies to get away with not doing homework, they may get away with being lazy. However, if they tell the truth, 'I couldn't be bothered', they get into trouble. Thus children learn to tell lies in school to survive.

Anti-school subculture

Children who feel rejected by schools may react by forming social groups that are negative towards school. If they can't be seen as good or clever, then children gain status with their **peer group** by getting a reputation for being a joker or badly behaved.

Check your understanding

Put the missing words in the sentences:

a)   Messages may be passed on to children unintentionally via the ••• curriculum.

b)   ••• subcultures form when children reject the values of the school.

c)   Self-fulfilling ••• occurs when something becomes true because it was believed that it would.

d)   Teachers may ••• pupils on the basis of how they look and behave.

e)   Teachers may ••• pupils as being hardworking and nice, or difficult and unpleasant.

f)   In many schools children are placed in ••• on the basis of teacher perceptions of ability and behaviour.

Exam practice

In 2006, Diane Reay studied working-class children in school. She observed a number of lessons and interviewed pupils and teachers. She found that teachers label working-class children negatively and assume they are low in ability. She found many teachers were originally working class themselves and sympathetic, but others were snobbish and did not like working-class parents. However, she also found that many working-class boys felt peer pressure to reject school and they expressed very negative attitudes, which would make it difficult for teachers to help them.

a)   Using the item, who carried out the study of children in school? (1)

b)   Identify one research method that was used in the study. (1)

c)   Using the item, identify and explain one teacher stereotype of working-class children. (2)

d)   Fully explain labelling theory using examples. (4)

e)   Identify and briefly explain one reason why working-class boys feel under pressure to act badly in school. (2)

Key terms

Labelling theory – people are given labels and then others act as though the labels were true.

Self-fulfilling prophecy – something that becomes true because someone said it would happen.

Dunce – negative term to describe someone who fails in school.

Hidden curriculum – messages that are passed on to children unintentionally.

Anti-school subculture – a social group in the school which rejects education and teachers.

Peer group – consists of people of a similar age and background.

Stretch and challenge

Suggest arguments for and against the view that all children should be tested for ability and then taught in classes or schools only with people who got the same grades in the examination.

Over to you

Why do you think some teenagers form anti-school groups or have anti-school attitudes? Can teachers or schools be blamed for how pupils act?

Topic 11: What are anti-school subcultures?

What am I going to learn?

- **Some whole groups of children appear to develop a culture that makes them reject schooling and disrupt the education of others**

Since the link between high earnings, a comfortable lifestyle and educational success is very clear to everyone, it is a matter of concern to recognise that some whole groups of children reject school. They seem to be making a conscious choice to fail. Sociologists have been debating the reasons for this for many years.

Over to you

What methods do teachers use to control disruptive pupils? Are these methods effective?

Personal research idea

You could conduct a small-scale and anonymous survey to find out how many children truant from school and why they do so. Is it to be with friends or because they dislike school? Think of closed questions that people can answer with ticks or circles so that they will feel that they can tell the truth without getting into trouble.

🔍 websites

tinyurl.com/clc9kvo

Read an article from the BBC News website, entitled 'Fewer pupils permanently excluded from school' about the number and types of children who are excluded from school for disrupting lessons. What does this tell you about patterns of underachievement in schools?

Subcultures in schools

Some groups of children in school form groups that have slightly different norms and values from the rest of the school. These groups are subcultures.

Colin Lacey, in the 1970s, said that if children were labelled in a negative way by teachers, they would rebel and reject the school. They would gain status from their peers as 'bad' by smoking, being rude and failing to do work. Some would drink and steal. Other sociologists also studied **anti-school subcultures** and found that they were particularly associated with working-class boys. Teachers often made the problem worse because they brought attention to these boys by banning their hairstyles and clothes. Willis in the 1970s studied an anti-school subculture and found that working-class boys felt school was a waste of time, but he was writing at a time when work was easier to get for unqualified people.

African-Caribbeans and anti-school cultures

Tony Sewell said that Black children formed anti-school subcultures because of teacher racism. Many other writers have claimed that teachers are racist, too. However, racism is illegal in British schools and most schools have strong equality and multi-cultural policies. Interestingly, many writers have said that negative labels and racism do not always lead to school failure. Some students succeed in school to spite their teachers and fight against the system.

Suggest reasons why boys are more likely than girls to form anti-school subcultures.

Lads and ladettes

Some writers have said that modern males are fighting the rise of feminism by behaving in a way that is traditionally male. They focus on drinking, football and sexism. Now, there is the rise of female 'lads' or 'ladettes' who behave in a way that is traditionally male and aggressive. Carolyn Jackson says that girls are getting increasingly cheeky. Both males and females are rejecting the idea of being a 'geek' or a 'swot'. The reason for this is fear of failure. Children are tested so much in school, they would prefer to be seen as lazy rather than stupid.

Check your understanding

Match the terms with their meanings:

a) What term means a girl who acts in a boyish fashion?

b) What term refers to a group of children in a school who reject the school's values?

c) What term refers to boys who behave in a masculine fashion?

d) What term refers to people who earn their living by their hands?

e) What term refers to a survey that is completed on a computer?

f) What term refers to a process where people are given labels and then others act as though the labels were true?

Lads
Ladette
Labelling theory
Anti-school subculture
Working class
Online survey

Exam practice

The Anti-bullying Alliance conducted an online survey of children in 2012. Over a thousand responded to the questions. More than half of the survey said that they had pretended to be less able than they were or had given up an activity they enjoyed for fear of being picked on or bullied. Girls were more likely than boys to deliberately fail in mathematics but many children also stopped singing, sport or dance lessons because of peer group pressure not to succeed.

a) Using the item, how was the study carried out? (1)

b) Fully explain the meaning of the term anti-school subculture. (2)

c) Fully explain the meaning of the term peer group pressure. (2)

d) Explain one possible reason why anti-school subcultures develop. (2)

e) Identify and briefly explain one reason why African-Caribbean children may develop anti-school subcultures. (2)

Key terms

Anti-school subculture – a social group in the school which rejects education and teachers.

Laddish behaviour – behaving in a very traditionally aggressive masculine way.

Ladettes – girls who copy male behaviour in terms of drinking, smoking and aggression.

Stretch and challenge

Suggest points for and against the view that schooling is very bad for children.

Extended writing

Explain reasons why children may form anti-school subcultures. (10)

Guidance: Focus on a range of different reasons why children form anti-school subcultures. You could look at two reasons in depth, or offer a lot of suggestions but just cover a few ideas. If you use actual sociologists or theories in your answer, then you will probably make the top mark band.

Education

Topic 12: How does material deprivation affect children's education?

What am I going to learn?

- There is a direct link between being poor and underachieving in school that is clearly understood by researchers and the government

Children who come from poor families are very likely to grow up to be poor themselves. They are more likely to be unemployed, and to experience poor health as adults. They are more likely to get a criminal conviction or to experience family break-up. The reasons for their problems are often linked to the fact that they do badly in school, regardless of their ability.

Grade boost

When people are asked about material deprivation, they often just talk about the fact that poor children do not have things such as books and computers. This is very narrow and shows very little understanding of how big an impact being poor can have on someone's life. Take a wider view and think of other issues as well in your answers.

Interesting facts

Material deprivation may contribute to the relative lack of success of children from some ethnic minorities as they are very likely to be from low-income families. Bangladeshi families traditionally have a larger number of children, and women are not expected to work outside the home. This means that there will only be one income for a large family to live on.

Material deprivation

People who are **materially deprived** are poor. Government statistics suggest that as many as one in five children in the UK comes from a family that has money problems, for example low pay or living on benefits. In the British system statistics are based on children who get free school meals (**FSM**).

Longitudinal studies that follow children through their lives all show that poorer children have worse educational experiences and more difficult lives as adults. The issues are more than a lack of resources; they have a whole range of other problems to deal with.

Location

Many poorer children go to schools where lots of other pupils have social problems. The school is more likely to be short of money, unpopular with parents and have poor results. Teachers often prefer not to work in difficult schools and so do not stay long.

Health

Many FSM children experience poor health linked to difficult living conditions or behavioural difficulties. Some are hungry or have a diet lacking in essential nutrients. Poor quality foods are linked to behavioural conditions such as ADHD. The children may therefore miss lessons and find it difficult to catch up.

Family breakdown and stress

People who are poor are more likely to experience stress-related problems such as depression. Children are therefore under pressure. They may have to care for their parents or other children in the family. They may have to work to support the family income.

Bullying

Children who are deprived are vulnerable to bullying from others for reasons such as lack of fashion items or even personal hygiene issues because they live in over-crowded homes or have no heating in the home. They develop **low self-esteem** problems and expect to experience failure.

Parenting

Children whose parents have low levels of educational attainment will usually have less support. Their parents may reject teachers because of their own bad experiences in school. They may pass these attitudes onto their children.

Key terms

Material deprivation – people lack the things that others in society have.

FSM – children who have free school meals.

Low self-esteem – lack of confidence in their own ability.

Stretch and challenge

Create a poster to encourage children to do their best in school. Explain the link between educational success and a comfortable life.

Check your understanding

Match the terms with their meanings:

Digital divide
Longitudinal
Poverty
Cultural capital
Material deprivation
FSM

a) What term refers to a lack of money in the home?

b) What term refers to a lack of the things that are needed and which other people in society have?

c) What term refers to studies which follow the same group of people over a long period of time?

d) What term is used to refer to children who are eligible for free school meals?

e) What term refers to the idea that richer parents know how to work the system in favour of their own children?

f) What term refers to the difference in access to knowledge between those with and those without access to the Internet?

Exam practice

According a study funded by the Welsh Assembly in 2008, nearly one in four children in Wales lives in a home where money is a concern. One in ten children lives in a home with serious problems because of the lack of money. This is often because no one in the home has a job, often because a parent is sick or disabled. The Welsh Assembly is committed to improving the education of such children because it gives them a chance of better lives than their parents. They support out-of-school clubs to help poor children catch up with others.

a) Using the item, what proportion of children in Wales live in a home where money is a concern? (1)

b) Suggest a term that can be used to describe lack of things that others in society have. (1)

c) Fully explain why children from families where mothers have no qualifications are very likely to be poor. (4)

d) Fully explain one reason why material deprivation can lead to a poor educational outcome for a child. (4)

Extended writing

Discuss reasons why material deprivation can affect educational outcomes for poorer children. (20)

Guidance: You will need to mention why people are poor and then to talk about how many children are poor, just to explain the importance of the discussion. After that, look at all of the possible reasons and think about how poverty affects children's lives. The discussion will be a consideration of which of the reasons is most important.

Education

Topic 13: How may cultural deprivation affect children's education?

What am I going to learn?

- **Many people believe that one of the reasons that working-class children fail to do well in education is because they have attitudes that make it difficult for them to learn**

This theory suggests that working-class people have a culture that is not as good as that of richer people. Their children are badly socialised and do not know how to behave. The parents are ignorant and do not understand how to support their children. They are aggressive to teachers and do not know how to behave properly.

Extended writing

Discuss reasons why cultural deprivation can affect educational outcomes for poorer children. (20)

Guidance: You will need to explain the meaning of the term carefully and then offer reasons why some people believe it. The discussion part of this essay may be to consider whether material deprivation or cultural deprivation is more of a problem for poorer children. It is difficult to prove whether a whole group of people (poor people) are worse than another whole group (rich people) and so the evidence for cultural deprivation is not clear. It is also a little insulting to poor people who are often doing their very best under difficult circumstances.

Cultural deprivation

Poor parents are bad parents?

In the 1960s and 1970s, it was widely believed by educational experts that poor children came from homes where parents did not support their children. Famous studies showed that they were less likely to read to their children and they did not go to parents' evenings in school. In America and in the UK, this led to the governments offering extra teaching to poorer children in nursery schools to make up for the lack of parenting skills in the home. It was also believed that poor people had different values from richer people. Poorer people wanted **immediate gratification** whereas rich people learned to work now for rewards in the future.

Some modern writers believe that poor children who come from single parent families are brought up without understanding the importance of hard work for success. Charles Murray, who was influential in the 1990s, said that poor children expected to grow up and have a life that depended on crime and welfare benefits.

Limited life experiences

Children from middle-class families are more likely to have had a wider variety of learning experiences. They may have been taken to out-of-school clubs or music lessons. They will have been on holidays abroad or taken to museums and events that give them a basic start. There will have been books and pictures in the home.

The British Museum is a top tourist attraction in London and entry is free. Do working-class people take their children to museums and art galleries?

Poor language skills?

Basil Bernstein suggested in the 1970s that poor people use language differently from richer people. He even thought that this might affect their ability to think. He certainly believed that poor children did not understand the way that teachers use language. Not everyone agrees with this idea, but it has been **influential**. It is known that some poorer children start school with limited language skills because they have not had much chance to talk to their parents and have spent more time watching television.

Check your understanding

Match the terms with their meanings:

a) Cultural deprivation	a category of children who qualify for free school meals
b) Material deprivation	working-class children fail because they lack possessions and money
c) Immediate gratification	working-class children have a culture that leads to failure in school
d) Vocabulary	middle-class people know how to work the system to benefit their own children
e) Badly socialised	lacking training in the skills for success in life
f) FSM	looking for pleasure in the present rather than putting it off
g) Cultural capital	language and words

Exam practice

In 2010, an educational charity known as the Sutton Trust found that children in the poorest homes were up to a year behind children from middle-class homes when they started school. They looked at language tests on 12,000 five-year-olds and found large differences in ability with words. They also said that good parenting such as reading to children, library trips and having a regular bedtime could help children improve. It urged the government to fund parenting classes in deprived areas. It also said that more nursery places with qualified teachers were needed.

a) Using the item, who conducted the survey? (1)
b) Using the item, how many children were surveyed? (1)
c) What did the research team consider was evidence of good parenting? (1)
d) How did the research team suggest that the government could help? (1)
e) Fully explain the meaning of the term cultural deprivation. (3)
f) Identify and explain the evidence from the item that suggests that working-class children have a different culture from middle-class children. (3)

Key terms

Cultural deprivation – the idea that working-class people have an inferior culture to middle-class people.

Immediate gratification – having pleasure in the present rather than putting it off, for example spending your money as soon as you get it, rather than saving up.

Influential – a lot of people believe it to be true.

Vocabulary – words that people understand and can use.

Cultural capital – middle-class people know how to work the system to benefit their children.

Stretch and challenge

What do you think are the main differences between the culture of poorer children and of teachers?

Grade boost

The evidence for material deprivation is quite good because the link between poverty and deprivation is clearly understood. The idea that poor people cause their own problems because they are bad parents may be a way of blaming the victim for their difficulties.

Topic 14: What happens in Further Education and Higher Education to cause inequality?

What am I going to learn?

- **There are very few jobs available for people on the basis of qualifications that they get in school at 16; education after school is important to people**

The statistics are clear. On average people who have been to university tend to earn more and live longer than other people. In the UK, most children go to school, so schools have a limited choice in who they teach. However, Further and Higher Education are different because they choose their students. Problems of inequality in schools are even more serious in universities.

Extended writing

Explain why working-class children tend not to apply for Higher and Further education courses. (10)

Guidance: A brief statement to explain that when Higher Education gives so many advantages in life, then people who do not apply put themselves at a disadvantage would explain the debate. Then move on to a variety of explanations; these can be to do with the failure to get qualifications, but to be in the highest mark bands, you need to know something specific about universities, so mention the effect of fees.

Education after school

School does not provide the qualifications for work. People usually go on to **Further Education**, to learn skills at a lower level or to **Higher Education** where they gain a qualification known as a **degree**. Getting a place at university is competitive, and some universities are harder to get into than others. People who have been to the universities with the best reputations can find it easier to get a job.

NEETS

There are about a million young people who do not go on to jobs or training. The government is very worried because these are likely to be the ones who will be poor in later life.

Higher Education

What advantages in life do you gain from getting a good degree from a good university?

It was argued that because going to university gives people such an advantage in life, they should pay for the education they gained. People were first charged for courses in 1998. Different levels of cost apply in Wales, England and Scotland. Students can take out a loan and then pay it back from their earnings. Families on very low incomes can get free education, but few people qualify. Numbers applying from poorer homes are dropping and universities are being set targets to get disadvantaged students. The money raised by fees for university funding is now being spent on attracting poorer children to apply.

Part of the problem is that poor children do not get the qualifications to apply. The qualifications required for courses such as Law or Medicine are high, and still, most people who apply will be rejected. Many or most of the applicants come from private schools or schools in wealthy areas where they are trained in the application process.

Poorer children are more likely to worry about debt. They are more likely to start courses and drop out and they apply for courses that may not lead to jobs. Many poorer children do not have the **aspirations** to go to university, even when they have the talent.

Key terms

Further Education – education after school for work and a career, e.g. A levels, BTEC Nationals.

Higher Education – education after school for professional work, e.g. degrees.

Degree – a qualification which is gained through university study.

NEETS – young people who are not in education, employment or training.

Aspirations – hopes and ambitions.

Check your understanding

True or false – what do you think?

a) Only rich people go to Oxford and Cambridge.
b) Getting a degree will guarantee you a good job.
c) Students can qualify for cheap loans to go to university.
d) Some universities have a better reputation than others.
e) Richer children are more likely to gain university places than poorer children.
f) Not everyone who has a successful career has been to university.
g) You must go to university if you want to work in medicine or architecture.

Stretch and challenge

Is an A-Level qualification gained by a poor, deprived child from a really difficult background worth more than the same qualification gained by a rich privileged child from a really good school?

Across the generations

Talk to someone much older than yourself, perhaps a teacher, about the decision to go to college. What made them go? Did others in their family go? What benefits did they get from going to university?

Exam practice

Gaining a university degree can significantly increase and improve your son's or daughter's career prospects. They will not only have a wider variety of career options to choose from once they have a degree, but they are likely to progress much faster up the career ladder. While it would be misleading to claim that a degree guarantees employment, an increasing number of organisations require people to hold degrees before applying. Some careers, such as those in medicine, nursing, architecture, law and pharmacy, cannot be practised without a particular vocational degree or relevant Higher Education experience.

a) Explain the meaning of the term degree. (1)
b) Using the item, identify four careers for which a degree is essential. (2)
c) Identify and explain two advantages of a degree qualification in life. (4)
d) Explain one reason why working-class children are less likely to gain a degree than children from wealthier backgrounds. (3)

Compulsory Core
Topic 1: What is inequality?

What am I going to learn?

● **To understand what the word inequality means**

There are several different kinds of inequality which can include differences in wealth, pay, status, health, jobs, houses, opportunities and quality of life. Sociologists call these differences 'life chances'. Inequality is at the heart of what sociology is about.

Famous people

Max Weber

Max Weber is a very important sociologist who had many good ideas. He took some of Karl Marx's ideas further. For instance, the idea of **life chances**, which is to do with how likely it is that a person will be successful in life. He said that a person's job was not the only thing that affected position in society. How important a person is seen as and the groups they belong to also affect a person's position.

Thinking skills

What would life in the UK be like if we had a perfectly equal society?

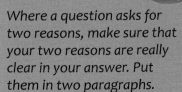

Grade boost

Where a question asks for two reasons, make sure that your two reasons are really clear in your answer. Put them in two paragraphs.

What is inequality?

Inequality is about the differences between the rich and poor. This difference can often be seen in all of those things listed above. Poor people will usually get lower pay than rich people, but also be seen as less important, have worse health and housing. These differences are what we call inequality.

Examples of inequality

Example 1

Joe is 15 and lives in a rented two-bedroom house with his mother and younger brother Sid. He shares a bedroom with Sid and they do not have a desk or anywhere quiet to work. The neighbourhood is very noisy. Joe does not get his homework done and is not expected to get many C grades next year. Joe's mother works part-time as a teaching assistant.

Joe does not have a garden and there are no playing fields nearby. He does not get much exercise. The house is damp so Joe gets lots of colds each winter, and has lots of time off school. The family have not been on holiday for three years. His mother has no savings and sometimes they do not have any money for food.

Example 2

Ben is 15 and lives in a large detached house with his parents, brother and sister. The house has a very large garden including an outdoor swimming pool. The house has six bedrooms and a study. Ben's father is a solicitor.

Ben belongs to a tennis club and is also learning to scuba dive. Ben plays piano and can ride a horse. Ben's family own a villa in Spain, which they visit several times a year. Ben has a large fund of money, already saved up by his parents, to go to university.

Sociologists are interested in all kinds of inequalities including **lifestyle**, **wealth**, health and opportunities.

Check your understanding

Complete the sentences below using the words in the word box.

reasons	rich	health
opportunities	inequalities	

Sociologists are interested in finding out about the ••• between different groups. Poor people tend to have a different lifestyle compared with ••• people. The poor are likely to have lower wages, worse ••• and live in poorer housing. Rich people are likely to have better ••• than poor people. Sociologists try to understand the ••• for these differences.

Exam practice

In 2011, the Office for National Statistics (ONS) revealed that workers in the worst paid jobs – such as dinner ladies, hairdressers and waiters – have seen their pay fall sharply. This has made families worry about being able to pay for food, heating and electricity bills.

The bottom tenth of earners saw their pay creep up just 0.1% between 2010 and 2011 while the top tenth saw their pay grow 18 times faster.

a) Using the item, identify why workers in the worst paid jobs are worried about being able to pay for food and heating. (1)

b) Using the item, identify which group of earners saw their pay grow 18 times faster than the bottom tenth of earners. (1)

c) Explain the meaning of the term inequality, using an example. (2)

d) Identify two areas of life in which there may be a gap between rich and poor. (2)

e) Describe two reasons why poor families may have worse life chances than rich families. (4)

Grade boost

Make this grid into your own revision card.
Add your own definition and example.

Key term	Definition	My own example
Inequality		
Life chances		
Wealth		
Status		
Lifestyle		

Key terms

Inequality – is where some groups of people have more wealth, better opportunities and may be seen as more important than other groups.

Lifestyle – the way that people live including their job, car, clothes, health and leisure activities.

Wealth – the amount of possessions that a person has. This may include money, property and other possessions.

Life chances – are about opportunities of enjoying the good things in life and avoiding the bad.

Status – how important a person is seen as.

Stretch and challenge

- Visit your local town. Look for evidence of inequality.

- Many people think that Britain is becoming more unequal. If you were the government, what laws would you introduce to try to make the UK more equal?

- Find out what functionalists and Marxists say about social inequality. You will find some information later in this chapter, but can also use other books and the Internet.

Compulsory Core

Topic 2: What are the causes of inequality?

What am I going to learn?

- **To understand different causes of inequality**

There are many different types of inequality. Sociologists have been very interested in racism, sexism and ageism as causes of inequality. In the UK all governments are concerned that too much inequality can cause social problems including crime and wastage of talent.

Over to you

What do you think could be done by the government to stop people having sexist, racist or ageist attitudes?

Grade boost

Using examples from your lessons, the media, and personal experiences will help you show your understanding and get better marks.

Equal opportunities

All societies have some kind of inequality. This may be about differences in wealth, power, property, lifestyle, how important people are seen as and their chances of enjoying the good things in life and avoiding the bad. The sociological phrase for these opportunities is life chances.

In countries like Britain and the USA, one of the values that is seen as important is the idea that everyone should have an equal chance of being successful. It is not expected that everyone will have the same amount of wealth or status, but everyone should have a fair chance. Therefore, an important type of inequality is a lack of equal opportunities. This is called **inequality of opportunity**.

Causes of inequality

In the history of different societies one of the main causes of inequality between social groups has been discrimination against certain groups.

In Britain and the USA one of the biggest inequalities has been between men and women. Treating another gender differently because of their gender is called **sexism**. In the early 20th century, suffragettes in Britain had to fight to win the vote for women. More recently, the film *Made in Dagenham*, set in 1968, shows how women had to battle for the same pay as men.

Racism has also been a cause of inequality. Racism is the belief that some races are better than others. Very few sociologists use the idea of race and see this as outdated. However, some people still may think there are differences between people based on their colour of skin or different cultures. They may then treat them differently causing inequality and unfairness.

In recent years there have been concerns about **ageism**. This is like racism and sexism but is directed against people because of their age. Elderly people may be discriminated against because they are old and considered to be 'past it'. Young people may be seen as troublemakers and discriminated against by police who target them.

Check your understanding

Match the correct word to the definition:

Racism	Sexism	Sample
Life chances	Ageism	Questionnaire

a) What term is used to describe the selection of people from a population for research?

b) What term is used to describe thinking or acting negatively towards someone because of their ethnic background?

c) What term is used to describe the different opportunities of enjoying the good things in life?

d) What term is used to describe treating someone differently because of how old they are?

e) What term is used to describe a list of questions on a piece of paper or online?

f) What term is used to describe treating someone differently because of their gender?

Key terms

Inequality of opportunity – people do not get an equal chance to be successful.

Sexism – the idea that one gender is better at or more suited to some activities than the other.

Racism – the idea that one race is better than others.

Ageism – the idea that some age groups are not as capable or act in a certain way.

Inequality of outcome – different people will finish with more money, better jobs or lifestyle than others.

Exam practice

Sexism in football

A football manager was in trouble with his club after making sexist comments that female referees and assistant referees shouldn't be involved in matches.

Mike Newell said: 'It's bad enough with the poor referees and assistant referees we have, but if you start bringing in women, you have big problems.'

Newell, the manager of Luton Town, later apologised for his comments. However, his club still wanted to talk to him about what he said, and made it clear they didn't agree with what he said about women.

a) Identify a sexist comment that Mike Newell the football manager made. (1)

b) Identify one effect that Mike Newell's comment could have on women interested in working in football. (1)

c) Explain the meaning of the term racism, using an example. (2)

d) Identify and explain one sociological reason why Mike Newell may have the view he expressed. (2)

e) Describe two different types of inequality. (2)

Stretch and challenge

- Find out who is responsible for equal opportunities in your school. Ask them to your class and find out what their job involves.

- Make a list of 10 ways in which young people (under 18) are treated differently compared with older people.

Compulsory Core

Topic 3: What are prejudice and discrimination?

What am I going to learn?

● **To understand the twin terms prejudice and discrimination**

Sociologists believe that understanding these two terms is really important to help get rid of racism, sexism and ageism.

Prejudice and discrimination

Martin Luther King

Famous people

Martin Luther King was a popular leader of the black community in the 1950s and 1960s. He is famous for challenging the laws and customs which discriminated against black people in the USA. Martin Luther King was assassinated on a hotel balcony in Memphis in 1968. Many people see him as an inspirational leader, and pop musicians like U2, UB40 and Stevie Wonder have all written songs about him.

In our lives we meet thousands of people, which can be a scary thing! Going somewhere new, such as a new class, school, town or workplace, we look for people who we are comfortable with. This often means people who we think are like either ourselves or people we know already. This is fine, but can make us less positive about people who are not like ourselves.

In one way this seems a fair enough thing to do. However, it can mean that we decide what people are like based on what they look like, their ethnic group, gender, or age. Sociologists call this **prejudice**. It means that we form an opinion based on appearances before we even meet them. We pre-judge them.

It may be a positive (good) judgement or a negative (bad) one. Prejudice only involves thinking in this way about other people. Most people probably do think like this at times, but realise that it is not a fair way to judge people. Prejudice may be based on stereotypes, which are exaggerated views of groups.

However, some people take it further and actually treat the person they are prejudiced about differently. This is called **discrimination**. It can include:

● Being unfriendly or ignoring them

● Abusing them

● Not including them

● Treating them unfavourably – not giving them a job, housing or the same chance as other people

● Institutions, such as the police, schools and courts treating them unfairly.

Discrimination can also be positive. As well as treating groups worse because of prejudice, some groups are treated better. This is called positive discrimination.

Sometimes the governments of some countries try to positively discriminate towards some groups. They do this to attempt to make up for the past disadvantages of the group. In Britain, extra resources have been targeted at schools in inner city areas to help poor children have a better chance.

Check your understanding

Match the terms with the definition:

> Prejudice   Inequality   Racism
> Discrimination   Ageism   Sexism

a) Treating someone differently because they are an elderly or young person.

b) Where some groups of people have more wealth, resources or a better lifestyle than other groups.

c) The idea that men are better at or more suited to some things than women.

d) When we decide what people are like based on what they look like, their ethnic group, gender, or age.

e) When we believe that our race is better than others.

f) The action of treating someone differently because they belong to a certain group.

Exam practice

> Up until the 1950s and 1960s, black people in the southern states of the USA were treated very differently. They had separate housing, schools, cafes and bars. Black people's places were much worse than white people's. They were unequal to white people in many ways, and it was made very difficult for them to register to vote.
>
> This was allowed to happen by most white people because they had grown up being prejudiced about black people. The long history of slavery in these states of the USA meant that white people had been socialised to think they were better than black people.

a) Using the item, identify one example of inequality between black people and white people in the southern states. (1)

b) Using the item, explain why white people allowed black people to be treated so unfairly. (1)

c) Explain, with examples, how people may be discriminated against. (2)

d) Explain the meaning of the term positive discrimination, using an example. (2)

e) Describe the difference between prejudice and discrimination. (4)

Key terms

Prejudice – an idea about what someone is like based on a pre-judgement about them.

Discrimination – an action for or against someone often because of a prejudice.

Stretch and challenge

- Speak to an elderly or disabled person. Find out how they feel about how they are treated in society.

- Find out about the Holocaust. YouTube has many useful documentaries. Movies like *The Pianist* are also worth viewing.

- Watch or read *To Kill a Mockingbird*.

Thinking skills

What could schools do to help children grow up to be less prejudiced?

Grade boost

Make sure you know the difference between prejudice and discrimination. Discrimination always involves an action, whereas prejudice is about the thinking behind it.

Compulsory Core

Topic 4: What are the reasons for prejudice and discrimination?

What am I going to learn?

● **To understand some of the sociological explanations for prejudice and discrimination**

Put simply, why do individuals not like other groups of people, and treat them differently? This can cause inequality. There are several different reasons for this, which sociology helps us to understand.

Famous people

Adolf Hitler

Hitler was the leader of Germany in the Second World War. Germany had a lot of money problems in the 1920s and 1930s. Hitler wrote a book called *Mein Kampf*, which means 'My Struggle'. In the book he blamed the Jews for Germany's problems. He stereotyped them as being greedy, and blamed them for Germany losing the First World War, the money problems and communism.

This made Hitler popular and helped to get him into power. The Jews became scapegoats for all of Germany's problems. The end result of this was prejudice, discrimination and the deaths of millions of Jews.

What are the reasons for prejudice and discrimination?

Some people are afraid when they meet people who are different from them. Other groups may look different and have different customs. They may not know much about the other group, and so not trust them. This may mean that they do not treat them fairly, e.g. not offering them a job, because they are from a different ethnic group. Alternatively, they may be rude or aggressive towards them.

Misunderstanding and fear

People may find different cultures hard to understand. For instance, in British culture it is seen as polite to look people in the eyes to show honesty. Some Asian cultures think that looking someone in the eyes is disrespectful. This can cause a **cultural misunderstanding**.

Socialisation

Unfortunately, racist ideas can be very strong and in some cultures young people can be socialised into prejudiced ideas. They will then grow up thinking that racism is the norm. In the 18th century when Britain was involved in the slave trade, prejudice and racism towards black people was seen as the norm.

Stereotypes

Stereotypes are another reason for prejudice. Stereotypes are oversimplified, exaggerated ideas about a group of people. For instance, one stereotype is the idea that the elderly have poor memories, and do not understand new technology. Even worse, in Nazi Germany stereotypes of Jewish people were used to show them in a bad way and blame them for all of Germany's problems. This is called **scapegoating**.

Scapegoats are often used when a country has economic problems. Minority groups, such as immigrants or ethnic minorities, are blamed for crime or unemployment. Prejudice is at the heart of this sort of thinking. Even though sociology has helped us understand prejudice, there have still been some terrible events caused by prejudice in the last hundred years.

Check your understanding

Complete the sentences using the words in the word box.

socialised	teaching	stereotyped
problems	culture	

a) Racism can be caused by not understanding another person's •••.

b) Some people are racist because they have been ••• that way.

c) Schools can help to stop racism by ••• people about other cultures.

d) Young people are sometimes ••• as troublemakers.

e) Scapegoating often happens when there are financial •••.

Key terms

Cultural misunderstanding – when a person may not understand something about another person's culture and so see them in a negative or confused way.

Stereotype – a fixed, exaggerated idea about a group of people.

Scapegoating – when a group of people are blamed for some of society's problems.

Thinking skills

Is a world without prejudice possible? How could it be achieved?

Stretch and challenge

- If you were the government think of three ways you would try to reduce prejudice against a particular group, e.g. young, old, disabled or ethnic minorities.

- Watch the film *Hotel Rwanda* and learn about the problems in Rwanda between the Hutus and the Tutsis in the 1990s.

Exam practice

In some shopping centres rules have been made about young people gathering in groups. Security guards have been encouraged to move them out of the centres and to break up groups of young people, even when they are not doing anything wrong.

The reason for this may be that older people feel worried that the young people may cause trouble or threaten them. They may be worried because when they see young people in groups they think of stereotypes they have seen on television and in the newspapers. The owners of large shopping centres want to keep the older customers happy.

The controversial ex-Manchester City striker Balotelli was told by security staff at the Trafford Centre near Manchester that he was breaking the rules by wearing a hoodie. He was hoping to keep a low profile so quietly left the centre.

Balotelli stereotyped.

a) Using the item, explain why older people may be worried when they see groups of young people gathering in shopping centres. (1)

b) Using the item, identify where older people may get their ideas about young people from. (1)

c) Identify two sociological explanations for prejudice and discrimination. (2)

d) Explain the meaning of the term scapegoating, using an example. (2)

e) Describe two ways in which prejudice can cause inequality. (4)

Compulsory Core

Topic 5: What are status and prestige?

What am I going to learn?

- **To understand the ways in which different groups enjoy different levels of status and prestige**

Sociologists are interested in the way that different roles are given different levels of status and prestige. Why are some people seen as more important than others?

Status

In simple terms **status** is about a person's position in society. Think about the different layers of a trifle. Societies are like this, with people placed in different layers of importance. Would you be jelly, custard or cream?

Unlike trifle, societies are organised in different ways. In medieval times, at the top there was the king, followed by barons, knights, freemen, and at the bottom, serfs. In India, there is a traditional caste system, where lower castes are seen as inferior to higher ones.

In both of these systems people were born into their social position. Sociologists call this **ascribed status**. This is seen by some as a very old-fashioned, and not very fair, way of deciding how important someone is.

In modern societies, like Britain, we aim to decide people's position in society based on what they achieve. For instance, important jobs like surgeon, MP and lawyer should go to the best qualified, brightest people as long as they work hard. Status achieved like this is known as **achieved status.**

In fact, in Britain there still exist a good many positions that are not earned. People like the Queen and some members of the aristocracy are born into their position. Kate Middleton came from a wealthy family, but 'achieved' even higher status by marrying Prince William. Some sociologists (Marxists and feminists) think that some groups (higher social classes and men) stand a better chance of gaining high status positions.

Prestige

Prestige is a similar idea to status. It is about a person's position in society being seen as special by other people. Certain positions in society are seen as especially valuable and are greatly respected. For instance, a doctor is seen as a position with a great deal of prestige. Most parents would be proud for their child to become a doctor or lawyer. In comparison, a labourer would have very low prestige and not be seen as special by others.

Over to you

- What is most important to you in your future life as an adult? Money or status?

- Can you think of five jobs that are well paid but have low prestige?

- Next try to think of five jobs that are low paid but have high prestige.

Thinking skills

- How do students in your school vary in status?

- Which students have the highest status?

- Are there possessions that give the students a higher status?

- What are they?

Interesting fact

The House of Lords is part of the system of government in the UK. THe House of Lords checks new laws that are passed by parliament and can stop or delay a new law.

Being a member of the House of Lords gives a person high status and prestige. It used to be mainly ascribed status. This meant that most lords were born into their position. In recent years this has changed and most of the lords are appointed by the Prime Minister or by special commission. People who are appointed are recognised for their achievements or contribution to the UK. So most members of the House of Lords now have achieved status.

Check your understanding

Complete the following sentences:

a) A position which is seen as special by other people may be said to have great •••.
b) A person who is born into their position has ••• status.
c) A person who has earned their position has ••• status.
d) How important a person is seen as is known as their •••.
e) Modern societies mainly give high status based on what people •••.

Exam practice

The BBC found in a survey that some features of people's houses are seen as status symbols. This means that they are signs that the person who owns them has a high status. The top status symbols were hot tubs, walk-in wardrobes and music piped through all rooms.

a) Using the item, identify one of the top status symbols. (1)
b) Explain what people may think of people who own the top status symbols. (1)
c) Explain the meaning of the term prestige, using an example. (2)
d) Identify and explain one advantage that having high status may have for the person. (2)
e) Explain two sociological reasons why some groups may not have a fair chance of getting into high-status positions. (4)

Key terms

Status – how important your position in society is.

Ascribed status – a position you are born into, e.g. gender, the queen.

Achieved status – a position you have earned, e.g. teacher, prefect.

Prestige – how special or important a position is seen as.

Stretch and challenge

- Do a survey of your class to find out what the top status symbols for young people at your school are.
- Make a list of what you think are the top ten most prestigious jobs in UK society. Compare them with others in the group.
- Is it possible to have a world where all people enjoy great prestige?

Grade boost

Make a revision card with the following table on it. Add your own examples.

Key term	Definition	My own example
Prestige		
Ascribed status		
Achieved status		
Status		

Compulsory Core

Topic 6: What is wealth?

What am I going to learn?

● **To understand what wealth is**

Sociologists highlight the difference between wealth and income. It is possible to have a high income and not be wealthy. Sociologists are interested in the way that patterns of wealth and income have changed in Britain. Are we becoming more or less unequal?

Across the generations

Interview a relative or family friend who had left school by the mid-1980s. Find out what it was like for people leaving school in the late 1970s or early 1980s. Report back to your class.

Famous people

Joseph Rowntree was a chocolate manufacturer in the 19th century. As well as running a successful business, he was very concerned about the lives of poor people. He wanted society to be fairer and to improve the lives of his workers. He set up the Joseph Rowntree Foundation which carries out research into poverty and tries to help the poor.

Wealth

Wealth includes property, savings, shares and any valuable items a person has. It is about how much money a person has stored away that they do not use in their everyday life. They may store it in the bank, own expensive houses, cars or works of art. All of these are stored assets that they could sell or use if needed, or leave to their children.

Income

Lots of people get wealth confused with **income**. Income means the money a person gets every week or month to live on. It could be wages, benefits or pensions. Someone could have a high income, but spend it all every month and so not have much wealth.

Some very lucky people might have an income from their wealth. For instance, if they own lots of property, people will pay them rent every month, which is an income.

Changing patterns of wealth

The American sociologist Robert K. Merton introduced an idea called 'The Matthew Effect'. Taken from the Bible, it means that the rich will get richer while the poor get poorer. How true has this been in Britain since 1945?

In the 1950s, working people's lives became much better. People had cars, televisions, better housing. Harold Macmillan, the prime minister of the time, is famous for saying:

'Indeed let us be frank about it – most of our people have never had it so good.

Go around the country, go to the industrial towns, go to the farms and you will see a state of prosperity such as we have never had in my lifetime – nor indeed in the history of this country.'

In the 1980s and onwards, most reports suggest that the rich are getting richer whilst the poor become poorer. The 1980s were seen as a time when being rich was an important value. Movies of the time, like *Wall Street*, *The Secret of My Success* and *Trading Places* focussed on wealth. The gap became wider and by 2007, the Joseph Rowntree Foundation reported that inequality of wealth was the highest it had been for 40 years.

So, even though inequality became less in the 1950s and 1960s, it seems that over time the Matthew Effect has happened in the UK.

Check your understanding

Decide which of the following are wealth and which income:

Wages

Interest on your savings

A holiday home

Pension

Jewellery

Stocks and shares

Benefits

Exam practice

The UK's richest people have become even richer over the past year, according to the *Sunday Times* Rich List in 2011. This is surprising when the country has been in a recession. A recession is when there are severe money problems in a country. This can cause people to lose their jobs, get into debt and businesses to go bust.

The newspaper's research found the total value of the country's 1,000 wealthiest people is £414 billion, up 4.7% since 2008.

It means their wealth, when added together, is even higher than in 2008, before the recession started. This is a new record. The poor have become poorer since the recession.

a) Using the item, identify how much wealth the top 1,000 people own. (1)

b) Explain one problem which can be caused by a recession. (1)

c) Explain the difference between the terms income and wealth, using an example. (2)

d) Identify and explain how the gap between rich and poor has changed since 1945. (2)

e) Explain two ways in which wealth may give the rich better life chances. (4)

Key terms

Wealth – includes property, savings, shares and valuable items.

Income – money that is received weekly or monthly as wages, benefits or pension.

Stretch and challenge

Imagine you were the government. Think of five laws you would introduce to reduce the gap between rich and poor.

Or

Imagine you are really wealthy. You want to make sure that you and your friends and relatives stay rich and get richer. What five laws would you encourage the government to make?

Grade boost

Keep a note pad by your television. Write down a brief note about any news items or programmes you see which link to your studies. Try to include them in your answers. They will make your work stand out.

Compulsory Core

Topic 7: Who are the elites? What power and privilege do they have?

What am I going to learn?

- **To understand what is meant by the term elite and the advantages they have over others**

Sociologists, especially Marxists and feminists, are very interested in discovering who has power in British society.

Elites

An **elite** is a small group in a society who are very powerful and wealthy. In the English football Premier League teams like Manchester United, Arsenal and Chelsea (and Liverpool!) are known as elite teams. They have more influence than other football clubs and are able to get their own way. Society also has a small group of individuals who are able to get what they want.

Power

Power is the ability to influence decisions in your favour. For instance, Rupert Murdoch, who owns Sky TV, *The Times*, *Sun* and other media interests, is very powerful. Some sociologists say that he has been able to influence the results of the last few general elections.

Privilege

Privilege is when a group of people in society enjoy special advantages over other groups. For example in the 2010 general election results, 504 MPs were male and 146 female. These numbers would be expected, by chance, to be roughly equal. The large numbers of male MPs show male privilege. Groups that enjoy privilege may not be treated as harshly by the police or courts as other groups. They may get the best jobs, health care and be seen as high status by other people.

Who are the elites in the UK?

Marxists would say that the most powerful elite are the **ruling class**. This would include the very rich, such as Alan Sugar and Richard Branson, who own the most important companies. Another part of this group is the aristocracy. This includes the royal family and people with titles.

There are other groups within the upper class who may have privileges, especially what is known as 'the Old Boys' Network'. These are people who went to the top fee-paying schools, such as Eton and Harrow. They are said to favour each other when top jobs are available. They are also mainly white and male.

Famous people

Steven Lukes wrote a book called *Power*. In the book he explained three ways in which powerful elite groups controlled other people:

1) They make sure decisions go their way, e.g. laws are passed allowing the rich to pay less tax.

2) They were able to make sure that some things are never discussed, e.g. in his study the powerful were able to stop discussions about changes in laws about pollution.

3) They make people want what they want them to, e.g. persuading people to want things like new phones through advertising.

Check your understanding

Complete the following sentences:

aristocracy	power	elite
	male	privilege	Marxism

a) A small group of people who have lots of influence are known as an •••.

b) The ruling class are seen by ••• as a powerful elite.

c) Groups of people that have ••• are more likely to get the best jobs.

d) The upper class are very rich, own important companies or are from the •••.

e) The elite are mainly upper class, white and •••.

f) The ability to get what you want is called •••.

Exam practice

Oxford and Cambridge universities dominate list of leading UK people

A third of the UK's leading people went to Oxford or Cambridge universities and four out of every 10 of them attended fee-paying schools, a report suggests.

The study of the backgrounds of nearly 8,000 people was carried out by a charity called the Sutton Trust.

Only 21% attended ordinary comprehensive schools. Eton, a top fee-paying school, educated 330 leading people on the list – some 4% of the nation's elite.

a) Using the item, identify what proportion of the UK's leading people did not go to Oxford or Cambridge Universities. (1)

b) Identify which type of school gives the best chance of becoming one of the nation's elite. (1)

c) Explain what is meant by the term privilege, using an example. (2)

d) Identify and explain which groups of people are more likely to be part of the elite. (2)

e) Explain two ways in which elites may have more power than other groups. (4)

Key terms

Elite – a small, rich and powerful group who control society.

Power – the ability to get what you want.

Privilege – having special advantages over other groups.

Ruling class – a Marxist term to describe the rich and powerful group who control society.

Stretch and challenge

- How might a sociologist find out who has the power in Britain?

- What benefits do members of the elite groups in Britain have?

Find out about

Find out who owns the main newspapers, radio and television stations in Britain.

Find out who the main newspapers told people to vote for in the last few general elections. See how many supported the parties that won in 1997, 2001, 2005 and 2010.

Compulsory Core

Topic 8: What are life chances?

What am I going to learn?

● **To understand what is meant by the term life chances**

The term life chance includes a huge range of possible outcomes in people's lives. This includes the lifestyle enjoyed (or not) by different groups in society.

Stretch and challenge

Design a life chances board game. It could be along the theme of the Game of Life or Monopoly. You could feature different groups in the game. Some groups may have different advantages or disadvantages compared with others. For example, you could make the course different for men and women, rich and poor or different minority groups.

Over to you

Write the opposite story from the one in the main text. This time telling the life chances story of someone who is rich.

Life chances

Life chances are used by sociologists to refer to the opportunities individuals have of having good things happen to them and avoiding bad things. Sociologists have found that some people in some groups enjoy better life chances than others. Life chances include the likelihood of being healthy, living in a nice house, being rich, living until you are old, good education, good job, travelling the world, going to prison or being a victim of crime.

Being healthy, happy and feeling good about your life are all part of what we call the **quality of life**. Quality of life is itself a key part of a person's life chances. Like other life chances it can be affected by a person's social class, gender and ethnicity.

A person's **lifestyle** may be linked to this and includes their attitudes, interests, possessions and what they enjoy doing. Rich people and poor people have very different lifestyles. This is partly due to differences in how much money they have. People get used to their lifestyle/way of life and may not want to change it even if it can have negative effects.

Life chances often link together and the best way to see this is as a story:

A baby is born into a poor family. The baby lives in poor housing, suffering poor health as a result. By the age of five, the young person is behind at school, because the parents are not able to support them, as they had poor experiences at school. They do poorly at school and gain low-grade GCSEs. They then leave school and get a low-paid job. They leave home and rent a cheap flat.

Poor housing results in bad health and time off work. They can only afford cheap food so their health becomes worse. It is difficult to manage and when they have children they have to work long hours. The prospects for the children are not good.

Check your understanding

Complete the sentences below:

life	improve	lifestyle
	quality	together

a) The opportunities that people have are known as ••• chances.

b) A person's ••• is influenced by how much money they have.

c) Feeling good, healthy and happy are known as ••• of life.

d) Life chances are often linked ••• and a good life chance can often lead to others.

e) Education can help ••• people's life chances.

Exam practice

Survey reveals best place to live in Britain

The town of Marlow, Bucks, which lies on the Thames.

Buckinghamshire residents have the best quality of life in Britain, according to research.

They are the healthiest, have the highest life expectancy and are among the highest paid, bringing home an average of £40,000 a year, according to the research.

About 77 per cent of those in the county own their own homes, and many are larger than average houses.

a) Using the item, identify which area of Britain enjoys the best quality of life. (1)

b) Identify what proportion of the people in Buckinghamshire own their own homes. (1)

c) Explain what is meant by the term quality of life, using an example. (2)

d) Identify and explain why poor people are likely to have the worst life chances. (2)

e) Explain two reasons why rich people may enjoy better health than other groups. (4)

Key terms

Quality of life – is to do with being happy and healthy, and feeling good about your life.

Lifestyle – is about a person's attitudes, possessions, interests and how they like to live.

Across the generations

Interview an older person, parent or neighbour. Ask them how they think life chances have changed. Do they think young people today have better or worse life chances than when they were growing up.

Find out about

The amount of money needed to be considered rich. What kind of lifestyle could you afford if you were rich?

www.thetimes.co.uk

www.moneywise.co.uk

Topic 9: What does social exclusion mean?

What am I going to learn?

- **To understand what is meant by social exclusion and appreciate how it affects different groups**

There has been a great concern in society about how different groups may be excluded from society in different ways. It is thought that this can cause problems for society as well as for those who are excluded.

Thinking point

Some people have suggested that the new technology of mobile phones/Internet, etc., has made some people more socially excluded. Do you think that this has made some people more socially excluded? Make a list for and against this statement and decide what you think.

source prweek.com

What is social exclusion?

Social exclusion means that some groups or individuals are being left out of society. The government are concerned that excluded groups may become a problem for society, in terms of higher crime rates and social problems.

Homeless

Homeless people are excluded from society in several different ways. Firstly, they are not part of a town or village community. They do not have access to the most basic things that people need to live a comfortable life. They may not be on a GP's (doctors) list. Furthermore, they may be isolated, as they do not have access to the modern means of communication such as phones and the Internet. Even if they wish to become part of society they may be unfamiliar with the current norms and values. To make it worse they may also be treated differently by other people who realise that they are homeless.

Unemployed

Unemployed people are those who do not have a paid job. These people will feel left out of society because they have no daily routine to get up for. Their lack of money will make it difficult for them to afford things that other people take for granted, such as holidays or entertainment. Since the 1980s **recession** there are groups of people who have become long-term unemployed. These people find it hard to be part of society.

Inclusion

The opposite way to look at this is to consider the idea of **inclusion**. The government, health service and schools are keen to make sure that everyone is included, and gets the opportunity to have a good life. As well as the homeless and unemployed, there are other groups that are in danger of being left out of society. These include the mentally ill, disabled, elderly and some ethnic groups. The government is trying to make sure that all these groups are included and get the opportunities others enjoy.

Check your understanding

Use the words below to complete the sentences:

opportunities	lifestyle	out
crime	ethnic	

a) One problem that the government think may be caused by groups that are excluded from society is more •••.

b) Homeless people are socially excluded because they do not enjoy as good a ••• as other groups.

c) Unemployed people feel left out of society because they cannot afford to go ••• like other people.

d) Groups that are in danger of being socially excluded are the mentally ill, disabled, elderly and some ••• groups.

e) Social inclusion means making sure that all groups have the same ••• as others.

Exam practice

Social exclusion: the real cost

In August 2011 there were riots across the UK. The riots involved looting from shops. Across London windows were smashed, and shops emptied. Experts said social exclusion and the breakdown of law and order could have caused looters not to follow social norms.

Experts said that young looters from poor estates did not feel part of society. Many have no jobs or low wages. They had nothing to lose and no reason to follow social norms.

Looters targeted large chain stores including JD Sports in Tottenham, north London.

a) Using the item, identify one cause of the riots. (1)

b) Identify and explain one reason why the young looters may not have felt part of society. (2)

c) Fully explain the meaning of social exclusion, using examples. (3)

d) Explain one method a sociologist could use to study social exclusion and explain why it is a suitable method. (3)

e) Write an open question that a sociologist could ask in a survey on social exclusion. (1)

Key terms

Social exclusion – being left out of society in important ways.

Recession – when many people are going out of business and losing their jobs.

Inclusion – the idea that all groups should be encouraged to be part of society and have the same chances as others.

Stretch and challenge

Why is social exclusion a problem for society? Try to think of 10 reasons why it could cause problems.

What solutions are there for social exclusion? Pick one of the groups below and think of five things that could be done to make them feel included:

- Elderly
- Homeless
- Disabled
- Unemployed

Grade boost

Always look for examples in the news about groups like the homeless and unemployed. These can be included in your answers and will breathe life into them.

Compulsory Core

Topic 10: What is poverty?

What am I going to learn?

- **To understand different definitions of poverty**

Poverty is a cause for concern across the world. In Britain, people disagree about whether there is any real poverty. Before you can decide this you have to think about what poverty is.

Famous people

Peter Townsend

Professor Peter Townsend was a pioneer in social research into poverty. He died in 2009 but was for 50 years the leading expert on poverty in the UK. His research was **qualitative**, which meant that he gained in-depth information through unstructured interviews and observations. He exposed the truth about poverty in the UK. His main focus was on exclusion and relative poverty.

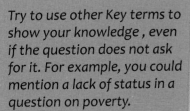

Grade boost

Try to use other Key terms to show your knowledge , even if the question does not ask for it. For example, you could mention a lack of status in a question on poverty.

Absolute poverty

Absolute poverty is when a person does not have their basic needs met. Basic needs could include food, clean water, shelter, clothes and warmth. These could also be seen as a part of a person's human rights. In the United Kingdom, the government supports people with benefits. This is supposed to make sure that nobody lives in absolute poverty in the United Kingdom.

Relative poverty

Even if the government were successful in stopping absolute poverty there are still groups who are deprived compared with other people. Being deprived means having to live without things which others expect. For example, not having access to the Internet may be seen as being **deprived** in modern society.

Sociologists use the term **relative poverty** to describe this situation. People may have their basic needs met, so are not in absolute poverty. However, compared with other people, they are in poverty. For example, they may not be able to go on holiday or eat out, even on a special occasion.

Subjective poverty

Subjective poverty is when you think you are living in poverty. Some people may live quite well, but may see themselves as living in poverty. This is still important to consider.

The problem is that people's expectations change all the time and the standard gets higher all the time. In the early 1960s many homes still had outside toilets and no central heating. That would now be seen as relative poverty. In the 1980s and even 1990s not all people were expected to have a computer or a mobile phone!

Poverty and social exclusion

Poverty links closely to social exclusion. A family without Internet may struggle to take a full part in society. Hobbies for children may cost a lot of money. For instance, a child playing football for a local team costs a parent money for subs and transport. Families who cannot afford this may be seen as living in relative poverty and are socially excluded.

Check your understanding

a) List five things that are a person's basic needs.

b) List five things that it would be difficult to manage without in our society. These should not be on the list for a), but things that are needed to play a full part in our society.

Exam practice

The website www.poverty.org.uk believes that relative poverty is important in the UK. They say that no one should live with money and a lifestyle, which is so far below the average, that they cannot take part in everyday life and customs. In other words, we believe that, in a rich country such as the UK, there should be certain minimum standards below which no one should fall.

As society becomes richer, norms change and the expectations about lifestyle change. Unless the poor keep up with the rich they will be excluded from the opportunities that others get. This could make the UK a community where people do not get along.

a) Identify one thing in the picture which suggests that the children may be living in poverty. (1)

b) Explain why the website believes that relative poverty is an important issue in the UK. (1)

c) Fully explain what is meant by poverty, using examples. (4)

d) Explain two reasons why poverty may lead to social exclusion. (4)

Key terms

Absolute poverty – when a person does not have the basics needed to live.

Relative poverty – when a person is poor compared with other people in the society.

Subjective poverty – when you think that you are living in poverty compared with others.

Deprived – not having things that are seen as important for a decent life.

Stretch and challenge

- Find out how much money a family of four would need to avoid living in absolute poverty.

- Find out how much money a family would need to avoid living in relative poverty.

- For both of these you need to work out a monthly budget. Teachers or other adults should be able to give you an idea of the cost of most things, but you could visit a supermarket or go online, to find out how much a basic weekly shop would cost.

- Find out what the government says is the minimum a family needs and compare with your findings.

Compulsory Core

Topic 11: What is social class?

What am I going to learn?

● **To understand what is meant by social class**

There are several things to think about when deciding a person's social class. The government has tended to group people based on their job, but there are other things to consider. Sociologists have to decide how they will classify a person's social class.

Interesting fact

Social class is really difficult for sociologists to study, as it is hard to pin down. John Major, the Prime Minister in the 1990s, said that he aimed to create a classless society. By this he meant that class would not affect people's life chances any more. Even though they disagree about how to measure social class, sociologists would say that class still has a big impact on people's lives.

Famous people

Peter Saunders, a New Right sociologist, has a different view about social class and inequality. Many sociologists have done research on how working-class students do less well at school. For society to be fair, working-class people should have the same chance of doing well.

This seems a reasonable idea. Peter Saunders argues that it is based on a false idea that ability is shared out equally. He suggests that middle-class children may be born more intelligent because they **inherit** their parents' intelligence. That is the reason they do better at school and work, not because society is unfair.

What is social class?

According to the writer George Orwell, Britain was a society divided by social class. At its simplest there were thought to be three main social **classes**:

Upper class – this includes the **aristocracy**, owners of big companies and the very rich. They have the highest status.

Middle class – people who are better off and usually do jobs where they do not work with their hands. This would include professions such as teachers, nurses and office workers.

Working class – people who work in manual jobs (using their hands). This included miners, factory workers and shipbuilders.

Occupational scale

In the 20th century a lot of this thinking was based on a government scale called the Registrar General scale. The scale had well-paid jobs at the top and lower-paid jobs at the bottom. Lawyers and doctors were at the top. Manual jobs such as factory workers and labourers were at the bottom.

Over time the scale became less useful. Many of the traditional working-class jobs in factories and mines were disappearing. There was no place for the **unemployed** on the scale. The scale was no use for the government or sociologists.

A new scale (NS–SEC) was introduced in 2001. The scale had 8 points. Generally the scale was similar to the previous scale, but there were new jobs working with computers and a space at the bottom for the unemployed.

Sociologists still have a problem with occupational scales. In a family do you base the social class on the man's or the woman's **occupation**? What about really wealthy people who do not work? What about people with no job?

Other factors

Other factors people think of when deciding on a person's social class:

- Are they wealthy?
- Accent
- Education – private school?
- Social circle
- What social class do they think they are?
- Lifestyle
- Area they live in.

So 'social class' can mean different things to different people.

Check your understanding

a) Which social class has the highest status?

b) What three problems are there with the occupational scales?

c) What was the old occupational scale called?

d) When was the new occupational scale introduced?

Exam practice

The idea of 'working', 'middle' and 'upper' class first appeared in the 19th century, as a way of describing the big differences between rich and poor that were found in Victorian Britain. But can a Victorian system still be useful to understand Britain today?

We simply don't know. It's clear that inequality has not disappeared and people still think about social class. So what does class really mean in Britain in the 21st century?

a) Identify when the terms working, middle and upper class first appeared. (1)

b) Explain what the item says has happened to inequality. (1)

c) Fully explain what is meant by the term social class. (4)

d) Explain what factors should be considered when sociologists are deciding a person's social class. (4)

Key terms

Class – a way of grouping people based on their job and status.

Aristocracy – includes high-status people with titles, such as dukes and earls.

Unemployed – people without jobs.

Occupation – a person's job.

Across the generations

Do some research on your family. See if you can find out what your grandparents and their parents did for a job. Has the social class of your family changed over the generations?

Stretch and challenge

Watch one of the British soaps on television. Make a list of the main characters and the jobs they do. Find the Registrar General scale and the new 8-point scale. Work out where they fit on the scale and which social class you think they are.

Compulsory Core
Topic 12: What is ageism?

What am I going to learn?

- **To understand what ageism is and how it can affect both young and old**

Sociologists have become more interested in age in recent years. They are interested in the way that different societies may treat people at a certain age differently. Sociologists also look at how age can significantly affect life chances through prejudice and discrimination. This is called ageism.

Across the generations

Interview your older relatives to find out how they feel about ageism. Do they feel that they are being treated differently as they become older?

Philippe Aries

Famous people

Philippe Aries was a French historian. The book he published in 1962 was called *Centuries of Childhood*. It was important because it was about ordinary people and started the study of childhood by other historians and sociologists. It shows how Sociology is connected to other subjects such as History.

Other interesting work by Aries showed how attitudes to death have changed. In medieval times people were not as fearful of death as they are in our society. They saw it as natural and inevitable. So even attitudes towards death are socially constructed.

Social construction of age

The way that people at a certain age are treated is not the same in all societies. For instance, nowadays children are treated as special and are protected in our society. A historian called Philippe Aries found that in the past children were treated as small adults and expected to work from a very young age. There was no special time set aside for education or play. In fact, our modern idea of childhood did not appear until Victorian times (late 19th century).

In Britain the elderly, although respected, are not seen as the most important members of society. In other societies, such as native American tribes of the Apache, Comanche and Sioux, the elderly have greater status and prestige.

These differences in thinking about what certain ages are like, shows that **age is socially constructed** or made by society.

Ageism

Unfortunately, different ideas about what different age groups are like can cause prejudice and discrimination. Having pre-judged ideas about different age groups, or treating them differently is called ageism.

Ageism, like sexism and racism, is often based on exaggerated, oversimplified ideas that we call stereotypes. Persistent stereotypes about the elderly in Britain are that they are bad tempered, poor at learning new technology and have poor memories. This can lead to discrimination and the elderly may be overlooked for promotion or not be given a job.

Young people may also be affected by this kind of stereotyping. Harry Enfield's character of Kevin* is a comedy stereotype which shows teenagers as argumentative, lazy and irrational. Young people may also be seen as troublemakers and the media often shows them in a negative way. Sociologists have called this the **demonisation of the young**. This can significantly affect their life chances.

*(Kevin becomes a teenager clip at tinyurl.com/6pnprc)

Check your understanding

Complete the sentences:

a) In the past the idea of ••• may not have existed.

b) Instead children were treated like ••• adults.

c) In ••• times the idea of childhood as a special time for play and innocence began.

d) The elderly are often victims of discrimination called •••.

e) Young people may also suffer from •••, which is an exaggerated, simplified view of a group of people.

f) Young people may often be demonised in the •••.

Exam practice

Ageism consists of a negative bias or stereotypical attitudes toward ageing.

Ageism: the final frontier for anti-discrimination laws

Hired   Not Hired
Age Discrimination?

Actor Patrick Stewart is starring in a short film for Macmillan Cancer Support that aims to tackle ageism in Britain's National Health Service. Macmillan is a charity that helps people suffering from cancer.

The film tells the stories of three older people who are defying the stereotypes often associated with their age.

Ena Mallet (79) is a 7th Dan jujitsu practitioner who teaches martial arts classes.

'Mamy Rock' (72) is a nightclub DJ who has toured all over the world since taking up DJ-ing at the age of 68.

And 72-year-old Geoffrey Palmer is a world-renowned grain scientist and university lecturer, who says there is no reason why an older person cannot still invent new ideas.

The *Age Old Excuse* film finishes with Star Trek and X-Men star Stewart, who is aged 72 himself, stating that 'age is just a number'.

The film will be used by Macmillan to campaign to improve the care and treatment of older people. The charity is worried that older people may not be offered treatment because of their age, even when they are fit. The film will try to change attitudes.

a) Using the item, identify one worry that Macmillan have about older people and the health care they are given. (1)

b) Briefly explain what Macmillan is hoping to achieve through making the film. (2)

c) Explain why age discrimination may be a problem for society. (3)

d) Outline two ways in which prejudice may affect the lives of young people. (4)

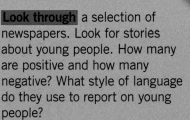

Compulsory Core

Topic 13: How does gender affect women's life chances?

What am I going to learn?

- **To understand how gender can affect life chances for women**

Gender has been a key focus for feminist sociologists since the 1970s and has changed the subject of sociology a great deal. In fact, feminists criticised sociology itself for being sexist and biased towards men! This topic links closely with the topic of family.

Social construction of gender

Just like age, our idea of gender has changed over time and place. At the start of the 20th century, women were not allowed to vote and were not expected to have a career. They lived in the shadow of the men they married and their main roles were traditional **feminine** ones as mothers, housewives and carers.

As the 20th century progressed, women fought for and gained greater freedom. Some gained the vote in 1918. The Second World War meant that they were able to show they could perform men's work roles. However, by the 1950s the common view was that a 'woman's place is in the home'.

Feminism

The rise of feminism has seen a constant push to gain equality for women. By the 1970s, women began to go out to work in greater numbers. The Sex Discrimination Act, 1975, meant that employers were not allowed to discriminate and that women had equal rights to do any job. The Equal Pay Act, 1970, meant that women could not be paid less money than men for doing the same job. Women had come a long way.

Are women equal?

Feminists still argue that women do not enjoy equality with men. Firstly, there is the **glass ceiling**. The glass ceiling is an idea to explain the way that women can see the top jobs but are still not able to reach them. There is an invisible barrier caused by sexism and discrimination.

Secondly, although women are able to have careers, they are still expected to be the main person responsible for housework and childcare. Feminists call this the **double burden**. Women work and still have to be housewives as well. Some Feminists go further and say that women do a **triple shift**; paid work, housework and emotional work. Women have to make sure everyone is happy when upset. Therefore, although women have greater equality, feminists argue that they are still overburdened.

Extended writing

Discuss how far have women achieved equality in Britain today. Paragraphs could include: in the family, at work, in the media, in government. (20)

Famous people

US writer Naomi Woolf called the shift in power that has happened between men and women a 'genderquake'. She thought that the balance had begun to shift away from men being in control.

Check your understanding

Use the words in the word box to complete the sentences below:

> glass   discrimination   equal   achieve
> equality   burden   vote

Three ways in which women made progress in the 20th century were gaining the •••, earning ••• pay and the act which made sexual ••• against the law. Feminism has helped women to ••• this. However, some feminists believe that women still do not have full ••• and are still disadvantaged compared with men. Two reasons they believe this are due to the ••• ceiling and the double •••.

Exam practice

Survey shows glass ceiling is yet to crack

A survey suggested that women are still one step behind when it comes to top-level promotion.

Nearly three-quarters of women say they still face barriers to top-level promotion in the UK, a survey suggests. Of the 3,000 managers questioned, 73% of women agreed that the glass ceiling still exists, whereas only 38% of men did.

The research was done in December 2012 by the Institute of Leadership and Management.

Despite gaining 57% of the highest university qualifications in the UK last year, only 12% of the top 100 company directors are female.

a) Using the item, identify where the survey came from. (1)
b) What percentage of women thought that the glass ceiling exists? (1)
c) Identify one reason why fewer men than women agreed that the glass ceiling still exists. (1)
d) A sociologist wants to research discrimination in the workplace. Suggest one research method that they could use. (1)
e) Explain two problems that a researcher could have using the method that you have chosen. (6)

Key terms

Social construction of gender – is the idea that the norms of gender vary from society to society and over time.

Femininity – is a set of norms for women traditionally including motherhood, housework, caring and looking beautiful.

Glass ceiling – an invisible barrier caused by sexism and discrimination that prevents women reaching the top jobs.

Double burden – is when women are expected to go out to do paid work and be in charge of the home and children.

Triple shift – is when women have to do paid work, housework and take care of all the emotional problems in the house.

Find out about

The sociologists who came up with the Key terms double burden and triple shift.

Grade boost
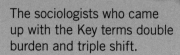

Make sure that when using the terms double burden and triple shift, you make clear that this is an extra burden that men (usually) do not have.

Compulsory Core

Topic 14: How have changes in gender roles affected men?

What am I going to learn?

- **To understand the effect that changes in gender roles have had upon men**

Feminist sociologists focussed upon trying to improve women's positions. However, some sociologists realised that big changes for women have meant changes for men, too.

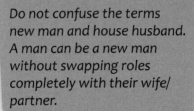

Grade boost

Do not confuse the terms new man and house husband. A man can be a new man without swapping roles completely with their wife/ partner.

Across the generations

Talk to an older male relative or neighbour about how the expectations of being a man have changed. Do they think there has been a change? Are changes for the better?

Men's traditional roles

Men were traditionally the head of the family and had a very clear role as **breadwinner**, decision maker, strong leader and protector. Men were expected to be strong, not show their emotions and leave the caring part of family life to the women.

From the 1960s, women's roles were changing fast. They were stronger and more independent. Women in relationships, and lone parents began to take on the roles mentioned above. Men have had to try to adapt their role as these changes have happened.

New man

Sociologists have tried to explain these changes. By the 1990s, the idea of the **new man** had appeared. New men were more caring and in touch with their emotions. They were helpers at home with housework and child care. New men worked in partnership with their wives or partners. Men and women were more equal. For example, David Beckham the footballer, presented himself as a hands-on dad who was in a partnership with Victoria, his wife.

House husband

There also appeared the idea of the **house husband**. This is where men and women swap roles. The man stays at home looking after the house and children, whilst the woman goes out to work.

Crisis of masculinity

Big changes were also happening in the world of work. Traditional men's jobs in mines, factories and shipbuilding were disappearing. More office and non-manual jobs were appearing. Some sociologists said that men were not sure how to act anymore. Their traditional power in the family has gone. This is known as the **crisis of masculinity**.

Confusingly, another male role appeared in the 1990s. The new lad was seen in comedy programmes, like *Men Behaving Badly* and men's magazines like *Loaded* and *FHM*. A throwback to an earlier kind of masculinity, new lads enjoyed football, being irresponsible, women and other traditional male pursuits.

The crisis of masculinity has meant that men and boys growing up have become confused about the norms of being a man in the 21st century.

Check your understanding

Complete the sentences below:

a) Women have grown stronger and more ••• since the 1970s.

b) Men's roles have changed as traditional male jobs in mines, factories and ••• have disappeared.

c) The ••• man who was more caring and in touch with his emotions, appeared in the 1990s.

d) Some men actually swapped roles with women and became house •••.

e) The confusion about the norms of being a man is known as the ••• of masculinity.

Exam practice

Men the main breadwinners? Don't bet on it in future!

The news this summer said that women were scoring higher in IQ (intelligence) tests than men.

Girls have long been doing better than boys in GCSEs, are more likely to go to university and get a job. More women are becoming the main breadwinner.

Britain, like many other countries, is seeing women taking over power from men. Boris Johnson, the Mayor of London, said that this is already happening in the USA and will be the biggest change Britain has seen for a long time.

a) Using the item, identify one way in which females are now doing better than males. (1)

b) Explain what is meant by the term breadwinner. (1)

c) Explain, with examples, what is meant by traditional male gender roles. (4)

d) Outline and explain two reasons why some sociologists say that there is a crisis of masculinity. (4)

Key terms

Breadwinner – the main wage earner in a family.

New man – a new set of norms which appeared in the 1990s for men, which included showing their emotions, being more caring and taking on some female roles.

House husband – is where a man takes on the traditional female role of looking after the house and children.

Crisis of masculinity – the idea that the norms for being a man are not clear anymore. Men are not sure of their place in society.

Masculinity – is a set of norms for men traditionally including being in charge, strong and aggressive.

Personal research idea

Find out from your class mates how many families have a male or female breadwinner, or is it a shared responsibility?

Stretch and challenge

There continues to be huge scientific and social change. What do you think will happen to male and female roles by the time that your grandchildren are born? Make a list of what you think that the main features will be for each gender. Will males and females become more similar or different?

Compulsory Core

Topic 15: How have norms about sexuality changed in the last 50 years?

What am I going to learn?

- **To understand how norms about sexuality have changed in recent British history**

There has been increasing sociological interest in the topic of sexuality. Sexuality is about whether a person is gay, straight or bisexual. It has become another important kind of difference in Britain and may have a big effect on a person's life chances.

Find out about

Your school's anti-bullying policy. Find out which senior teacher is in charge of anti-bullying. Does your school have a policy about homophobia? Are students aware of it?

Also find out about the work of Stonewall, the lesbian, gay and bisexual charity.

🔍 websites

To find out about recent changes to the laws about discrimination against all groups go to: www.homeoffice.gov.uk/ equalities/equality-act/

If you wish to find out more about an organisation that has promoted rights for gay and lesbian groups go to: www.stonewall.org.uk/

Homosexuality and the law

In 1962, the Beatles made pop music history and became one of the top selling groups of all time. Few people knew at the time that their manager Brian Epstein was gay. He faced the risk of arrest if his secret got out, as having sex with another man was against the law in 1962. On the outside, Epstein was a respectable businessman, famous for promoting the Beatles. He was forced to hide his lifestyle.

In 1967, a new law appeared which made being gay (**homosexuality**) legal; as long as it was in private and the people involved were over 21. This was still not equal compared with **heterosexual** couples (men and women having sex together). Eventually the age for gay couples was changed to 16 in 2001, making it equal.

Social norms and sexual orientation

The law has changed, but social norms may still vary on this subject, according to where you live and your age. Young people may be more open minded than older people as they have grown up in a different time with different media influences.

Pop stars such as Elton John and Boy George, who have all declared themselves gay, may also have influenced people as role models. Movies like *Brokeback Mountain* may also have helped people become more tolerant.

Despite this, homophobic attitudes are sometimes found. **Homophobia** is fear of, or hostility towards, homosexuals. This can result in prejudice and discrimination.

Laws continue to change. In 2005, civil partnerships were introduced. Civil partnerships gave gay or lesbian couples the same rights as married couples. In 2013, The Marriage (Same Sex Couples) Bill was introduced to parliament.

In 2010, the Equality Act was passed to protect gays, lesbians and people changing sex (**transgender**) from discrimination. The law now makes discrimination on the basis of sexual orientation illegal. This is still controversial but norms continue to change.

Check your understanding

a) Homosexuality became legal in the UK in •••.

b) The age of consent for homosexuality was not made 16 until •••.

c) The 2010 Equality Act made discrimination against people on grounds of ••• illegal.

d) Fear of or hostility towards gay people is known as •••.

e) People changing gender are called ••• and are also protected by the 2010 Equality Act.

Key terms

Homosexual – when people are attracted to people of their own sex.

Heterosexual – when people are attracted to people of the opposite sex.

Sexual orientation – whether someone is gay, straight or bisexual.

Homophobia – fear of or hostility towards gay people.

Transgender – when someone is changing or has changed their gender.

Exam practice

What is homophobic bullying?

Any hostile or offensive action against lesbians, gay males, bisexual or transgender people, or towards people because they are thought to be lesbian, gay, bisexual or transgender.

These actions might be:

- Verbal, physical, or emotional (social exclusion) harassment, insulting or degrading comments, name calling, gestures, taunts, insults or 'jokes'.

- Offensive graffiti.

- Humiliating, excluding, tormenting, ridiculing or threatening, refusing to work or co-operate with others because of their sexual orientation or identity.

Coronation Street and other soaps have regularly run storylines featuring gay and lesbian characters, like the one shown on the right.

Brooke Vincent as Sophie Webster and Sacha Parkinson as Sian Powers in Coronation Street, ITV

a) Using the item, identify two examples of homophobic bullying. (1)

b) Explain what effect storylines with gay or lesbian characters in soap operas may have on viewers. (2)

c) Outline two sociological reasons why some people may be homophobic. (4)

d) A sociologist is researching into why some people may be more likely to be victims of homophobia than others. Suggest one ethical problem with this topic. (3)

Stretch and challenge

The media has changed the way that gay news stories are reported and storylines on soaps have included gay and lesbian characters. Has this happened because social norms have changed? Or did the media cause social norms to change? In the same way have changes in the law changed social norms or did the law change because norms had changed?

Compulsory Core
Topic 16: What is racism?

What am I going to learn?

- **To understand the different forms that racism can take**

Sociology provides very useful insights into the subject of racism. In British society the issue of racism is very topical. High profile footballers, such as John Terry (Chelsea and England) and Luis Suarez (Liverpool and Uruguay), have been accused of racism. Norms about racism have changed dramatically in Britain over the last few decades.

Thinking skills

Look at the item in the exam practice feature.

Why do you think the information about free school meals is included?

What other information would you like to know about the pupils on the database? What other factors might affect an individual's level of success?

Stretch and challenge

Find out about political correctness in the 1980s. What effect did this have on television programmes, school text books? Ask older people if they remember this and see what they thought of it. Try to find people who thought it was good and people against it.

Race

Firstly, it is very important to be sure of the key terms here. **Race** is a term which sociologists do not use anymore. Race is linked to the idea of biology (the way people are born). **Ethnicity** is the preferred term now.

Ethnicity

The term ethnicity is used to describe the different groups found in a society like the UK. Ethnicity is about the shared culture of a group. This may include religion, language, nationality, a shared history and customs.

The key difference between race and ethnicity is that race is about biology. Ethnicity is about culture.

Racism

When people are prejudiced and discriminate against different ethnic groups this is racism. People may mistrust people who are different from themselves. They may have grown up in an area where most people are racist. Parents and peers may have socialised them to be racist.

Racism is often in the news. Racism has been an issue that the government has tried to tackle through laws against racial discrimination. Schools have also tried to introduce an anti-racist curriculum.

Scapegoating

Racism often becomes worse when society has problems. Ethnic minority groups are sometimes blamed for social problems, such as unemployment and crime. This is called scapegoating and means blaming groups for things which are not really all their fault.

The Stephen Lawrence case has been a challenge to how organisations like the police operate. Stephen Lawrence was a black teenager who was stabbed to death in April 1993. The police who investigated the murder did not bring any of the murderers to justice until 2011. An inquiry called the Macpherson

Report found that the police had failed badly. The police officers did not listen to witnesses or investigate properly because of **institutional racism**, according to the Macpherson Report. This meant that the whole organisation was full of racial stereotypes and racist thinking. The officers assumed that Stephen and his friends were involved in gangs.

Check your understanding

Complete the sentences below:

a) Ethnicity is about the cultural group a person ••• to.

b) Ethnicity may include a group's way of life, religion, nationality and shared •••.

c) The government have introduced ••• to try to prevent racial discrimination.

d) Scapegoating happens when a group is ••• for society's problems.

e) The police investigating the Stephen Lawrence case were criticised for ••• racism.

f) The report which found the police to be institutionally racist was called the ••• Report.

Exam practice

The Welsh can be seen as an ethnic group based on their shared nationality, language and history. Welsh people who live in Australia may still, over many generations, see themselves as Welsh. In fact, they may join together the new place they live with their ethnic origins and call themselves Welsh Australians! Ethnic identity can become very complicated, especially in modern-day multicultural Britain.

Ethnicity can affect educational success. Recent statistics showed that ethnic minority groups, such as Africans, Pakistanis and Bangladeshis generally were less likely to pass 5 A*–Cs. However, the other factor that had an effect on this was whether students had free school meals or not. Students with free school meals were less likely to gain 5 A*–Cs compared with other students in their own ethnic group.

a) Using the item, identify one group of 16-year-olds with less chance of getting 5 GCSEs at A*–C including English and Maths. (1)

b) Using the item, identify what other factor, apart from ethnicity, affects educational success. (1)

c) Explain, with examples, the term ethnicity. (4)

d) Outline and explain two sociological reasons why some ethnic groups may have worse life chances than others. (4)

Key terms

Race – an outdated way of dividing people into groups often based on skin colour.

Ethnicity – is about the cultural group a person belongs to and may include religion, nationality and way of life.

Institutional racism – is when the culture of an organisation is racist.

Political correctness – was the idea that people needed to be careful when using words that could be seen as sexist, racist or offensive to people.

Over to you

1. Describe your own ethnic identity.

2. Try to come up with five examples of different ethnic groups found in the UK.

3. What effect do you think the Macpherson Report will have had upon the police force in Britain?

Grade boost

Do not see the different topics you study in Sociology as different subjects. Ideas you learned about for Paper 1, such as norms and socialisation, will help to understand a topic like racism.

Compulsory Core

Topic 17: How does disability affect life chances?

What am I going to learn?

- **To understand what disability is and how it affects life chances**

Disability is a relatively new topic area for sociology. It is important to know the range of conditions that are classed as disability. Also, remember that people with disabilities may also be affected by their age, gender, class and ethnic group.

Erving Goffman was a Canadian sociologist. He was very interested in the everyday interaction between people rather than grand ideas about the whole of society. His book *Stigma* looked at how identity could be spoiled. This could be because of something a person had done, e.g. murder or rape. However, disability could also spoil a person's identity and have stigma attached to it. Stigma is a mark of social shame. Disabled people, through no fault of their own, may suffer this in society.

What is disability?

The Equality Act 2010 says that **disability** is a when a person is not able to do everyday tasks, due to physical or mental impairment. Most people think of the disabled as someone in a wheelchair. Disability includes many more conditions including blindness, mental health problems and learning disabilities. People who are not disabled are known as **able-bodied**.

Prejudice, discrimination and disability

The British Social Attitudes Survey found that although attitudes towards people with disabilities have changed, many people still feel uncomfortable. People were not deliberately negative towards people with disabilities but thought they were not as capable as able-bodied people. They were most uncomfortable when people with mental health conditions or learning disabilities were in authority positions. This shows prejudice and may lead to discrimination.

Social model versus Medical model

There are two main ways of looking at the situation of people with disabilities. The **Medical model** sees disability as an illness or something bad. This model sees people with disabilities as needing to be helped. People with disabilities will probably have worse life chances, so they need help from society.

The other view is the **Social model**. This view sees disability as just another kind of difference, like being male or female, old or young, or black or white. Being disabled is just part of who someone is (identity). It is society that needs to change and make things accessible for people with disabilities, for example providing ramps or lifts.

In the Social model view, people with disabilities have worse life chances because of society. Being disabled is not a bad thing, but people with disabilities find it difficult to get on in a society which is hard for them to fit into.

Check your understanding

Complete the sentences using the words in the word box.

educated	mental	prejudice
illness	intelligent	wheelchairs

a) Disability does not simply mean people in •••. It also includes people with a range of physical and ••• conditions. They may have been born with them or have become that way due to •••.

b) People with disabilities may suffer worse life chances because of ••• and discrimination.

c) Some people assume that people with disabilities are not ••• and are not independent.

d) People need to be better ••• about disability.

Exam practice

Paralympics: opinion split

The opening ceremony for the 13th Paralympic Games renewed the British feel-good factor started by the summer Olympics. The message about people with disabilities was very clear. Professor Stephen Hawking spoke at the start of the games, this was followed

by the high-wire arrival in the stadium of a double-amputee serviceman, and topped off by the lighting of the cauldron by the winner of Britain's first Paralympic gold medal over 50 years ago. This showed that people with disabilities excel in many areas, and not just sport.

Despite this, the disabled charity Scope found in a survey that lots of people with disabilities are worried about society's attitude towards them. The government are cutting welfare benefits for them and they think that the media are linking people with disabilities with the idea of being 'benefit scroungers'.

However, many thought that the media coverage of the Paralympics might help the image of people with disabilities.

a) Using the item, identify one positive message about people with disabilities that may come from the Paralympic games. (1)

b) Explain why the survey said that some people with disabilities were worried about society's attitudes towards them. (2)

c) Outline two sociological reasons why people with disabilities may be victims of prejudice and discrimination. (4)

d) A sociologist is researching disability and uses unstructured interviews. Explain why this would be a good method to use. (3)

Key terms

Disability – when a person is not able to do everyday tasks, as well as other people, due to a physical or mental impairment.

Able-bodied or non-disabled – means other people who are not disabled.

Medical model of disability – sees disability as a problem that the person has.

Social model of disability – sees society as causing disability.

Personal research idea

Do a content analysis of the daily newspapers. See what stories you can find which are about disability or feature disabled people. Try to find a way of classifying these stories into categories. For example, are they positive, negative, novelty or do they involve stereotypes, prejudice or discrimination?

Grade boost

Try to remember the acronym CAGED. This stands for Class, Age, Gender, Ethnicity and Disability. If you are stuck for a way of answering a question, especially one about inequality and life chances, these may give you a lead in.

Topic 18: Why is there an underclass?

What am I going to learn?

● **To understand what is meant by the term underclass**

The term underclass has been used much more since the 1980s. One of the main reasons for this is that since the early 1980s Britain has always had significant numbers of unemployed people and most ways of looking at social class are based on the jobs people have. Different sociologists disagree about why we have an underclass.

Grade boost

In Section A of both papers your knowledge of sociological theory will make your answer stand out. Make sure that you relate it closely to the question.

Interesting facts

● Conservative MP Kenneth Clarke thought that the British rioters in August 2011 were a feral underclass. How right was he?

● The Ministry of Justice figures show that 21% of the rioters were aged between 10 and 17. The remaining 79% were adults, 18 or over. A huge 91% of all rioters were male.

● 61% of the adults had previous brushes with the law – either cautioned or convicted for a previous criminal offence. It is not clear how effective the courts are at stopping people reoffending.

What is the underclass?

The **underclass** are seen as groups of people who have such low status and poor quality of life, that they are not part of the social class system. They are not part of the working class and are in a position below them. This may include the long-term unemployed, homeless, and some disabled people.

The culture of the underclass – the underclass are to blame!

These groups have low status and do not take a full part in social life. Lack of money may be part of the reason for this. However, these groups may also create their own way of life with very different norms from the other social classes. This may include having no job, and finding other ways of having fun and making a living. It may start with truancy from school and later include alcohol, drugs and crime.

The New Right support this view. They blame the underclass themselves for being poor and also blame the government for giving them benefits. The New Right say this means that they learn to depend on benefit and do not want to get jobs.

The New Right are concerned about the effect of the underclass on society. High rates of teenage pregnancy, crime and bad parenting are linked to the underclass according to the New Right.

Cycle of deprivation

This view sees the underclass as lacking the basics for a happy and successful life. The underclass grow up in poor areas with bad housing. Children copy the parents and socialise their own children in the same way. This continues the **cycle of deprivation**. The way of life of the underclass becomes a **culture of poverty**, trapping them in poverty.

Winners and losers – someone has to end up at the bottom of society!

A different view, held by Marxists, is that society is so competitive and greedy that someone will end up at the bottom of society. Not all will get a good job and be successful. There will always be some people who are very poor.

Check your understanding

Complete the sentences below:

a) Some sociologists call the group below the working class the •••.

b) The New Right blame the underclass themselves for being poor, but also blame the •••.

c) The New Right also think that the underclass are ••• parents for their children.

d) Marxists think that our society is ••• and greedy.

e) Marxists believe that the gap between ••• and poor has become greater since the 1980s.

f) The underclass are caught in a poverty trap known as the cycle of •••.

Exam practice

The underclass are back again!

The Conservative Party's spokesperson for social affairs Iain Duncan Smith believes Britain has witnessed the growth of a 'more menacing underclass'.

Duncan Smith thought that young people in the underclass were doomed to carry on repeating the mistakes of their parents.

The Labour government under Tony Blair set up a group to end the problem of the underclass. Unfortunately, they are still here – hundreds of thousands of people, workless, skill-less, often homeless and hopeless; a group **marginalised** and cut off from mainstream society – 5% who are unlikely to change.

a) Using the item, identify two features of the group referred to as the underclass. (1)

b) What does the item suggest will happen to the children of the underclass? (1)

c) What proportion of the population does the item suggest belong to the underclass? (1)

d) Explain what is meant by the term cycle of deprivation. (3)

e) Outline and explain two sociological reasons why there may be an underclass in Britain. (4)

Key terms

Underclass – group below the working class and left out of society.

Cycle of deprivation – the idea that people who are poor cannot escape poverty and their children will also continue the pattern.

Marginalised – left out of society.

Feral – people who are unsocialised and wild.

Culture of poverty – is the way of life of the underclass which dooms them to remain in the underclass.

Stretch and challenge

If you were the government, how would you go about helping the underclass? Think of five changes you would make to society through laws, education, benefits, media, and children's services.

Over to you

What do you think about Duncan Smith's view in the item? Why do you think we had riots in Britain in the summer of 2011?

135

Compulsory Core

Topic 19: How do class, age, gender, ethnicity and disability affect people in the world of work?

What am I going to learn?

- **To understand how different social groups' life chances are affected at work**

Sociologists are interested in all five of the issues above and how they affect life chances. The last forty years have seen lots of laws passed to protect groups and give equal opportunities. How effective have these been in the world of work?

Class

A BBC news report in 2011 called *Who gets the best jobs* found that Britain was still a very unequal place. In fact, the documentary said that Britain had not been such an unequal place since before World War One. Young people wanting to join the top professions needed to have contacts and money behind them to stand any chance. The working classes may be finding it more difficult than ever to break into medicine, law and the media.

Age

Prejudice can still work against older people and can be hard to prove. At the other end, young people may be **exploited** by being paid low wages. Exploitation means that a person is being taken advantage of.

Gender

Feminists argue that the glass ceiling still blocks women from being successful at the highest levels. A *Daily Telegraph* report from 2012 showed that there was still a **gender pay gap**, despite the Equal Pay Act, 1970. A gender pay gap is when men are paid more than women for doing the same job

Ethnicity

A story in *The Guardian*, 2008, showed that ethnic minority groups may also have a pay gap. This is very complicated as different ethnic groups may on average vary a lot. However, in 2008 non-whites doing the same job as whites earned 18p an hour less. They also found it more difficult to get into well-paid jobs and professions.

Disability

A disability pay gap also exists and this is 22% less for women, but only 11% for men. This situation is known as a dual disadvantage for women with disabilities.

Find out about

Find out about the minimum wage. When was it first introduced and how much is it for different age groups? How fair do you think this is?

🔍 **websites**

To find advice about people's rights at work go to:
www.adviceguide.org.uk/england/work

For more information about discrimination at work go to:
www.gov.uk/discrimination

www.acas.org.uk
has a wealth of information about all work-related issues including health, employment rights, etc.

Personal research idea

Design a questionnaire for employers. Find out what they think of the minimum wage.

Check your understanding

Match the terms in the box to the explanations below.

Race	Gender	Ethics
Ethnicity	Exploitation	Discrimination

a) Which term is used to describe when a group is treated differently because of prejudice?

b) Which term is used to describe the set of norms that go with the role of being male or female?

c) Which term is used to describe when one group takes advantage of another?

d) Which term is used to describe whether research is right or wrong?

e) Which term is used to describe an outdated way of dividing people according to biological features, such as skin colour?

f) Which term is used to describe groups based on culture including religion and nationality?

Exam practice

Women's pay: hot on the heels of men's

The 'gender pay gap' between full-time workers is closing as women's wages rise at a faster rate than men's, official figures show.

The Office for National Statistics (ONS) found that the pay gap between men and women is now below 10% for the first time this century. Experts suggested that this shows that the 'glass ceiling' is starting to crack. The rise in women's hourly pay was 2% in 2012 compared to a 1.1% rise for men.

The gender pay gap – which compares men and women's pay is now only 9.6%. This is a drop of around 1% from the year before. In 2000, the gap was over 16%.

The film Made in Dagenham *told the story of female workers at the Ford Dagenham plant who campaigned for equal pay in the 1960s. Some 50 years on, the gender pay gap still exists, although it is closing.*

Film still from *Made in Dagenham*, director Nigel Cole, Sony Classics/BBC Films (2010)

a) Explain what is meant by the term gender pay gap. (2)

b) Identify what percentage women's hourly pay grew by in 2012. (1)

c) Fully explain what is meant by the term glass ceiling. (3)

d) Outline and explain two sociological reasons why any group, other than women, may be disadvantaged in the work place. (4)

Key terms

Exploitation – when people are treated unfairly and taken advantage of.

Minimum wage – a figure agreed by the government which is the lowest hourly rate of pay that employers can give.

Gender pay gap – the difference between the amount men earn compared with women.

Stretch and challenge

Think of 10 reasons why laws against discrimination, such as the Equality Act 2010 and previous laws about racial and sex discrimination are a good idea.

Interesting fact

A new law, the Equality Act was passed in 2010. This law strengthened laws about age discrimination at work. It also protected against discrimination due to sexuality, disability and other differences.

Compulsory Core

Topic 20: How do class, age, gender, ethnicity and disability affect health life chances?

What am I going to learn?

- **To understand how different social groups' health life chances vary**

Sociologists are interested in all five of the issues above and how they affect health life chances. Some individuals are lucky to naturally enjoy good health. However, sociologists would argue that our social characteristics will also have a big influence on our chances of being healthy.

Find out about

Find out about private health care. How does it compare with the NHS?

websites

www.ageuk.org.uk/
for information about age-related concerns.

www.mencap.org.uk
is a useful source for finding out about issues for people with learning disabilities.

www.poverty.org.uk
has more information about poverty in the UK.

Personal research idea

Carry out a piece of research amongst your class mates. Compare boys' and girls' attitudes to healthy eating and exercise. If possible interview some older people to compare attitudes.

Class and health

The NHS was set up in 1948, and was expected to eliminate inequalities in health. However, the Black Report, a government health report published in 1980, found that a person's chance of dying younger and the chance of becoming seriously ill were greater for working-class people. More recent studies show that this pattern continues.

Healthier lifestyles are popular now, but this may not be true for all social classes. A group of experts, called The King's Fund, found in 2012 that the middle classes were exercising more, eating healthily, avoiding smoking, and drinking less alcohol. In comparison, poorer people were still risking their health by drinking too much, smoking and doing less exercise. Overall the nation's health may be getting better, whilst health inequalities are getting worse.

However, this report puts the blame on people's lifestyle or culture. Other sociologists would say that poverty and poor living conditions cause ill health.

Age and health

Issues of **health** affect youth, and young people today are not always enjoying happy lives. One in ten young people in Britain suffer from a mental disorder, which may include depression or anxiety. Between 1 in 12 and 1 in 15 self-harm and each year 25,000 are admitted to hospital because their injuries are so severe.

Some older people complain that they are given second-class health care. They may not be given treatment because of their age.

Gender and health

Although women report more illness than men, **life expectancy** is higher for women (82.5 years) than men (78.5 years) , although the gap is closing. This may be because men take part in more risky behaviour including dangerous jobs. Ethnic minorities also suffer more ill-health than other groups.

Ethnicity and health

Ethnic minority groups generally suffer worse health than the rest of the population. However, there are big differences within and between groups. Also differences may be because more ethnic minority people are found in the working classes.

Check your understanding

Complete the sentences using the words from the word box.

poorer	treatment	discrimination	healthy
mental	cost	life	five

a) The nation has overall become healthier in the last few decades. However, some groups are still not eating a ••• diet. The government have tried hard to convince people through campaigns, such as the •••-a-day fruit and vegetables.

b) Smoking is not as popular as it was, but ••• people are still risking their health through this. The government are concerned about the huge ••• of providing healthcare for people not looking after themselves.

c) As well as this there are other concerns that vulnerable groups, such as the elderly and disabled may not get the same ••• as other groups. This is an example of •••. Children in today's society are suffering many ••• health problems. Social characteristics can play a strong part in deciding a person's health ••• chances.

Exam practice

Working-class way of life under attack by ideas about healthy living

Public health **toffs** want to destroy the pleasures of working-class communities simply for being 'unhealthy'.

Working-class culture is under attack. Public health toffs are trying to pass laws to stop parts of working class culture.

The target of the public health toffs is Average Joe, the stereotypical, overweight, working-class male who's a junk food addict and a betting shop regular, when he isn't a beer-swilling, chain-smoking couch potato – and they're also not fond of Average Jane's artificial tan.

Joe and Jane are the target of a plan to improve the nation's health. Working-class pleasures are seen as not worthwhile and a risk to health.

a) Using the item, identify one aspect of working-class culture. (1)
b) Using an example, explain what is meant by the term stereotype. (2)
c) Explain why the government want to stop parts of working-class culture. (2)
d) Outline and explain two sociological reasons why any social group may have worse life chances regarding health. (4)
e) Write a closed question which could be used in a research project into healthy lifestyles. (1)

Key terms

Health – means being free from illness or injury, both mental and physical.

Life expectancy – the average age that a person may be expected to live to.

Social characteristics – could include your gender, ethnicity, age, class or other significant parts of your identity.

Toff – a slang word for the rich.

Stretch and challenge

- Try to think of five reasons why some poorer people may take more risks with their health by drinking, smoking, eating unhealthy food and not exercising.

- What could the government do to change the lifestyle of people who are unhealthy?

- Is it right to make laws that force people to be healthy and do exercise?

- Is it reasonable that people who can afford private health care get treated more quickly than others?

- Why do the government want to make people healthier?

Topic 21: What do the major sociological theories say about inequality?

What am I going to learn?

● **To think about what the theories say about inequality**

Sociologists will always disagree with each other. They often do so because they have a different theory or idea about how society works. Understanding theory will give you an advantage and may make you want to learn more at a higher level of study. You may think about which theory makes most sense to you.

Betty Friedan

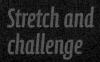 *Famous people*

In 1963 Betty Friedan, an American feminist writer, wrote a book called *The Feminine Mystique.* The book was very important in making women think that they did not have to be stuck in their traditional roles of mother and housewife. They could be successful outside of the family. It may sound tame now, but at the time her ideas shocked people and helped to start massive social changes for men and women.

Stretch and challenge

What would happen if everybody in the UK was paid the same amount whatever their job? Would this work?

Functionalists

Functionalists are always interested in what job any part of society does. Inequality is part of society and so functionalists believe it does a job. Inequality creates a society of winners and losers. Some people are rich, powerful and have high status. Some people are poor, have little power and are low status. Inequality helps to motivate people to be winners. If we were all equal, nobody would try to do anything. Therefore, functionalists say that inequality is needed by society and helps society to run well.

The **New Right** would agree with a lot of this but would go further and blame the poor themselves for inequality.

Marxists

Marxists think that inequality is not a good thing. They believe there are two main social classes: the ruling class and the working class. The ruling class have all the power and own big businesses, factories, the media and control what happens. They have such a lot of power they are able to control how the working class think. This ensures they will never realise how they are being used by the ruling class.

For Marxists, inequality is unfair. However, they think that one day the workers will realise their situation and overthrow the ruling class.

Feminists

Feminists believe that the most damaging inequality is between men and women. They call our society **patriarchal**, which means that it is ruled by men. Feminists are concerned that women have been trapped in the traditional roles of mother and housewife. This has suited men, who control the world, not even allowing them to vote until they fought for the right.

Feminists also are concerned about the way that girls are socialised. They think stereotypes about beauty and being sexy are not helpful for women growing up and are to suit men.

Some feminists believe that progress has been made and laws like the Sex Discrimination Act (1975) have helped. Others called **radical feminists** think that men will never change and want to see bigger changes.

Check your understanding

Identify the quotation. Name the theory:

a) 'The ruling class control everything and have all the power.'

b) 'The underclass are lazy and do not want to work.'

c) 'Inequality is needed in society or nobody would try and there would be no one to do the most important jobs.'

d) 'Women were stuck at home for too long. It suited men to stop them from getting careers.'

Exam practice

Gender divide starts to affect men

The government equality watchdog found yesterday that women are more likely to do better at school and less likely to lose their jobs. They are healthier and eat a better diet including their five-a-day fruit and vegetables. Women are less likely to be overweight, and live longer than men.

There may still be a gender pay gap, but in other things men have worse life chances.

a) Using the item, identify two ways in which the report says that women are doing better than men. (1)

b) Using examples from the item, explain what is meant by the term life chances. (4)

c) Explain what is meant by the term inequality. (1)

d) Outline and explain one sociological reason why we have inequality in our society. (4)

Key terms

Theory – an idea about how society works.

Functionalism – a major theory in sociology which looks at the way different parts of society help to keep it healthy.

New Right – a theory which is concerned that things are going wrong in society and changes need to be made.

Marxism – a conflict theory which sees society as divided into two classes.

Feminism – a theory which sees the biggest conflict in society as between men and women.

Patriarchy – a society dominated by men.

Radical feminism – a more extreme type of feminism.

Interesting facts

Marxist ideas about how to have a more equal society were tried in many countries such as Russia, Cuba and lots of Eastern European countries. Marxism is often known as communism.

In the USA, people were very strongly against Marxist/ communist ideas in the 1950s. The USA saw Russia as its main enemy in the world as Russia was communist. This led to the Cold War, which was not actually a war, but tension was very high and lots of weapons were built, including nuclear ones.

Very few countries would now claim to be Marxist/communist, but Marxist ideas are still influential.

Compulsory Core

Topic 22: Is Britain an equal society?

What am I going to learn?

● **To consider whether British society is an equal society**

As we discussed in Topic 2, Britain is not an equal society. There is lots of sociological evidence to show there is a great deal of inequality. However, is British society fair? Do people get a fair chance of being successful? This topic will try to consider these questions.

Interesting facts

Pop music is now dominated by people who went to fee-paying schools. In 2012, the *Daily Mail* reported that 60% of the British artists in the pop charts went to fee-paying schools. This includes Chris Martin (Coldplay), Pixie Lott, Mumford and Sons, Florence Welch (Florence and the Machine), La Roux and Lily Allen.

Some of the great British bands of the past including Oasis, The Beatles, Stone Roses, The Kinks and The Smiths were all working class.

Working-class children go to schools with fewer resources for music provision. State schools had half the money in 2011 compared with 1990.

Meritocracy

The idea of **meritocracy** links to this topic. The idea of a meritocracy means that the most successful people in society have achieved this because they have worked hard and are very able. So, the top jobs in the country, such as lawyers, doctors and scientists, should go to the cleverest people providing they work hard. Education is the key to enabling this to happen.

If you think about this Sociology exam, the A's and A*'s should go to the brightest students providing they work hard. This is what will happen. Some students who are not the most able may still achieve high grades because they work hard and are well organised. Imagine if the grades awarded had nothing to do with ability or hard work. How unfair would that be? Some students would get an A* who were not able and didn't work hard.

This sounds very unfair, but if British society is not a meritocracy then this is what happens in people's lives. There is lots of evidence to show that Britain is not a meritocracy.

The 'isms'

Racism, sexism, ageism and treating people differently because they are not able-bodied or are working class will stop Britain being a meritocracy. There is lots of evidence in this book to suggest that these things go on. People have different chances of getting a good job, keeping a job, being healthy, staying out of jail, being a victim of crime or living to a good age depending on class, age, gender, ethnicity and disability.

It is important to realise that sociologists are not saying that being working class or belonging to any group means you are doomed to failure. Individuals can overcome difficult circumstances. However, there is lots of evidence to show that the odds may be stacked against some people.

Finally, there are always sociologists who do not agree.

Check your understanding

Complete the sentences.

discrimination	work	talent		
	gender		working	fair

a) Meritocracy is the idea that success should come to those who are most able and who ••• hard. There is a lot of concern from many people that Britain is not a very ••• society.

b) Prejudice and ••• may stop many talented and hardworking people from being successful. This is bad for our society as we are wasting the best •••.

c) Life chances vary considerably based on your class, age, •••, ethnicity and whether you are disabled. It is important to remember that we all belong to more than one of these groups. The life chances of an upper-class woman are very different from those of a black •••-class woman.

Exam practice

MPs, actors and sports stars are more likely to be from private schools, according to Gove.

Michael Gove warned that **privately educated** people are gaining all the best positions of wealth and power in Britain.

The Education Secretary, Michael Gove, raised concerns at the start of 2013 that Britain was a very unequal society with poor children likely to stay poor while the rich remain rich.

He said that this was not acceptable and is a waste of the nation's talent. The majority of the most important MPs attended fee-paying schools, he said.

This is also true for doctors, lawyers, media, university and business. Even in sport, half of Britain's Olympic medallists went to fee-paying schools. Only 7% of people go to fee-paying schools in Britain.

Mr Gove said that 'Those who are born poor are more likely to stay poor and those who **inherit** privilege are more likely to pass on privilege in England than in any comparable country.'

He called for big changes, especially in schools, to change this.

a) Using the item, identify which group of people it says is dominating British society. (1)

b) What percentage of people go to fee-paying schools in the UK? (1)

c) Explain what is meant by the term privilege. (2)

d) A sociologist wants to research the reasons that people who attend fee-paying schools get the best jobs. Identify a suitable research method and say why it is a suitable method. (3)

e) Explain how you would obtain a sample of people to use in the research. (3)

Key terms

Meritocracy – the idea that ability and hard work should bring success in a fair society.

Privately educated – students who go to schools where you have to pay.

Inherit – is when things are passed down from your parents.

Stretch and challenge

Look at the source for the exam question. Michael Gove thinks Britain is too unequal and unfair. How do you think the situation could be changed? What would you do if you were the government?

Extended writing

Discuss whether Britain is a meritocracy. Write an essay collecting together as many different ideas and evidence as you can find. This should sum up the whole chapter. Include as many sociological terms as you can. (20)

Grade boost

Practise thinking about research methods and design research projects thinking about the difficulties involved.

Topic 1: Why do people work?

What am I going to learn?

● **To understand what work is and why people do it**

People have to spend a large proportion of their lives at work. It has a huge impact on their quality of life and on their identity. Sociologists have tried to understand the reasons for people working. Some of these seem obvious but human beings are never simple.

Extended writing

Describe reasons why people work. (10)

Personal research idea

Carry out some interviews with people in different jobs about their level of job satisfaction. Design either questions for a structured interview or topic areas for discussion in an unstructured interview. Start with your teacher!

Grade boost

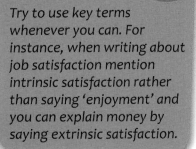

Try to use key terms whenever you can. For instance, when writing about job satisfaction mention intrinsic satisfaction rather than saying 'enjoyment' and you can explain money by saying extrinsic satisfaction.

What is work?

Work is something that we do to achieve a purpose. Most people think of work as paid employment or a job we are paid for. However, we also think of mowing the lawn or homework as work, which are not usually paid.

To make things even more complicated some people do things as paid work which others do for enjoyment. A professional footballer plays football for money, yet thousands of people play every weekend for enjoyment. Things we do for enjoyment are called leisure. So, work is not easy to pin down, but sociologists have tended to focus on paid work as something that has to be done.

Income

Paid work is done to earn an **income** or wages. Most people primarily work to gain an income because they need it to live. Workers need to make enough money to pay their monthly living costs, but also need to put money aside for retirement. The pleasure the worker gets from the money they earn and what they can buy with it is known as **extrinsic satisfaction**. In this view work is a means to an end – getting money!

Job satisfaction

Although money is the most obvious motivation, work also is an important part of people's lives. **Job satisfaction** is the pleasure that a job brings the worker. Does the job make the person feel pleased with what they have achieved? Does the job allow the worker to express themselves? Creative jobs may allow this but jobs which involve organising and fixing things may also be rewarding. The pleasure the worker gets from the job itself is known as **intrinsic satisfaction**. In other words, the job is satisfying in itself, regardless of money.

Social rewards

The other reasons for people working are social ones. Workers gain a sense of identity and purpose from their jobs. People also find a sense of community at work and meet new friends.

Check your understanding

Complete the sentences below:

a) Work includes jobs that we are ••• for but also unpaid work.

b) Most people work mainly to earn •••.

c) The actual physical rewards that we get for work are known as ••• satisfaction.

d) The pleasure that people get from doing a job well is known as ••• satisfaction.

e) People also meet others and feel part of a ••• through work.

f) Work can also become an important part of a person's sense of who they are, which is known as their •••.

Exam practice

I can't get no job satisfaction

Job satisfaction among UK workers has gone up since 2006 even though the **recession** means that workplaces are struggling. The study was done by the Chartered Institute of Personnel and Development (CIPD).

But the organisation said its survey may reflect people simply being happy to have a job during the recession and being 'less likely to grumble'.

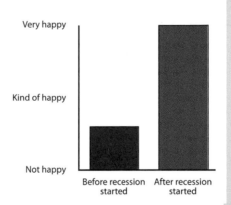

How happy I am with my job

More than a third of the 3,000 people quizzed worried about losing their jobs. Most said finding new work would be tough.

The percentage of people made 'tense' by their job had also risen since 2006. This could make workers feel unhappy and unhealthy in the near future.

a) Using the items, suggest why workers may be 'less likely to grumble' during a recession. (1)

b) Why does the item suggest that workers may feel unhappy and unhealthy in the near future? (2)

c) Explain what the term work means. (3)

d) A researcher is studying workers' job satisfaction in a factory using questionnaires. Outline two problems that there may be using this method for this. (4)

Key terms

Work – jobs that we do for a purpose, often but not always paid.

Income – the money people are paid as wages, pensions or benefits.

Extrinsic satisfaction – the rewards that we get for working, such as wages.

Job satisfaction – how much happiness and sense of worth a worker is feeling about the job that they do.

Intrinsic satisfaction – the enjoyment that people gain from the work itself.

Recession – a time when there are money problems, jobs are lost and many businesses close down.

Stretch and challenge

- Make a list of 10 jobs and score each one out of 10 for how much intrinsic and how much extrinsic satisfaction you think is involved in those jobs.

- What do you think is the ideal job which gives both intrinsic and extrinsic satisfaction?

- How much satisfaction do you get out of being a GCSE student? How would you score your position as a student on the same scale?

Topic 2: What is leisure and non-work?

What am I going to learn?

● **To understand the role that leisure and non-work also play in people's lives**

Sociologists have also tried to understand how people spend the rest of their lives outside of paid work. This is also an important part of people's lives and is greatly affected by experiences at work. Sociologists have been interested in how leisure has changed and how it will change in the future.

Stretch and challenge

What will leisure be like in the future? Will there be more or less?

Find out about

Stanley Parker was one of the most famous sociologists who wrote about leisure. He found that leisure was closely linked to work. People who enjoyed their jobs tended to do leisure activities that were extensions of their working day. Others saw their work as boring so made sure that they spent quality time with their families and enjoying themselves out of work. The third kind are people with very tough physical jobs who tended to do the complete opposite in their spare time, such as drinking and letting off steam.

Non-work

Non-work includes all the things that people do outside employment. This includes **leisure**, sleeping, eating, washing and travelling. Some aspects of non-work may possibly be seen as work. For instance, gardening could be seen as non-work or more precisely leisure.

Leisure

Leisure means the things we do for relaxation or enjoyment and has been the focus for sociologists. So many household tasks may not be seen as leisure; although DIY is leisure for many and work for others.

Leisure can include both physical activities such as sport, walking or travelling and less active pursuits such as sunbathing, reading, watching television or chatting. If work is about things you *have* to do, leisure is about choice.

The past

Before the growth of the **factory system**, the idea of the workplace as somewhere to go for a set number of hours a day was not the norm. Most people worked at home, on the land or in **cottage industries**. Cottage industries were where people worked at home, possibly spinning, weaving or other trades. Leisure time and work were not clearly divided. When people started going out to work in factories or offices the need for leisure became important. In the 19th century work was tough and the working days were long.

Leisure and identity

In the 20th century leisure became increasingly important. People looked forward to their leisure time, and the things they did in their leisure time became an important part of their identity. The growth of the teenager in the 1950s was about young people developing an identity based on how they spent their leisure time.

Life chances and leisure

Leisure links closely to the topic of life chances studied in the previous chapter. Sociologists have found that a person's background, which includes job, social class, gender, ethnicity and age, will have a huge impact on how much leisure time they have and how they spend it. Money, time and a person's social network will affect how they spend their leisure time.

Check your understanding

Match the correct term to the definitions below:

Leisure	Work	Identity	Validity	Non-work	Income

a) What is the term for a person's sense of who they are?

b) What is the term used to describe all the things that people do when they are not at a paid job?

c) What term is used to describe how close a research study is to describing the truth of what is being studied?

d) What term is used to describe the money that people use to live on each week or month?

e) What term is used to describe a task that is done for a purpose?

f) What term is used to describe things that people do for enjoyment or relaxation?

Exam practice

Men take it easy

An international survey found that men spent longer watching television, meeting friends, playing sport or doing hobbies than women.

The report, done by the Organisation of Economic Co-operation and Development, was released to mark International Women's Day and called for greater equality for women. It said that 'governments and firms need to do more to tackle the gender equality gap'.

There were some problems in deciding what counted as leisure. The OECD decided that shopping, soaking in the bath, grooming, having a lie-in or taking a long lunch all count as work rather than leisure. If these are counted as leisure, British men have only 10 minutes more spare time a day than women.

The report said: 'Men universally report spending more time in activities counted as leisure than women'.

a) According to the item, which gender has the most leisure time? (1)

b) Using the items, explain one problem that the researchers had. (2)

c) Explain what is meant by the term leisure. (3)

d) Outline and explain two reasons why some social groups may have less access to leisure than others. (4)

Key terms

Non-work – all of the time spent not doing work.

Leisure – activities that are done for relaxation or enjoyment.

Factory system – the system that meant people went to work in huge buildings specially designed for manufacturing goods on a large scale.

Cottage industry – historical term to describe a system where people worked in their own houses.

Stretch and challenge

Collect pictures from magazines/advertisements about leisure. Make two or three sociological points about leisure beneath each one.

Across the generations

Find out how your parents, grandparents or older family friends spent their leisure time as children or teenagers. Compare it with your own leisure time.

Extended writing

Describe how the social group a person belongs to may affect their leisure time. (10)

Topic 3: What are the different types of work?

What am I going to learn?

- **To understand the different sectors of work and how these have changed over time**

This section will outline the three main sectors of work in Britain. It is also important to see how these have changed and think about the social impact of this.

Interesting fact

Sociologists (and geographers) now also use the term quaternary sector to describe another type of job. The advance in communications and information technology has led to many new jobs. Jobs involving communication, information, knowledge and computers are known as the quaternary sector. This sector has become very important in Britain.

Over to you

Find out how many of the parents of students in your class work in primary, secondary and service sectors. Do any of them work in a quaternary industry? There may be parts of the country where primary and secondary industry are still common.

What is the economy?

The **economy** is about how people make and use money. Work is the main way that people make money to live on or to save as wealth. The economy is usually divided into three main areas.

Primary sector

The first of these is the **primary sector** and includes all the jobs which involve taking things from the earth's resources. Mining, farming and fishing are examples of this. They all involve taking raw materials in some way. In Britain up until the **Industrial Revolution**, these were the most common types of job that people did, e.g. mining in Wales. Most of these industries are in decline and fewer people now work in the primary sector in Britain.

Secondary sector

The Industrial Revolution was a huge change in the way people worked and lived. It happened in the 18th and 19th centuries in Britain and made the **secondary sector** the most important part of the economy. The secondary sector involves making things. For instance, car factories make cars out of raw materials which include metal, rubber and lots more. Therefore, car factory workers are working in the secondary sector.

Since the 1970s, British manufacturing has been in decline and the number of people working in the secondary sector has become less.

Service sector

Even before these changes, the **service sector** had grown larger. Since World War Two ended there were more service sector jobs appearing. The service, or **tertiary, sector** is when people provide a service for other people. This includes people who work in schools, hospitals, shops, offices, restaurants and thousands of other jobs. In most areas of Britain this is the sector that most people work in.

Check your understanding

Complete the sentences below:

a) Farming is an example of a job in the ••• sector.

b) A person serving in Burger King is an example of a job in the ••• sector.

c) A person working in a tyre factory is an example of a job in the ••• sector.

d) At the start of the 21st century most people in Britain work in the ••• sector.

e) Before the Industrial Revolution most people in Britain worked in the ••• sector.

f) During the Industrial Revolution most people worked in the ••• sector.

Exam practice

Mary Portas's kinky knickers to save Britain?

Mary Portas is making a new programme called *Mary's Bottom Line*. It is about a factory that makes knickers in Middleton, England. Mary suggests that Britain has lost part of its identity as a manufacturing nation.

Mary is trying to help the factory be successful and wants to encourage viewers to buy British goods. Mary believes that this will help the secondary sector in Britain do better.

But when her team asks the seemingly innocent question, 'So when and why did we stop buying British?' she should not forget that millions of British people still work in the manufacturing industry.

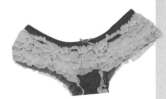

Although British firms cannot produce as cheaply as Chinese ones because of the low cost of Chinese workers, they can still produce high quality goods.

a) Using the item, identify one reason why British factories cannot produce goods as cheaply as Chinese ones. (1)

b) Explain why Mary Portas wants viewers to buy British goods. (2)

c) Explain, with examples, what is meant by the term service sector. (3)

d) A sociologist wants to carry out interviews to find out how workers feel about their bosses. Explain two problems that he may have in conducting the research. (4)

Key terms

Economy – is the way that people make and use money.

Primary sector – means jobs where people take natural resources from the planet.

Industrial Revolution – a huge change which happened in the 18th and 19th centuries which changed work and peoples' lives completely.

Secondary sector – jobs which involve making or manufacturing something.

Service sector – jobs which involve doing something for other people or providing a service.

Tertiary sector – another term for the service sector.

Stretch and challenge

- Brainstorm ways in which Britain could revive its secondary sector.

- The service sector continues to change. Try to imagine 10 jobs that do not exist now but might in the future.

Extended writing

Describe the different sectors of the economy. (10)

Topic 4: What other changes have there been to the economy?

What am I going to learn?

● **To understand that there have been global changes in the world of work that have impacted upon British work**

Sociologists have been interested in the impact of changes in technology. These have had a huge impact on the way we live and work in Britain. One of the most important changes is that of globalisation, which has made new ideas spread more quickly and led to fast-paced change.

George Ritzer

Famous people

George Ritzer developed the idea of the McDonaldization of society. Globalisation has also led to ideas spreading quickly across the world. McDonald's the fast food chain is a powerful multinational company which has spread its restaurants across the globe. In addition it has a model of business organisation that has spread.

McDonald's burgers are predictably the same wherever you go. This idea of standardisation of products has spread and is part of the McDonald's idea. The uniform that staff wear is part of this idea. Also part of this is the efficiency of service. Ritzer said that the idea of McDonaldization had influenced all of society. Other businesses and organisations followed the McDonald's model.

Global media

On 25 June 1967, fourteen countries of the world got together to produce the first global satellite broadcast. The Beatles sang 'All you need is love' for the British contribution. The song's simple message of love was watched by 400 million people in 26 countries. This was technically very difficult to do but was the start of the global media that we now take for granted.

Globalisation

The global media has developed because of changes in technology for communications and transport. It was just part of a huge change to the world that sociologists call **globalisation**. Globalisation is the idea that parts of the world are being brought increasingly closer together by exchanging ideas, technology, products and services. It is more than simple international links. The different parts of the world have become linked closer and closer.

Globalisation and work

Globalisation has had a huge effect on work. For instance, the biggest companies are now **multinational** companies. Multinational companies are not based in any one country and cannot be controlled by any one government.

Multinational companies, like Ford, Sony and Nestlé, move their bases of operations around the world to make their businesses more efficient. Poorer countries are often used for both raw materials (primary sector) and manufacturing because workers are given low wages. This has meant that there are fewer manufacturing (secondary sector) jobs in wealthier countries like Britain. There are fears that workers in poorer, developing countries are made to work in poor conditions by multinational companies. Workers in rich developed countries may lose their jobs as multinationals move factories to other countries.

Globalisation brings good things for consumers as there is more choice in the shops. Internet sales from companies like Amazon have also given greater choice but are said to be destroying traditional British high streets. Internet companies may employ people overseas costing British workers jobs.

Check your understanding

Match the following terms to the definitions:

| Technology | Globalisation | Ethics |
| Multinationals | Employment | Participant observation |

a) What term is used to describe the issue of whether research is right or wrong?

b) What term is used to describe the jobs people do?

c) What term is used to describe the idea that the world is becoming increasingly interconnected through communications and technology?

d) What term is used to describe large companies based in more than one country?

e) What term is used to describe inventions?

f) What term is used to describe a method which involves watching people whilst joining in with their activities?

Exam practice

Technology-driven workforce

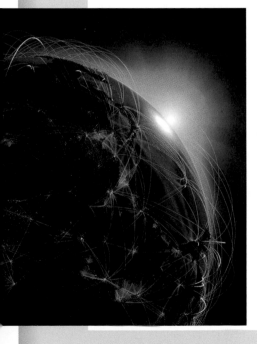

New computer and scientific technology will continue to change the workplace. This will reshape the workforce as we know it today. There will be less need to go to the office. Video conferences, working from home and teams of workers who only meet in virtual reality will be the norm along with increased remote access to offices, video conferencing and virtual work teams.

The old ideas of time and space will disappear. A person can do business 24 hours a day with someone 10 time zones away. A worker's boss may be 10,000 miles away. Globalisation will become a force for improvements to computer technology and a result of more advanced technology in the workplace.

a) Using the item, identify two changes in work as a result of changing technology. (2)

b) Suggest one effect that this will have on workers. (1)

c) Explain how globalisation has affected workers. (3)

d) Outline and explain two ways that new technology may have affected leisure. (4)

Stretch and challenge

Make a list of 10 good things that globalisation has brought and 10 things that are negative.

Explain whether you think that globalisation has made the world a better place.

Extended writing

Explain what the impact of globalisation has been on the workplace. (10)

Grade boost

Do not confuse the terms globalisation and McDonaldization. Globalisation is a general idea about the changes and McDonaldization is a more specific idea.

Topic 5: How has work changed in the UK?

What am I going to learn?

- **To consider the many changes affecting work in Britain since World War Two**

Britain has faced a difficult economic time since the end of World War Two. There have also been huge global changes which have had dramatic effects on work and social life in general. The changes have brought some positive things but also some concerns.

Across the generations

Ask your older relatives what it was like during the power cuts in the 1970s or the dustbin strikes of the late 1970s.

Also find out what it was like to leave school in the 1950s, 60s, 70s, 80s and 90s. What sort of employment opportunities were there?

Famous people

Marshall McLuhan

Marshall McLuhan has become famous for coining the term 'global village' in 1962. He had a lot of ideas about how media and communications were developing. He predicted correctly that new technology would shrink time and space making the world like one village. The Internet and the process of globalisation have proved him right.

After World War Two

Britain finished World War Two as victors but **weak economically**. However, changes after the war included the new NHS, expanded **civil service** and secondary schools for all. Lots of new jobs were created in teaching, nursing and offices. New building also created work in the building industry. The 1950s were a time of boom for Britain.

Economic crisis

By the mid 1970s, the British economy was beginning to struggle. The manufacturing base that had made Britain rich was beginning to have problems. There were lots of arguments between bosses and workers. Power cuts were a regular thing as miners went on strike. By the late 1970s the industries of coal and steel that whole communities had been built around were in **decline**. The good times seemed to be over. Unemployment rose (see Topic 8).

Coal to oil

Coalmining was a very important work area for Britain around which whole communities were built. The availability of oil as an alternative made the coal industry go into decline. In the 1980s, a fierce conflict between Margaret Thatcher's government and the miners over pit closures divided the nation. The miners were defeated and many pits closed. Britain's industrial past was becoming history.

Globalisation

Globalisation was another reason for this. Globalisation brought many exciting changes including the availability of goods from all over the world and undreamt of communication improvements. However, the higher wages expected by British workers made British industry uncompetitive compared with developing countries like China and India.

Growth of the service sector

Britain has had to change its economy to adapt to this new world. The service sector has become much more important along with newer industries, including computers, **financial services** and communications. Since 2008, the recession which was started by the 'credit crunch' has bitten hard. Many of the work areas that were expanded after World War Two have been cut back. The future for British workers looks tough and they will need to adapt.

Check your understanding

True or False?

a) Britain was really rich after winning World War Two.

b) There were no power cuts in the 1970s.

c) Margaret Thatcher was one of the Prime Ministers who had conflict with the miners.

d) British manufacturing has gone into decline since the 1970s.

e) British companies can produce goods as cheaply as countries like China.

f) The service (tertiary) sector is where most people now work.

Exam practice

Globalisation hits Britain in the pocket

Rich European countries like Britain and France have soft laws on retirement and working hours. No European country is going to compete with China, Brazil and India in a time of globalisation with this sort of attitude.

British businessmen trying to run a business in France cannot ask people to work more than 35 hours a week. India and China have no such laws protecting their workers so their businesses will win.

In some ways, British jobs are particularly at risk because many people speak English. You think you are talking to someone in Dagenham, paid at least the minimum wage. In fact, you are speaking to someone in Delhi, paid much less.

Globalisation brought cheap products from overseas, but now the lack of jobs means there is no money to buy the products.

a) Using the item, suggest one reason why British firms cannot compete with India and China. (1)

b) Which law protecting workers does the item say that India and China do not have? (1)

c) Explain two effects that globalisation has had on the British workplace. (4)

d) Outline and explain two ways that the economy of Britain has changed since World War Two. (4)

Key terms

Weak economically – when there is not enough money and/or money is owed to other people.

Civil service – workers who help the government carry out their ideas.

Decline – get worse.

Financial services – people who help people choose how to invest their money.

Credit crunch – a term used to describe the problems caused by governments, businesses and people borrowing too much money.

Extended writing

Describe how work has changed in the UK since the end of World War Two. (10)

Stretch and challenge

- If you were the government list five changes that you would make to try to make Britain more competitive with emerging nations like India and China.

- What would be the possible consequences if Britain stopped allowing goods from other countries into Britain so that more British goods were sold?

Topic 6: How has the experience of work changed?

What am I going to learn?

● **To understand how changes in technology and the organisation of work have changed the experience of work**

Sociologists have analysed the changes that have happened in the workplace and tried to understand what effect this has had upon workers. Do workers feel less powerful, skilled or happy at work when changes have occurred? Technology and new ideas about how to organise the workplace have influenced these changes.

Famous people

Henry Ford

Henry Ford was an American who started the famous Ford motor car company. He developed the use of the production line to make a cheap user-friendly car that Americans could afford. The Model T Ford was the first mass-produced car and Ford's method of production line manufacture became known as Fordism. Famous for his quotes, Ford said 'Any customer can have a car painted any colour that he wants, so long as it is black'.

One quote you might like to think about in terms of your approach to GCSE Sociology is this Henry Ford quote: 'If you think you can do a thing, or think you can't do a thing, you're right!'

The coming of machines

The word Luddite has survived into the computer age as a word for someone who is resistant to new technology. The word comes because of the actions of a group of weavers in the 1800s. New machinery made it possible for them to be replaced with low-skilled workers paid much less money. The weavers were angry and vandalised machinery. They were named after a legendary figure called Ned Ludd who was said to have smashed machines earlier.

Deskilling

The workers concerns in both cases were about their jobs being **deskilled**. Their skills would no longer be valuable and their wages would drop. Harry Braverman is a sociologist who developed this idea. The process of jobs being deskilled is linked with **mechanisation**. Mechanisation is when jobs are taken over by machines. The computer age has seen this process develop even further. Some jobs are deskilled because a machine can do the job. Some jobs may be lost as a result of mechanisation. Either fewer workers are needed or none at all.

Automation

Linked to mechanisation and deskilling is the idea of **automation**. The work process becomes automatic and is controlled by machines. At its extreme, workers work on a production line and have no control over the pace of work. The work is also broken down into small tasks so that the worker does not take part in the whole production process. A person in a car factory may just fit a wheel before it moves down the production line. This may be very repetitive and not enjoyable.

Division of labour

This way of dividing a job up into small parts is known as the **division of labour**. Factory owners liked it because it was more efficient and wasted less time. Each worker became very good at their specific part of the job so products became better. The Model T Ford was one of the best examples of this.

Check your understanding

Complete the sentences below:

a) The people who smashed the machines in factories were known as •••.

b) The process where jobs that workers do require less skill is known as •••.

c) ••• is when jobs are taken over by machines.

d) The organisation of work when individual workers only complete a small part of the whole process is known as a production •••.

e) A work process controlled by machines is known as •••.

f) Factory owners set up their factories as production lines because it saved time and was more •••.

Exam practice

Teleworking – blessing or curse?

Working from home can, for many people, mean finding it hard to know when work ends and life begins

There are strong arguments in favour of **teleworking**. Time saved not having to commute into a central office can result in higher **productivity**, better quality of life, and give people with families more flexibility over how they organise their time. Less traffic also means less pollution and congestion.

High-speed broadband and secure virtual private networks now make teleworking possible and information secure. More workers at home and flexible hours mean smaller offices and lower costs for businesses.

Most importantly, workers seem to like it.

Vodafone, the mobile phone company, did a survey of the London area in 2012. 24% of respondents said they had changed their normal working arrangements over the Olympics period, either working from home or somewhere else, to avoid travel problems. They had done more work as a result of time saved.

But what are the disadvantages? Humans like face-to-face contact. Will people be as creative without working face-to-face?

a) What percentage of workers in the survey changed their normal working arrangements over the Olympics period? (1)

b) Using the item, suggest two benefits of working at home. (2)

c) Outline and explain two effects that working from home could have upon society. (4)

d) Describe one problem that changes in technology may bring for workers. (3)

Key terms

Deskilling – the way in which jobs need less expertise to do.

Mechanisation – when jobs that were done by hand are now done by machines.

Automation – when machines begin to control the work.

Division of labour – when tasks that make up a job are split between many individuals.

Teleworking – when people use computers and phones and modern technology to work at home or away from the office.

Productivity – the amount of work completed.

Stretch and challenge

Imagine what work will be like by the year 2050. Consider future technology, where will it be done, hours worked, organisation of businesses, working conditions, number of jobs available. Will it be better or worse? Write a magazine article or produce a PowerPoint about your vision.

Extended writing

Discuss the impact of technology on the workplace. (20)

Topic 7: What is the experience of work like for workers?

What am I going to learn?

- **To know about sociological insights into the experience of work**

Working conditions have changed drastically since the time of the Industrial Revolution. However, sociologists have drawn attention to the aspects of work that are not an enjoyable part of being human. Marxism, in particular, has provided a view of work that is interesting and helps to explain why work is not always enjoyable.

Personal research idea

Find out whether people you know are alienated at work. Use Robert Blauner's four parts of alienation to devise questions for an interview. Ask people who do different jobs to do the interview.

Over to you

Are you alienated at school? How alienating is the school as a workplace for students? How could it be improved? Take your ideas to the School Council or Student Voice.

Extended writing

Explain what is meant by the term alienation. (10)

Work and being human

Nearly all humans have to do some kind of work whether it is paid or unpaid. At its best, work can be rewarding and satisfying. At its worst, work can make us feel exhausted, ill, out of control, lonely, stressed or miserable. Work is an important part of being human and our identity.

Working conditions

The situation in which we work is known as our **working conditions**. This includes:

- Are we working with others or alone?
- Do we see the completed **product** we help make or the service we are providing?
- Are we in control of our work? Is the work worthwhile?
- Hours worked and breaks, pay and holidays.
- Relationships with co-workers and bosses.

Alienation

Karl Marx thought that work was the most important thing that humans did. The terrible working conditions of the 19th century were making work **dehumanised**. This means that humans were losing touch with their real selves.

Marx noticed that people working in factories had no control over their work and did not even own the end product that they were making. He compared this with a time when a craftsman, such as a carpenter making a table, would have had the pleasure of making a whole product. Before the Industrial Revolution, workers were closer to nature. They could appreciate where the products they were making came from.

The workers were losing the pleasure of work, which is a key part of being human. The industrial work process is not natural and unsatisfying. Marx called this **alienation**.

Modern work

21st-century work may be more alienating than in Marx's time. Workers now use technology that they do not understand and are further away from nature than ever.

Check your understanding

Match the terms below with the correct definition:

Alienation	Globalisation	Employment
Mcdonaldization	Automation	Deskilling

a) What term is used to describe the paid work that someone does?

b) What term is used to describe the way that machines control the process of work?

c) What term is used to explain the way that work has become unnatural and unsatisfying?

d) What term is used to describe the way jobs now need less expertise?

e) What term is used to describe the way that a fast food chain's style of organisation has spread around the world?

f) What term is used to describe the way that the world has become increasingly closely connected through communications?

Exam practice

Farmers, forestry workers and fishermen happiest of all

Results from the government's first ever survey of National Well Being, published by the Office for National Statistics, are likely to show that people who work in farming, forestry and fishing are happier than others.

The government want to use the information to help young people choose their jobs – asking whether they will be happy, rather than whether they will earn a lot of money.

The study – published in 2012 – found that at the top of the satisfaction list were people who work in agriculture, forestry and fishing. The least satisfied were those working in admin, transport, hotels, catering and car repairs.

a) Using the item, identify the work areas that were most satisfied with their jobs. (1)

b) What does the item say that the government want to use the survey for? (1)

c) Which two sectors of the economy do the jobs with the highest and lowest levels of satisfaction come from? (2)

d) A sociologist wants to research alienation in the workplace using observation. Outline and explain two problems that the researcher may have using this method. (6)

Key terms

Working conditions – what it is like at work.

Product – is the thing that the worker makes.

Dehumanisation – the idea that humans are acting in a way that is not natural for humans.

Alienation – Marxist term to describe the way that work has become unnatural and unsatisfying for workers.

Famous people

Robert Blauner

Robert Blauner was an American sociologist writing 100 years after Marx. He decided to try to find a way of measuring alienation for sociological research. He identified four parts to alienation. These were:

- Powerlessness – the amount of control workers had over their work.

- Meaninglessness – did the work have any meaning for the worker. Did they see a finished product?

- Isolation – could the worker talk to other workers?

- Self-estrangement – as a result of the other three does the worker feel distanced from their true selves and from society?

This is called operationalising a concept. Blauner turned the idea of alienation into a form that could be measured.

Topic 8: What are the effects of unemployment?

What am I going to learn?

● **How unemployment has a damaging effect on individuals, their families and society**

Unemployment has been a steady feature of life in Britain over the last 30 years. Sociologists have studied the effects of unemployment. There are other times when people do not work, such as retirement, which will also be considered in this topic.

What is unemployment?

Unemployment is when a person is of working age and is unable to find work. The government has used many different methods to decide who to include in the figures, but generally it would be fair to say that unemployment has remained a lot higher than in 1971.

Retirement

Another group who do not work but are not classed as unemployed are people who have retired. **Retirement** is the time when a person's working life ends and they expect to relax and enjoy life. As people are living longer, the cost of pensions is increasing. One way of controlling the cost is to delay retirement and the official age for retirement has just been raised to 67. The retirement age may rise even higher by the time you come to retire!

Retirement can be a difficult time as people lose their main role in life. Work is an important part of identity and retirement can be a difficult life change.

The effects of unemployment

Unemployment affects a person's identity as they lose one of their main roles in life. The unemployed can suffer from **depression** damaging their whole life including their relationships. Money is an obvious problem and families can find themselves losing their homes and suffering from poverty. All of these things can affect family health. Their children may not eat a good diet and may be denied opportunities that other children get.

Men, in particular, may find losing their job and being unable to find work particularly tough. This may be because of their traditional role as the breadwinner.

Society and unemployment

Society itself suffers because the economy may become worse as fewer people are able to spend money. Crime rates may rise and the unemployed may misuse drugs and alcohol. Since the 1980s there have been a group of long-term

Interesting fact

During 2012 the BBC, *Daily Mirror*, *The Guardian* and *Daily Telegraph* all reported that there was a growing unemployment gap between the north and south. The south of England has less unemployment than the north, Scotland and Wales.

Grade boost

Think carefully about the links between this topic and the core topics on Paper 2: prejudice, discrimination, inequality, life chances all link closely to this.

unemployed who are seen by some as not wanting a job. The term underclass has been used since then to describe this group (see Chapter 4).

Check your understanding

Complete the sentences below:

a) The government have used several different ••• to calculate how many people are unemployed.

b) Being unemployed means being of working ••• and unable to find paid work.

c) Retirement is different from being unemployed as people have ••• their working life.

d) Unemployment affects people's finances and may result in them living in •••

e) Unemployed people may suffer from •••.

f) The group of long-term unemployed are sometimes call the •••.

Exam practice

Breadline Britain: unemployment in Britain among the worst in Europe

The UK has some of the worst figures in Europe for households where no one is working. The latest statistics also indicate that Britain's unemployment rate may hide a sub-class who prefer a life on **benefits**.

Even Greece and Spain, who have had riots in 2012, have fewer jobless households than Britain.

Figures, which are from the EU's statistical arm, Eurostat, and cover 2011, raise particular concern over the number of single mothers who are not working in the UK; 43% of single mothers in the UK do not do any work for more than one day a week.

Furthermore, a report by the Trades Union Congress (TUC) revealed that 1.4 million men in Britain are taking on low-paid part-time work because they can't find a full-time job; the highest since records began in 1992.

a) Using the item, identify the proportion of British single mothers who do not work more than one day a week. (1)

b) Explain why 1.4 million British men are taking on low-paid part-time work. (2)

c) Outline one sociological reason why any group is more likely to be unemployed than others. (2)

d) Explain how being unemployed may have a negative effect on life chances. (5)

Key terms

Unemployment – being of working age and unable to find paid work.

Retirement – is the time when a person's working life ends.

Depression – a mental health condition where people feel extremely low and cannot cope with life.

Benefits – money that is paid to people who are unemployed or in other difficulty.

Stretch and challenge

- What should be done about the long-term unemployed?

- What would you do to get them back to work if you were the government?

- The answer is benefits. What are five possible questions?

Extended writing

Describe the effects of unemployment on individuals and families. (10)

Work

Topic 9: How has work changed for women?

What am I going to learn?

● **To understand the changing world of work for women**

Feminist sociologists have been concerned with the experience of women at work and legal changes that have protected women in the workplace. However, the unpaid work that women do in the home has also been a focus.

Women in the workplace

Women's traditional role was doing unpaid work strongly linked to **femininity**. This included housework, cooking, cleaning and child care. This was women's main working role with the exception of wartime. In the 1950s women's traditional role as housewives in the nuclear family seemed stronger than ever.

Women go out to work

There were many changes during the 1960s which altered this situation. Feminism raised women's ambitions and more women wanted to work. The availability of the contraceptive pill gave women more control over when they had children and enabled them to plan to work or finish education. By the 1970s women went out to work in their numbers.

Women in the workplace

Despite changing social norms, there were still problems for women going out to work. Working women with younger children had to find child care arrangements. Although norms had changed, some people still criticised women who put their children into nursery as being poor parents. Men escaped this criticism as they were seen as the natural **breadwinners**. The New Right still argue that this is not the best start for children.

Prejudice and discrimination

Women also faced prejudice in the workplace. Women tended to do jobs that fitted the feminine role, such as nursing, cooking, cleaning or working as secretaries serving male bosses. This is called **gendered work**. Even when they did equivalent jobs to men, they were often paid less. The Equal Pay Act tried to address this problem in 1970.

Women have also not been given jobs or promotion on account of their gender. The Sex Discrimination Act was introduced in 1975 to tackle this problem. Despite this, there is still a gender pay gap and feminists have developed the idea of the glass ceiling which stops women reaching the very top jobs.

Personal research idea

Interview women who have been in the world of work. Ask them about their hopes, experiences, conditions and treatment.

Interesting fact

According to Unison, an important trade union, 50% of working women in the UK have experienced sexual harassment at work.

Sexual harassment means comments or actions that are related to the persons' gender and are unwelcome and offensive.

Statistic from Unison.org.uk

Check your understanding

Complete the sentences:

a) The traditional work role for women was in the •••.

b) During the Second World War women tackled all kinds of •••.

c) In the 1950s women went back to their tradtional role as housewives in the ••• family.

d) The 1970s saw large numbers of women go out to •••.

e) The availability of the ••• meant that women could plan their families and have careers.

f) Women have not always been treated fairly at work and suffer from prejudice and •••.

Exam practice

Women losing out this time

Men used to suffer most during a recession. This time women are also being affected.

Wome go to work for money, enjoyment, achievement or to stand on their own two feet. Women work for all sorts of reasons: achieving their best, love of the job, a desire for independence – or simply because they need the money. Women may be out at work now but they are feeling the downside of this, just as men did in the past.

Two-thirds of women were in paid employment in 2010, compared with just over half in 1971 — and 7.6 million, or 56%, work full-time. Females losing their jobs on a large scale is a new thing.

The impact on men of losing their job is well known, with many men experiencing upset at being stripped of their role as breadwinner and provider. Films like *The Full Monty* deal with this.

Work might not be so central to most women's identity and how good they feel about themselves. But the effect of the first large-scale female job losses the British economy has seen is still likely to be great.

a) What percentage of women were paid employment in 2010? (1)

b) Using the item, identify two possible reasons for women working. (2)

c) Explain one reason why women may not feel as upset as men at losing their work. (2)

d) Explain one reason why women may not reach the top jobs. (2)

e) Explain, with examples, what is meant by the term gendered work. (3)

Key terms

Femininity – is the roles linked to being female including housework, caring and looking beautiful.

Breadwinner – the role of the main wage earner in the family.

Gendered work – is when men and women do jobs that are linked to traditional male and female roles respectively.

Stretch and challenge

What could this picture have to do with the sociology of work?

Extended writing

Describe problems that women have experienced with regard to work since World War Two. (10)

Topic 10: How has work changed for men?

What am I going to learn?

● **To understand how changes in the workplace have affected men**

Feminism was a driving force for change in the workplace and for sociological research from the 1960s onwards. The changes that happened for women also had an effect on men in the workplace. In addition to this, great changes were happening for men in the British workplace as the economy changed. Sociologists did not begin to write about men until the 1990s. Strangely this was what feminists had said about women in sociology in the 1960s!

Across the generations

Ask older male family members about how work has changed since they first started work.

Find out about

Find out about changing gender patterns of employment, managing directors of top companies, professionals, headteachers, unemployed, gendered occupations. Find some simple statistics that you could learn for exam use!

Grade boost

Make sure if a question asks about changing gender patterns at work, that your answer includes men as well as women.

Men in the workplace

Traditionally men have dominated the workplace and enjoyed the best paid, highest status jobs and some of the worst too. Many traditional trades, such as carpenters, builders and miners are seen as male jobs. They were linked closely to ideas about **masculinity**. For instance, being physically strong, smart and skillful.

Other men dominated the workplace as managers and this closely linked to ideas about males being in charge. Women were expected to be the 'weaker sex' and stayed at home. There was lots of pressure on men to be the breadwinner and provide for a family. This pressure may have become stronger in the second half of the 20th century as families were expected to have better and better houses, cars and consumer goods.

Dual income families

As discussed in the previous topic, women began to go out to work more in the 1970s. This enabled families to buy a better lifestyle and made the male role as breadwinner less prominent. Many families now expect a lifestyle which needs both parents to go to work to maintain it.

Decline of traditional industry

From the late 1970s onwards traditional jobs went into decline. The factories, mines and shipyards started to shut down. The masculine style jobs became less important. Even labouring jobs that required a man's strength were less common as machines continued to take over.

Feminisation of the workplace

Women became more prominent in the workplace. Laws were in place to help protect them from discrimination and harassment. More women began to become managers themselves in charge of men. The skills that women had became more valuable. By the 1990s, women's understanding of emotions (**emotional intelligence**) was being recognised as an important workplace skill.

Men were no longer able to dominate the workplace. Many men suffered the shame of being made **redundant** and were often unemployed for a long time. This was a huge blow for men whose role as breadwinner was a vital part of their identity. The workplace was now a less masculine and more **feminine** place.

s anot sure

Check your understanding

Match the correct term with the definition below:

Masculine	Gendered work	Alienation
Respondent	Femininisation	Breadwinner

a) What is the term used to describe a person answering questions for research?
b) What is the term for women's ideas and skills taking over the workplace?
c) What is the term used to describe the norms of being male?
d) What is the term used to describe the role of main wage earner?
e) What is the term used to describe work that is seen as suited to one gender?
f) What is the term used to describe the way that people's work is not natural?

Exam practice

Are males on the way out?

Men may not know it but their days on top are numbered. Soon many women with top qualifications and earning big money will take over! A new book by Hanna Rosin called *The End of Men* is spreading this idea in America and Britain.

Women on top: Writer Hanna Rosin thinks women are taking over

Men are being left out in the cold by social changes. Women don't need a man as they can get **IVF treatment**. They are happy to have one night stands and prefer being lone parents. Many are ambitious, wanting good careers and are becoming the family breadwinners.

a) Using the item, suggest one reason why Hanna Rosin thinks that women may be doing better than men. (1)
b) What does the item suggest that women prefer to living with men? (1)
c) Explain one reason why men may not be doing so well in the 21st-century workplace. (2)
d) A female researcher wants to interview men about how they feel about work. Outline and explain two problems that she may have. (6)

Key terms

Masculine – norms linked with being male.

Emotional intelligence – understanding how other people are feeling.

Redundant – when a worker loses their job as it is no longer needed.

Feminisation of the workplace – when women's ideas and skills begin to be valued at work.

IVF treatment – a way that women can become pregnant without having sex with a man.

Stretch and challenge

- If the workplace becomes increasingly feminised, consider some of the problems/consequences that society may have.

- Imagine what a workplace of the future will be like. Think of what it will look like, the norms, rules and how the different genders will behave. Who will be in charge?

Extended writing

Discuss how changing gender patterns have affected the British workplace. (20)

Topic 11: What is work like for different ethnic groups?

What am I going to learn?

- **To consider issues affecting ethnic groups in the workplace**

A range of issues affect ethnic groups in the workplace. These include experiences of racism in the workplace and legal changes to prevent this. Globalisation has also meant that people are moving around the world to find work and so the workforce in Britain is more and more diverse. Some groups are more successful than others in the workplace.

Find out about

Investigate the cockle pickers disaster in Morecambe Bay, 5 February 2004. Find out what happened.

Over to you

Imagine you are an employer, what measures would you put in place to make sure that there is no racism in your workplace? What rules would you have? How would you encourage workers from different ethnic backgrounds to mix?

websites

To find out more about human rights in the workplace go to: **www.equalityhumanrights.com**

www.onewkplace.org.uk is a useful website that provides information and advice about discrimination at work. It focusses on discrimination based on race, sex, disability and sexual orientation.

For further information about the laws on discrimination, go to the Equality Challenge Unit's website: **tinyurl.com/cr6j7fy**

Ethnic groups in the workplace in Britain

First of all it is important to recognise the range of ethnic groups living in British society since before England, Scotland or Wales existed as nations. Romans, Angles, Saxons and Vikings were here before the Norman invasion in 1066. Britain has always had a wide ethnic mix. Britain explored, traded with and took over other parts of the world. This has resulted in a great deal of **migration** to Britain. Therefore, the British workplace has always had a range of ethnic groups.

After World War Two

When World War Two ended, Britain, although bankrupt, borrowed money from the USA and our economy began to boom. People from the West Indies, Asia and other parts of the **British Empire** were invited to Britain to take the jobs that people already here did not want. They were tempted to come here by an advertising campaign. Some highly skilled workers also came here to work in the National Health Service as doctors as well as working in other jobs.

Racism in the workplace

The workers who came here were shocked to find racist attitudes in 1950s Britain. Prejudice and discrimination were not uncommon in the workplace and were not illegal. There was also an **ethnic pay gap** which still exists despite laws being passed to protect ethnic groups.

Legal changes

The Race Relations Act was originally introduced in 1965, but was seen as too weak and the most well-known law was the Race Relations Act 1976. This made it illegal to discriminate against people because of nationality, race or ethnicity. It was strengthened further in 2000. Race equality laws are now covered by the Equality Act 2010.

Migration and the workplace

At the same time as laws against racism there have also been laws limiting **immigration** to allay fears that Britain is becoming over populated and that the country is changing too much. Immigration laws passed in 1962 and 1968 made it more difficult for workers to migrate to Britain, unless they had a proven family background linking them to Britain.

Check your understanding

Complete the sentences below:

a) Britain has had a wide range of ••• groups working here since Roman times.

b) After World War Two, workers came here from various parts of the British ••• to find work.

c) Workers from the West Indies and Asia were invited to Britain and convinced to come by •••.

d) The Race Relations Act 1976 made racial discrimination at work •••.

e) Immigration laws were passed making it more difficult to come to •••.

f) Some workers experienced ••• attitudes in the workplace.

Exam practice

Report shows the exploitation of migrant workers

Migrant workers in Scotland, from various ethnic groups, are often abused by their bosses. Several migrants were interviewed for a report on forced labour in the food industry.

The research revealed that one restaurant boss called a Russian cleaner a prostitute for wearing make-up, hit a cook with a pot and told a Polish woman to clean the floor on her knees. The Joseph Rowntree Foundation, who did the study, found that most migrants were legally in the UK, but their working conditions were not legal.

Holding back pay, reducing the amount paid and not having a break were regular events. The workers had no power and were afraid of their employers. The report compared the work to modern slavery.

a) Using the item, identify one way that migrant workers are being treated that is unfair. (1)

b) Suggest how the migrant workers in the study may have felt about their employer. (2)

c) Explain two reasons why migrant workers may be easy for employers to exploit in this way. (4)

d) A researcher wishes to carry out interviews with migrant workers who may be exploited. Outline and explain two problems that may need to be overcome. (4)

Key terms

Migration – moving from one country or area to another.

British Empire – all the countries that Britain used to rule over.

Ethnic pay gap – the difference in pay between different ethnic groups.

Immigration – is when people are coming to a country.

Migrant – a person who has moved from another country or area.

Ethnic minority – a group of people with their own way of life, nationality or religion that are few in number compared with the rest of society.

Stretch and challenge

- What do ethnic minorities and women have in common in the workplace?

- List words associated with the sociology of work A–Z.

Extended writing

Describe problems experienced by ethnic minority groups in the workplace. (10)

Topic 12: How are different age groups treated at work?

What am I going to learn?

- **To understand how different age groups may experience ageism**

Age has become an increasingly important area of Sociology. Sociologists have been interested in how elderly people are treated differently at work and youth is also important.

Across the generations

Ask any pensioners you know what it is like being retired.

Grade boost

Remember to think about ideas like life chances and inequalities which are part of the Core for Paper 2, but also may be included in the work topic.

Personal research idea

Investigate whether people in your class are ageist. Use questionnaires or interviews to find out how they feel about having teachers of different ages.

An ageing population

There are many reasons why Britain's population has begun to be older. Contraception and changing norms around family size have meant that people have had fewer children. At the other end of life, better diet, health care and lifestyle have meant that people are living longer. Therefore, there are more elderly people than young people.

An ageing population means that health care costs the government more each year. Generally elderly people require more medical care than other age groups. Pensions for elderly people also cost the government a great deal of money.

Retirement changes

This has meant that the government is encouraging people to carry on working longer. There used to be a retirement age of 65. Workers could be forced to retire at this point. This is now seen as discrimination and workers can carry on working if they choose to.

As well as this the age that people qualify for the **state pension** has increased. It will soon be 66 for both men and women and go up to 67 in 2026.

Discrimination

So, in the past elderly people were worried about ageism. Ageism could result in their being overlooked for promotion or forced out of their jobs at 65. Now the concern is that they may have to carry on working for much longer and may never get to enjoy a retirement.

Younger people still have to worry about **discrimination** at work. They may also be exploited. The minimum wage is designed to protect against exploitation, but does not protect workers under 21 as fully as adults. Some workers may be employed in **casual work** and may not receive the **minimum wage** and not feel confident enough to stand up for their rights. Young people may also be treated poorly as a result of stereotypes.

Check your understanding

Match the term with the correct definition:

Stereotyping	Ageism	Discrimination
Pilot study	Exploitation	Ethics

a) Which term is about whether research is right or wrong?

b) Which term is about the action of treating people differently because of prejudice?

c) Which term is about a test of your research method?

d) Which term means being prejudiced or discriminating against someone because of their age?

e) Which term is about taking advantage of a person or group of people?

f) Which term is about an exaggerated view of a group of people?

Key terms

State pension – the money that people are given by the government when they retire.

Age discrimination – treating people differently because of their age.

Casual work – temporary work that is not permanent.

Minimum wage – the lowest hourly rate that a worker can be paid.

Exam practice

Ageism at work affects young and old

DWP research shows perceptions towards those aged over 70 are more positive than towards those in their 20s, unless they are in senior roles.

Age discrimination at work remains a problem for both young and old, according to research by the Department for Work and Pensions.

The report, based on a survey by the Office for National Statistics, compared attitudes towards people in their 20s and those over 70.

Views towards those aged over 70 were more positive than towards those in their 20s, with older people viewed as being more friendly, having higher moral standards and as being better at their job than younger workers.

However, when respondents were asked whether they would prefer a suitably qualified 30-year-old or 70-year-old boss, the results showed a bias towards younger workers. While most were accepting of either age, three times as many thought that having a 70-year-old boss would be 'unacceptable' compared with having a 30-year-old boss.

a) According to the item, which age group would people prefer to have for a boss? (1)

b) What does the item suggest are two qualities that older people may have? (2)

c) Explain one problem that either old or young people may have in the workplace. (3)

d) Outline and explain two sociological explanations for age discrimination. (4)

Stretch and challenge

Should there be a fixed age for retirement? Think of arguments for and against.

What age do you think it should be?

Should the minimum wage be the same for all age groups?

Extended writing

Explain how age can affect work. (10)

Topic 13: Are workers exploited?

What am I going to learn?

- **To understand changes in the way that work has been organised which can result in exploitation**

This topic will explore ways that employers have tried to get more work out of workers. There has been a tension between laws to protect workers and the need to make profits. Globalisation has also affected work as multinationals move production around the world to boost their profits.

Interesting fact

Marxists do not think that there is such a thing as a fair day's pay in our type of society. The owners of businesses will always make money out of the workers and will always try to make as much as possible at the workers' expense. Marxists do not think our society can ever work without conflict between bosses and workers and that one day there will be a revolution.

Famous people

Frederick Taylor

Frederick Taylor (1856–1915) was the man who invented scientific management at work. He noticed that some workers did more than others. He said that work processes had to be analysed to make sure that the least wasteful and most efficient systems were put in place. His ideas have been used all over the world and are known as Taylorism.

All workers needed to follow the same system and steps to make sure that as much work as possible was completed.

Conflict between workers and owners

A simplisitic view of the world of work suggests that workers want to do as little work as possible for as much pay as they can get, while employers want as much work as they can get out of the workers for the least pay.

As employers usually have the most power, many sociologists, especially Marxists, argue that the workplace is often exploitative.

What is exploitation?

According to Marxists, **exploitation** means that workers are being used or taken advantage of just to make bigger profits for the owners. This may involve unacceptable working conditions, hours and pay so low that it leads to poverty.

Piecework

Piecework was introduced in some workplaces by bosses to make sure that workers complete as much work as possible. Instead of being paid an hourly rate, workers are paid for each item they produce or complete. In theory, it sounds as though this could be good for workers who are encouraged to complete more work and earn more money. In reality, rates paid can be low, and delays in work which are not the worker's fault, stop the worker from earning a fair day's pay. However, the minimum wage should still protect pieceworkers in this country.

Sweatshops

Piecework is often linked to the idea of **sweatshops**. However, they are not necessarily the same and some workplaces are called sweatshops because of the low pay and poor conditions. The concern in Britain is that multinationals are exploiting workers in developing countries to produce cheap goods for sale in Britain. This has included well-known companies and is said to involve child labour and conditions that are like modern slavery. In Britain workers have Health and Safety laws to protect them, as well as the minimum wage. However, migrant workers may not know their rights or be protected as well as other people.

Check your understanding

Match the correct term with the definition below:

Minimum wage	Unstructured interview	Income
Piecework	Alienation	Sweatshop

a) What term is used to describe the money that people get to live on?

b) What term is used to describe a workplace with unreasonably low pay and poor working conditions?

c) What term is used to explain the least amount of money a person should receive each hour they work?

d) What term is used to describe a research method which is like a conversation?

e) What term is used to describe when workers are paid per unit of work they complete?

f) What term is used to describe the way a worker feels the work they are doing is unnatural?

Exam practice

Chinese electronics factories fit suicide nets after several suicides

Chinese sweatshops pay workers £1.12 an hour to make iPhones for Europe and the USA

Apple have opened the doors to their Chinese 'sweatshop' factories where employees are paid as little as £1.12 an hour. Many workers perform boring tasks like wiping down screens or shaving aluminium from the edge of the Apple logo. This can be for a ten-hour shift.

ABC TV showed the conditions inside the factory in Shenzhen – where 18 employees have killed themselves. It would take two months' wages to pay for an iPad.

a) Using the item, identify how much the Apple workers were paid per hour. (1)

b) Suggest one reason why British workers are unlikely to be paid such low wages as the Apple workers. (1)

c) With examples, explain what is meant by the term piecework. (4)

d) Outline and explain two reasons why sweatshop workers may feel alienated. (4)

Key terms

Exploitation – is where people are taken advantage of and used.

Piecework – is where an employee is paid per unit of work completed.

Sweatshop – a workplace with unreasonably low pay and poor working conditions.

Stretch and challenge

What would be the impact if the minimum wage was introduced all around the world?

Do you think it is reasonable to buy goods from companies that have used sweatshops to produce their goods? Make a list of reasons for and against.

Extended writing

Discuss what is meant by exploitation. (20)

Over to you

Find out about sweatshops. Which big companies have been accused of this? What is their response?

Topic 14: What are trade unions?

What am I going to learn?

● **To understand the role of trade unions in the workplace**

Individual workers are not usually in a strong position if there is a dispute with their bosses. This has led workers to join together, to form trade unions. Working together, or collectively, workers are stronger. This section is concerned with relationships between workers and their bosses. Trade unions have been the main focus of this but workers do protest in other unofficial ways, too. Trade unions are meant to protect workers against exploitation.

What are trade unions?

Trade unions developed in the early- to mid-19th century, as the economy became more industrial and factory based. The growth of unions was not always welcomed and the law often made it difficult for workers to organise themselves.

Trade unions try to bargain for better wages and working conditions. They also protect workers from unfair treatment, offering legal advice when workers are disciplined or are at risk of losing their jobs.

History

In the 19th century employers did not want workers to form trade unions. The 1800 Combination Act made trade union activity illegal. After 1825 unions were not illegal, but their activities were limited. Union leaders and members risked prison or worse, **deportation**. Workers risked this to continue the trade union movement. Trade unions are now an accepted part of the workplace in Britain.

What action do trade unions take?

Trade unions protect workers' interests by offering them legal advice and support. They also bargain on behalf of all workers for pay rises and improvements in working conditions. At the extreme end they may organise **collective action**, such as strikes, to get their views across.

Conflict

The 20th century saw trade unions grow stronger, by the 1970s most workers were members. Some trade unions had a great deal of power and could influence the government, for example, the coal miners. Coal was the main source of electricity in the 1970s and the miners were able to bring the country to a standstill if they went on strike. Power cuts were put in place at these times disrupting all workplaces and homes.

Find out about

Find out the story of the Tolpuddle Martyrs. Why is their story remembered?

Interesting fact

Workers also show their unhappiness in unofficial ways. They may 'go slow', which means deliberately not producing enough work. Sometimes workers sabotage machinery to prevent work being done. Nowadays workers may waste time on their mobile phones or social networking. Unhappy workers may also take time off for illness when they are not unwell.

Workers also used to do 'wildcat strikes' which were unofficial strikes without trade union go ahead. These were used in national strikes in Paris in 1968.

Trade unions for different sets of workers could come out in support of each other. This could be very disruptive. In the 1980s, the Conservative government of Margaret Thatcher passed laws which weakened the trade unions. Some people think this is a good thing as they thought that trade unions were too powerful and stopped British workplaces being successful. Others would say that the trade unions are not strong enough to protect workers now.

Check your understanding

Complete the sentences below:

a) In 1800 the Combination Act made trade union activity •••.
b) Union members risked being sent to ••• or deported.
c) Trade unions offer their members legal ••• and support.
d) Collective bargaining is where the trade union try to get better ••• and conditions for all workers.
e) Trade union members may vote to go on ••• if they do not agree with bosses' decisions.
f) The Conservative government of the 1980s passed ••• which weakened the trade unions.

Exam practice

Trade unions: still strong?

Trade union membership numbers are falling and unions have less power. The figures suggest that this is true. In 1979 some 13.5 million workers in the UK were members of a union; today that figure is about 6.5 million.

In London in March 2011 teachers' unions and others went on strike about cuts to public services.

However, recent strikes have had large turnouts, suggesting that the unions are not finished. The national strike by public sector workers that took place on 30 November in 2011 saw up to two million workers striking in protest against changes to their pension schemes. This was the biggest stoppage seen in the UK in decades.

Prime Minister David Cameron at first said the day of action had been a 'damp squib' but later described it as a 'big strike'.

a) Using the item, identify how many UK workers are members of a trade union. (1)
b) Suggest what has happened to trade union membership since 1979. (1)
c) Explain two ways that workers may show they are unhappy at work. (4)
d) Outline and explain two reasons why workers may join a trade union. (4)

Key terms

Trade union – an organisation that protects the interests of a group of workers.

Deportation – being sent to another country to live.

Collective action – is when the trade union as a group work together to improve their pay or conditions.

Collective bargaining – is when the trade union tries to make a deal with bosses for all the workers.

Extended writing

Explain what is meant by the term trade union. (10)

Stretch and challenge

Imagine you are a boss. Try to list 10 reasons you would not like trade unions. Are there any positives about trade unions for bosses?

Imagine you are a worker. Try to list 10 reasons you would like being in a trade union. Are there any negatives about being in a trade union?

Crime and deviance

Topic 1: What are crime and deviance?

What am I going to learn?

- **To understand the difference between crime and deviance**

Sociologists are interested in the difference between these two terms. It is important to recognise how they overlap with each other. Sociologists are also interested in the way that what is seen as deviance and the law changes over time and place.

Extended writing

Describe what is meant by the term deviance. (10)

Find out about

How laws on alcohol have changed over time and in different countries.

What is deviance?

Deviance means actions that break the social norms of society. This could include a wide variety of things, from not saying please or thank you, to wearing unusual clothes to stealing or even murder. If people broke social norms all the time then life would become very difficult to manage as there would be uncertainty, chaos and disorder.

What is crime?

Some deviant acts are against rules that people have written down. The most important rules that can be enforced by the police are called **laws**. Laws are enforced by agencies of social control, such as the police and the judiciary. **Crime** means actions that break the laws of society.

Social construction of crime and deviance

What is seen as criminal or deviant changes over time and varies from place to place. In medieval times, it was seen as the norm to marry girls who were under 16. A person who did this now would be seen as a paedophile. Laws change over time as well. Abortion was illegal in Britain until 1967. Examples of **polygamy**, in places like Kenya, show that deviance can vary from place to place.

The way that crime and deviance vary from society to society is known as the **social construction of crime and deviance**.

Crime and deviance

Crime and deviance are not the same thing. Most crimes are seen as deviant. For example, murder is normally both criminal and deviant.

On the other hand, some crimes are not seen as deviant, there are some laws that many people break. Speeding just over the speed limit is against the law, but many drivers see this as the norm. However, a driver travelling 25 miles over the speed limit would be seen as criminal and deviant.

Some behaviour may be seen as deviant but not against the law. For example, a man wearing a swimming costume in the snow is deviant but it is not a crime.

Check your understanding

True or false?

a) Crime and deviance are the same thing.
b) Some acts may be criminal and deviant.
c) Some acts may be criminal but not seen as deviant.
d) Acts which are against the law are against the law everywhere.
e) Deviance is always against the law.
f) Deviant acts break social norms.

Exam practice

Clampdown on teachers

The dress code at an American school has been accused of being too strict. But it's not the students at risk of breaking the rules, it's the teachers.

Litchfield Elementary School District's 600-strong staff have been banned from wearing 'extreme' hairstyles, 'excessive' earrings or facial piercings in the classroom. They also must not dye their hair blue or display distracting tattoos.

The authorities said that they had had lots of complaints that teachers did not look professional. Some are saying that this is not needed as edgy hair colours and piercings are the norm now.

Distracting tattoos and facial piercings banned.

a) Using the item, identify one part of the dress code for teachers. (1)
b) Suggest two reasons why the authorities have banned some items of dress. (2)
c) Explain, using examples, how what is seen as deviant can change over time. (4)
d) Outline and explain two sociological reasons why attitudes to piercings may have changed over time. (4)

Key terms

Deviance – actions which break social norms.

Laws – formal rules made by the government.

Crime – actions which are against the law.

Polygamy – marrying more than one person at the same time.

Social construction of crime and deviance – is the way that what is seen as criminal or deviant varies from time to time and place to place.

Stretch and challenge

- Try to think of actions that are seen as deviant in every society.

- For any you think of try to look for examples of when they are seen as acceptable.

Personal research idea

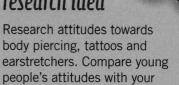

Research attitudes towards body piercing, tattoos and earstretchers. Compare young people's attitudes with your teachers or parents.

Crime and deviance

Topic 3: What is formal social control? – The police

What am I going to learn?

● **To understand the role of the police in formal social control**

It is a challenge for sociology to understand the role of the police in keeping social order. Some answers to this question are practical ones and others are about sociological theory.

What role do the police play in formal social control?

The police are one of the most important agencies of social control. The British police were the first police force and were a model for police forces all over the world. Practical roles of the police include:

● Controlling traffic and roads.
● Keeping order in society.
● Investigating crime, collecting evidence and catching criminals.
● Protecting and serving the public.
● Educating the public about crime.

Public relations and styles of policing

The role that the police play may vary considerably according to the style of **public relations** they are trying to have. Public relations is to do with how the police are trying to get on with the public.

The first of these is called **community policing**. This has been a popular style of policing and involves making links with the community. This type of policing may be useful when the police have to deal with ethnic minority groups.

A harsher style of policing started in New York. This involves the police being really strict on even the smallest crime. The idea is that people will not commit big crimes if they are worried about being arrested for unpaid parking fines or litter. This is called **zero tolerance** policing. It has been successful in some parts of Britain and has made people in dangerous communities feel safer.

Functionalism and the police

Two main theories take opposite views of the police. Functionalists see the police as doing a good job for society. They socialise the public through teaching them about speeding, drink driving and other issues. The police keep society healthy by keeping social order.

Marxism and the police

Marxists see the police as keeping the ruling class in charge. They protect the ruling class from the workers who may try to steal their wealth. They help to stop any working-class protest.

Check your understanding

Complete the sentences using the words in the word box.

ruling	protect	zero
control	style	community

The police are an important agent of social •••. They have many practical roles in society, but are seen as there to ••• and serve the public. There are different ideas about what ••• the police should use to carry out their role. One of these is called ••• policing which means making strong links with local people. At the other extreme, a harder style of policing is called ••• tolerance. Functionalists see the police as a positive force, whereas Marxists think the police help the ••• class stay in control.

Exam practice

What does a police officer do?

I, as a Police Officer, have a range of powers ranging from issuing speeding tickets to powers of stop and search and entering premises with or without a warrant. The variety of roles and powers of police officers is wide. I work on the neighbourhood team and police a very close-knit community. On a daily basis I will deal with a number of issues that have been raised by residents as their priorities. For example, issues of anti-social behaviour, youths causing a nuisance to local residents and also moving youths on if the area has a Dispersal Order.

As a police officer I have a number of powers. These include:

- Searching people, vehicles and property.
- Seizing property.
- Power to arrest a criminal/suspected criminal and take them into custody with or without a warrant.
- To stop a driver in a vehicle and request to see documents such as driving licence, insurance certificate, and vehicle registration document.
- To request a 'breathalyser' (ask you for a breath test).

a) Using the item, identify a power that police officers have. (1)
b) Suggest one duty that police might do as part of community policing. (1)
c) Explain, with examples, what is meant by anti-social behaviour. (4)
d) Outline any two styles of public relations that the police might employ. (4)

Key terms

Public relations – is about how the police get on with the community.
Community policing – is about the police working with local people.
Zero tolerance – is when the police are really strict about the smallest crimes to stop bigger ones happening.

Extended writing

Describe how the police help to enforce social control. (10)

Find out about

How do the police work in your community? See if you can organise for the local community officer to come into your school. Talk to the person in school who liases with the police.

Interesting fact

Big Brother Watch found that schools were using CCTV more than other organisations including local councils. There are over 100,000 cameras in schools today.

Topic 4: What is formal social control? – The judiciary

What am I going to learn?

- **To understand the role that the courts and other parts of the judiciary play in maintaining social order**

This topic will cover the various parts of the judiciary and their role in keeping social order. The views of two main sociological theories will be considered.

Interesting fact

Community service has been used increasingly to avoid prison for all ages. Prison places cost a lot of money. Unofficial warnings and official reprimands are also used by the police. Anti-Social Behaviour Orders (ASBOs) were introduced in the 1990s by New Labour and aimed to control individuals who acted in anti-social ways. They used strategies like tagging, curfews and banning people from going to certain places. The new Coalition government is going to replace these with Criminal Behaviour Orders and Crime Prevention Injunctions.

Extended writing

Explain the role of the judiciary. (10)

websites

To find out more about how the criminal justice system works go to: www.gov.uk/browse/justice

There is lots of information about the work of the youth offending team at: www.gov.uk/youth-offending-team

What is the judiciary?

The **judiciary** includes all the legal institutions that work together to decide what happens when laws are broken. The police investigate crimes and collect evidence. From that point on the judiciary take over. The police have a role in deciding how seriously a crime is taken when reported. However, the CPS (Crown Prosecution Service) decides whether there is enough evidence and whether to prosecute.

The courts

There are a range of courts to enforce the law. These include Youth Courts for young people, which work with the Youth Offending Team. **Magistrates' Courts** are the place where less serious crimes are dealt with. Magistrates are volunteers and have the power to send people to prison for up to 6 months and fine up to £5000. Where crimes are more serious they are sent to **Crown Court.** Crown Courts are controlled by a judge, assisted by 12 members of the public chosen at random. These twelve are known as the jury. The jury decide if the person is guilty or innocent of the crime. They all have to agree the verdict or at least have a 10–2 majority. The judge then decides on the sentence.

Functionalism and the judiciary

The two theories disagree about how they see the judiciary. As usual functionalists see it in a good light. Functionalists see the judiciary as playing an important role in society taking bad individuals out of society and trying to make sure they are resocialised, as well as punished, to become useful members of society. The judiciary reminds everybody about the boundaries of behaviour, especially when reported in the media. Functionalists would also say that courts shape the way the law is used and respond to changing norms.

Marxism and the judiciary

Marxists take a negative view of the judiciary. They believe that the courts favour the rich and powerful. The law itself is mainly about protecting property, which favours the rich. Marxists would argue that the poor are treated more harshly by the judiciary.

Check your understanding

Complete the sentences below:

a) The institutions that enforce the law are known as the •••.

b) There are special courts for people aged 10–18 called ••• Courts.

c) Less serious crimes are dealt with by ••• Courts.

d) The more serious crimes have to be dealt with by a ••• Court.

e) The twelve members of the public who decide the verdict are known as a •••.

f) Marxists believe that the courts favour the ••• and powerful.

Stretch and challenge

- Suggest ways that courts could stop people reoffending.

- Prisons are becoming overcrowded. Some people think that fewer prison sentences should be given. Try to think of reasons to support this argument.

- Some countries still have the death penalty. Make a list of reasons for and against it.

Exam practice

Law too tough on rioters

MPs and justice campaigners say that some sentences given to rioters were too harsh. Two men were jailed for four years for using Facebook to incite riots and another was given 18 months for having a stolen TV in his car.

The former chair of the Criminal Bar Association, Paul Mendelle QC, said sentences were too long and harsh. But Communities Secretary Eric Pickles said tougher sentences would show there were consequences to disorder.

More than 2,770 people have been arrested in connection with last week's riots in a number of English cities.

By Tuesday afternoon, 1,277 suspects had appeared in court and 64% had been kept in prison. The normal rate kept in prison for serious offences was 10% the year before.

a) What percentage of those arrested for the riots were kept in prison? (1)

b) Suggest a reason why so many people were kept in prison. (1)

c) Explain what is meant by the term judiciary. (4)

d) Outline and explain two ways that the courts help to maintain social control. (4)

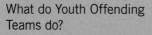

Find out about

What do Youth Offending Teams do?

How are youth courts different from adult courts? Is it right that young people get treated differently?

The Jamie Bulger case – what happened to the boys who killed Jamie Bulger?

Crime and deviance

Topic 5: How do the media help keep social control?

What am I going to learn?

- **To understand how the media can act as an agency of social control**

In recent years sociologists and other researchers have spent much time examining the effect the media can have upon the general public. The mass media can influence our behaviour but there is debate about whether the inflence is positive or negative.

Sarah Thornton

Sarah Thornton wrote a book called *Club Cultures*. She studied the clubbing and acid house scene of the late 1980s and found that there was a moral panic about acid house. However, she thought that some youth cultures enjoyed the negative attention of the media and tried to be rebellious to be cool.

Find out about

See if you can produce a fact file on other moral panics. Past moral panics have been binge drinking, guns and knives. See what others you can find out about.

Extended writing

Discuss the effect that the media can have on crime and deviance. (20)

What is the media?

Sociologists use the term **media** to refer to all the methods of mass communication. This includes television, books, radio, films, Internet and social networking sites. These reach huge numbers and can have great influence.

Media representation of crime

One issue that particularly interests sociologists is the way that crime is presented in the media. The media have been accused of focussing on some crimes more than others, for example crimes committed by young people and the working classes.

Another concern is how newspapers, especially tabloid ones, may sensationalise crime, focussing on the extremes.

Moral panics

A sociologist named Stanley Cohen studied the way media reported bank holiday violence in Clacton at Easter bank holiday 1964. Although there was some violence between youths, Cohen said the newspapers exaggerated the events. The media drew everyone's attention to the events and called out for greater punishment for the young people involved. Cohen said that the media created a moral panic about the events. A **moral panic** means that the worry was exaggerated as though the whole of society was going to break down.

Folk devils

The young people involved were part of two popular **youth cultures** of the time, the Mods and Rockers. The Mods and Rockers became known as **folk devils**. This means that they were shown by the media as the modern terrors of society. What happened is similar to stereotyping. There was an exaggerated unfair view of these groups. Cohen's ideas of moral panics and folk devils have been used by sociologists to understand other fears shown in the media.

Deviancy amplification

In the case of the Mods and Rockers the media were trying to help keep society under control. However, Cohen said that they actually made things worse. They predicted trouble at future bank holidays, which actually advertised the events to young people. The publicity actually made the events worse at future bank holidays. Cohen called this **deviancy amplification**.

Check your understanding

Match the terms with the correct definition below:

Folk devils	Moral panics	Deviance
Sanctions	Media	Deviancy amplification

a) What term describes behaviour that breaks social norms?

b) What term describes a group that the media make everyone afraid of?

c) What term describes the way that media reporting can make crime worse?

d) What term describes the ways of communicating with a mass audience?

e) What term describes the actions taken to stop further deviant acts?

f) What term describes the way the media exaggerate and make everyone worry about a problem?

Exam practice

British teens – Europe's worst?

A new report suggests that British teens are the worst behaved in Europe. They are more likely to binge-drink, take drugs, have sex at a young age and start fights.

Its study found that 44% of British youngsters had been involved in a fight in the previous year – compared with 28% in Germany, 36% in France and 38% in Italy.

Also 27% of British teenagers admitted to getting drunk regularly. In Italy, the figure is 5% and in France it is just 3%.

The researchers found that UK children do not communicate well with their parents and there are few regular shared family meals. The report also says British adults are becoming afraid of trying to control youngsters.

a) Using the item, how do British teenagers' drinking rates compare with other countries? (1)

b) What percentage of British youngsters does the item say have been involved in a fight during the past year? (1)

c) Using examples, explain what is meant by the term moral panic. (4)

d) Suggest two ways that British youngsters might be affected by reading the report above. (4)

Key terms

Media – are the ways that people have of communicating with large groups of people.

Moral panics – are when the media exaggerates an issue and makes the public worry about it.

Youth cultures – are groups of young people with their own set of norms and values.

Folk devils – are groups that the media make people afraid of.

Deviancy amplification – is when the media makes a problem worse by the way they report it.

Stretch and challenge

- How should the media report on British teens to avoid creating a moral panic? Make up five guidelines for journalists to follow.

- After the riots in 2011 the media printed pictures of some of the rioters. What effect do you think that this could have? Why do you think they did this? Do you think it is a good idea?

Grade boost

Complete a revision card for all the key terms for crime and deviance so far. Add examples and definitions next to each one.

Topic 6: What is white collar crime?

What am I going to learn?

● **To understand the term white collar crime**

This section will examine the view that society has focussed on some types of crime and ignored others. It will also link the idea of blue collar crime and consider recent events, such as the MPs' expenses scandal.

Stretch and challenge

Does white collar crime matter? Who are the hidden victims of white collar crime?

Occupational crime is crime that is linked to a person's job. The idea of occupational crime is closely linked to that of white collar crime. Make a list of all the crimes that a doctor could commit as part of their job. Do the same for:

● a high-ranking police officer

● a bank manager

● a shop manager.

Find out about

The MPs' expenses scandal.

The phone hacking scandal involving the *News of the World*.

Watch the movie *Wall Street* – which is all about insider trading.

What is white collar crime?

White collar crime, at its simplest, is crime committed by middle-class people. It usually refers to certain types of crime which may be linked to a person's job. White collar crimes are not obvious and for several reasons may be hard to detect and may not be reported. Examples of white collar crime are **fraud**, **bribery**, **insider trading** and **embezzlement**. White collar crimes are non-violent and usually committed for money. The term comes from the fact that middle-class workers traditionally wore a white collar and tie.

Why is white collar crime hard to detect?

White collar crime is difficult to detect because it is committed by middle-class people who are usually respected members of society. The people who do it are not suspected and tend to be intelligent and in a position to hide their criminal activity. Sometimes there is no obvious victim of the crime or the victim may be unaware that they have lost money. Also, the media tend to focus on more sensational crimes involving violence or theft.

Blue collar crime

The term that links to white collar crime is **blue collar crime**. Blue collar crime, an American term, refers to crimes committed by members of the working class. They are usually less planned than white collar crimes and may involve damage to person or property. It would also include drug abuse, prostitution and illegal gambling. In many ways, blue collar crime is the opposite extreme to white collar crime.

Why is it hard to know how much white collar crime there is?

Firstly, many white collar crimes are not discovered for the reasons shown above. To add to this, many companies that discover white collar crime are frightened of bad publicity. An item in local papers about criminals working for a business may put customers off. So bosses may ask workers to resign and in return not involve the police. The media has tended to focus on blue collar crime, which can be easier to report but this may have changed in recent years with the MPs' expenses scandal.

Check your understanding

True or false?

a) White collar crime is crime committed by the working class.

b) Armed robbery is a white collar crime.

c) Bosses always involve the police when they catch employees committing white collar crime.

d) Blue collar crime is working-class crime.

e) White collar criminals are usually from the underclass.

f) White collar criminals are often very respectable people.

Exam practice

Over £70 billion lost through fraud

Fraud is costing the country around £73bn a year, according to a watchdog's new report.

Broken down, each UK adult over the age of 16 is £1,441 a year worse off because of fraud, the group estimates. But the National Fraud Authority says the figures are higher than in the past

because they are better at measuring it, not because there is more.

NFA chief executive Stephen Harrison said: 'From large businesses and high street retailers to pensioners in their own homes, we are all at risk of becoming victims of fraud.' The effects are not always obvious but can be dramatic.

a) Using the item, identify the amount that each individual person can expect to be worse off as a result of fraud. (1)

b) What does the item suggest is the reason for the increase in fraud since the previous year? (1)

c) Suggest reasons why fraud is often a hidden crime. (4)

d) A researcher wants to investigate white collar crime, suggest a method they could use and explain why it is a suitable method. (4)

Key terms

White collar crime – crimes that are committed by the middle classes, usually linked to their jobs.

Fraud – is when money is gained by telling lies or giving false information.

Bribery – is when people are given money in return for breaking the rules when they are in a position of trust.

Insider trading – an illegal practice when people working for a company use their insider knowledge to make money on stocks and shares.

Embezzlement – workers taking money without the people affected realising.

Blue collar crime – crimes that are committed by the working classes.

Occupational crime – is a crime that is connected to your job.

Edwin Sutherland

Famous people

Edwin Sutherland was the person who first used the term white collar crime. He challenged the idea that most crime was committed by working-class people. He had a very wide definition of white collar crime and also included corporate crime (see next topic) which is crime committed by big companies. Sutherland said in his book published in 1949 that white collar crimes were committed by high status and respected people.

Crime and deviance
Topic 7: What is corporate crime?

What am I going to learn?

● **To understand the difference between corporate crime and other terms**

Sociologists often try to look behind the surface of things. This topic will consider the way that sociologists have tried to uncover crimes that are committed by powerful people.

What is corporate crime?

Corporate crimes are those committed by people working for big companies and businesses. Like white collar crime there are respectable and high-status people who commit these. The crimes are usually motivated by greed. However, the aim is to get rich by making the company rich. Individuals will benefit, but through the company making more profit, not by individuals taking money from the company.

Sometimes the company may not be actively making money, but could allow sloppy working practices that risk people's health to continue.

Examples of corporate crime

One of the saddest cases was that of Thalidomide in the early 1960s. Thalidomide was a drug marketed by a German chemical firm. The drug was supposed to relieve morning sickness, which pregnant women may suffer from. Many women took the drug. Unfortunately, the drug caused as many as 10,000 children to be born with missing limbs and other problems. The company had done tests on animals but not on the possible effects on pregnant women. After many years of campaigning, the company eventually began to pay money as compensation to the families affected.

What does corporate crime include?

Corporate crime can have some overlap with white collar crime. Some corporate crimes may include activities like fraud and insider trading. The key point is that it is the company that can be held responsible, not just individuals. It may be individuals working for the company who commit the offences, but the company itself can be punished. Individuals may also be held to account. The victims of corporate crime may be the public or the **employees** of the company. Multinational companies are difficult to catch as they are not under the control of any one government. Recently, supermarkets and frozen food companies have been accused of selling horsemeat as beef.

Corporate crime includes **negligence**, false advertising, lying about the contents of a product, bribery, financial fraud and many other things. Marxists have been involved in researching this as they see it as ruling-class crime.

Find out about

Find out more about the following:

- Herald of Free Enterprise
- Hillsborough disaster
- Horsemeat scandal

Famous people

Frank Pearce

Frank Pearce in his book *Crimes of the Powerful* linked the crimes of big business with organised crime. Organised crime run by gangsters ran alongside corporate crime and little attention was given to this by the law. Frank Pearce was a Marxist sociologist.

Extended writing

Describe what crimes high-status people are more likely to be involved in. (10)

Check your understanding

Complete the sentences below:

a) Corporate crime includes crime committed by large companies and •••.

b) White ••• crime is about individuals who commit crime for their own gain.

c) With corporate crime the ••• is held to account for the crime.

d) Thalidomide was a drug that had side effects on ••• women.

e) The victims of corporate crime may be employees or the •••.

f) Corporate crime and white collar crime are not the •••.

Exam practice

Corporate manslaughter: key cases

Herald of Free Enterprise

One of the most famous corporate **manslaughter** cases was in the late 1980s, when the Herald of Free Enterprise – a Townsend Thoresen car ferry owned by European Ferries – capsized in 1987 off the Belgian

coast. A total of 193 lives were lost after the bow doors of the ferry failed to close and the car deck was flooded.

An inquest jury returned verdicts of unlawful killing in 187 cases. However, the corporate manslaughter case failed because the negligence could not be blamed on one person.

Clapham rail disaster

Britain's worst rail disaster in recent years claimed 35 lives after three trains collided on 12 December 1988. The British Rail Board admitted fault for the accident, which was because of careless work by signal engineers. The board was held responsible and paid compensation reaching £1m in some cases, though no one was prosecuted for manslaughter.

a) According to the item, why did the Herald of Free Enterprise manslaughter case fail? (1)

b) What does the item say was the reason for the rail disaster? (1)

c) Explain two reasons why corporate criminals may not be prosecuted successfully. (4)

d) Explain what is meant by the term corporate crime. (4)

Key terms

Corporate crime – crimes that are committed by big businesses.

Employees – people who work for a company.

Negligence – is when a company does not keep the public or its workers safe through a lack of care.

Manslaughter – when a person is killed unlawfully because of a lack of care.

Stretch and challenge

Imagine you are in a key position in a large company selling a global product. Think of ways that you could break the law to give your company an advantage to make bigger profits.

Invent a simple law that would help to control corporate crime in Britain.

Grade boost

Make sure you are clear about the difference between white collar and corporate crime. There is crossover between the two but Frank Pearce noted the big difference between the employee fiddling his expenses and the big corporation damaging the lives and welfare of thousands.

Crime and deviance

Topic 8: What does sociology tell us about youth crime and street crime?

What am I going to learn?

- **To understand the way that youth crime and street crime may dominate society's fears of crime**

This topic will consider the way that society has often focussed on youth crime and street crime. This will also link to the previous two topics on white collar crime and corporate crime. Marxists believe that the media, police and judiciary tend to focus on youth and street crime.

Across the generations

Ask older relatives or neighbours what crime was like in the past. Were young people more respectful? Was society more or less violent? Were people as worried about crime in the past?

Famous people

Geoffrey Pearson

Geoffrey Pearson published a book called *Hooligan: A History of Respectable Fears* in 1983. Britain had had riots in 1981 and many people thought that street crime and youth crime were out of control. The New Right thought that Britain had gone soft on people who broke the law. The New Right looked back to a golden age when Britain's streets were safe and people respected the law.

Geoffrey Pearson's book challenged this idea. He looked back to Victorian times and found that street crime was a problem even then. There were robbers known as footpads prowling the streets waiting to rob you. All through the 20th century there were problems on Britain's streets. Pearson found that the golden age when everything was rosy was a myth.

What is youth crime?

Youth crime is simply crime that is committed by young people. In England and Wales 10 years old is the age at which a person can be held criminally responsible. In order to be classed as a young offender by law, you need to be aged between 10 and 17. After this age, in legal terms, a person is considered an adult.

Youths are associated with **delinquency** and crime including theft, vandalism, intimidation, fighting, and drug-related crime and joyriding.

What is street crime?

Street crime is crime that takes place in public places. It is associated with youth, working-class and ethnic minority groups. It involves mugging, prostitution, drugs offences, **anti-social behaviour**, gun and knife crime or any other crime committed in public places.

How does society view youth crime and street crime?

Many people see these two as the main concerns for society. The media may play a big part in this as they focus on these types of crime. Marxists believe that the media focus more on these crimes. The public may then be more concerned about these issues and call for tougher punishments. Youth crime and street crime are seen as the big problems, and white collar and corporate crime are overlooked. The forces of social control, the police and the judiciary, may also spend more time and energy in bringing these issues to justice.

Gangs, gun and knife crime have been a great focus in the UK in the last few years. There has been a moral panic about these issues. In addition, hoody-wearing youths and 'chavs' have been seen as folk devils making our streets unsafe. The New Right would see these as real causes for concern. They would like to see tougher punishments from courts, but also stricter discipline from parents and in schools.

Check your understanding

Match the definitions with the terms below:

Street crime	Corporate crime	White collar crime
Occupational crime	Youth crime	Folk devils

a) What term means crime committed by the middle classes?

b) What term means a group that the media make everyone afraid of?

c) What term means a crime that a person commits connected with their job?

d) What term means crime committed by people under 18?

e) What term refers to crime committed in public places?

f) What term means crime committed by big businesses?

Exam practice

Britain's feral youth: a minority who commit an incredible 86 crimes by age 16

A tiny band of delinquents, who commit around 86 crimes by the age of 16, are responsible for most of **youth offending**, according to a study.

It also found that nearly half of young people's offences can be traced back to a small number of thugs who make up less than 4% of the teenage population.

The research by Cambridge University has been seen as a vital study into Britain's feral youth, as it suggests for the first time, that not knowing right from wrong is the most important factor influencing whether people commit crime.

Most children, in the study, knew the difference between right and wrong. Knowing this was what stopped them from offending. The small group who did commit the crimes had no idea of right and wrong.

Researchers studied 700 teenagers over five years from the age of 12 to 16 in Peterborough, which was chosen for its average size, crime level and social make up.

a) Using the item, identify what percentage of young people the study says commits most of the crime. (1)

b) What does the study suggest is the main reason for the small group of young people offending? (1)

c) Using sociological ideas, explain how young people are presented in the media. (4)

d) Explain reasons why Peterborough was chosen for the study. (4)

Topic 8: What does sociology tell us about youth crime and street crime?

Key terms

Youth crime – means crime committed by 10–17 year olds.

Delinquency – means anti-social behaviour by young people.

Street crime – refers to crime committed in public places.

Anti-social behaviour – means behaviour that breaks social norms and is a nuisance to other people.

Chav – a stereotype of working-class youths who behave in a loud anti-social way.

Feral youth – young people that are not socialised.

Youth offenders – young people who break the law.

Stretch and challenge

- If the item in the Exam practice is correct, what solutions would you suggest for the small percentage who do not know right from wrong?

- The answer is street crime, what are five possible questions?

Extended writing

Discuss which types of crime are the greatest problems in 21st-century Britain. (20)

187

Crime and deviance

Topic 9: What are the nature explanations of crime and deviance?

What am I going to learn?

- **To understand non-sociological explanations of crime and deviance**

This topic links with the work in Chapter 1. Understanding crime is useful to help understand the nature/nurture debate. This topic will examine nature explanations of crime, which include psychological and biological explanations. As a point of comparison we will also consider labelling, a sociological explanation of crime.

Stretch and challenge

- If a person is influenced to be a criminal by their genes, is it their fault?

- Make a list of arguments for nature (biological/ psychological) explanations of crime.

- Make a list of nurture explanations of crime.

- What do you think? Is crime caused by nature or nurture? Give reasons.

- The topic is crime. The answer is socialisation. What are five possible questions?

Extended writing

Explain whether socialisation is an important cause of crime. (10)

Biological explanations

Nature explanations see crime as caused mainly by something that a person is born with. An early explanation was that of Cesare Lombroso, a late 19th-century Italian army doctor. He worked with criminals and noticed their physical features. They could be identified by their distinctive features including large ears, jaws, flat nostrils, dark skin and their high threshold to pain.

Although Lombroso's ideas sound far-fetched to us, other theories have developed linking criminal behaviour to the way we are born. Chemical imbalances have been blamed for people's behaviour. This is taken seriously and drugs such as lithium are used to treat mental health problems, such as **bipolar disorder**. In recent years, research into **genes** has tried to identify behaviour caused by certain genes.

Psychological explanations

Psychological explanations believe that criminal behaviour is connected to a person's mind or personality. Hans Eysenck believed that extroverts, who are risk taking and outgoing, are more likely to become criminals than introverts. Introverts have quiet personalities and do not take risks. Therefore, personality type was linked to criminal behaviour.

Psychology has developed other explanations for people's behaviour. This includes ADHD, schizophrenia and many others.

Biological and psychological theories focus on the individual and their characteristics as the explanation for criminal behaviour. Sociologists emphasise nurture when explaining crime. A person is influenced into following a life of crime by their experiences. **Labelling** theory is one example of that.

Labelling theory

Labelling theory sees individuals as influenced by the labels other people give us. If others call a person a thief, they may live up to that label. This is called a **self-fulfilling prophecy**. A person caught shoplifting may go on to commit worse crimes if they accept the label of thief or criminal. A '**deviant career**' as a criminal may be the result of labelling.

Check your understanding

True or False?

a) Nature explanations say that criminals are born likely to be criminals.

b) L'ombroso thought that criminals had had a bad upbringing.

c) Chemical imbalances have been blamed for some criminal behaviour.

d) Eysenck believed that quiet, shy people are more likely to be criminals.

e) Biological explanations see criminals as born that way.

f) Labelling is a biological explanation.

Exam practice

Psychopaths: born evil?

When Brian Dugan pleaded guilty to the brutal rape and murder of a seven-year-old girl, Jeanine Nicarico, he seemed to be a typical brutal serial killer.

She was murdered in 1983, though Dugan only pleaded guilty in 2009. He was also convicted of rape several times over, and two other murders. This included a seven-year-old girl and a 27-year-old nurse whom he forced off the road before raping and killing her.

Dugan would have been executed, but the death sentence was now no longer used in Illinois.

Yet, he showed no regret for any of his murders or crimes. Scientists now believe this lack of regret may in fact be linked to the reason he committed these acts.

A neuroscientist, Dr Kent Kiehl of the University of New Mexico, scanned Dugan's brain, and found that Dugan didn't understand why people cared about what he had done. He found that there was little activity in the part of Dugan's brain that controls emotions.

a) Using the item, identify how Dugan felt about his crimes. (1)

b) Suggest what the item says is the cause of Dugan's crimes. (1)

c) Explain, using examples, what is meant by the term deviance. (4)

d) Describe any two ideas about why people become criminals. (4)

Key terms

Non-sociological theories of crime – ideas about why people become criminals based on psychology and science.

Bipolar disorder – a mental disorder that can make people very active or depressed.

Genes – the basic unit of DNA that decides what your physical characteristics are.

Psychological – ideas about how the mind works.

Labelling – the view that people are influenced by the words other people use to describe us.

Self-fulfilling prophecy – the idea that the labels people are given will turn out to be true.

Deviant career – the path that a person labelled a criminal follows.

Personal research idea

Investigate your classmates. Interview them to find out whether they think criminals are born or made.

Grade boost

Remember to use sociological key words from Unit 1 to answer crime questions. Norms and socialisation are particularly useful.

Crime and deviance

Topic 10: How do subcultures help to explain crime and deviance?

What am I going to learn?

● **To understand the contribution that subcultures have made to our understanding of crime and deviance**

The idea of subcultures has been used by many sociologists to try to understand the nature of crime and deviance. This section will consider some of the most well-known ones.

Extended writing

Describe what is meant by the term criminal subcultures. (10)

Across the generations

Ask older people you know whether there were gangs when they were young? What were the subcultures or gangs like then?

Walter Miller

Famous people

Walter Miller explained crime through male working-class subculture. Men want to be cool, smart, have excitement, be tough and have fun. They also do not want to be told what to do. When these are all added together, a wild Saturday night can result in men being involved in crime.

Walter Miller was one of the first to study gang culture and did it through observing gang life first-hand giving his work great validity.

What is a subculture?

As you will know from Unit 1, culture is a shared, learned way of life. A **subculture** is another different way of life within that. Subcultures have different norms and values from the rest of society. They may look and speak differently.

Some subcultures may be criminal in nature and even criminal subcultures may be very different from each other.

Strain theory

Robert K. Merton thought that crime got out of control when there was no balance between the goals people wanted and the chances of achieving them. People are socialised to want to be rich, have a big house and car. Some people cannot get this through legal means so turn to crime. Merton explained that there were five possible responses including crime, drugs, giving up, rebelling or continuing to try for success even when it's unlikely. The overwhelming desire to be successful puts a strain on individuals, putting pressure on them to commit crime. Cohen and Cloward and Ohlin developed these ideas further.

Status frustration

Albert Cohen had the idea that in America there is a strong value on success. Working-class people may fail to be successful. They are frustrated. So they invent their own subculture – with the opposite norms and values; gaining success and respect in the subculture. This may cause them to do badly at school and take part in a criminal lifestyle.

Criminal subcultures

Cloward and Ohlin took Merton's ideas a stage further and explained why criminal subcultures take different forms. People turn to a criminal subculture but it depends on the area you live in. Some areas have different opportunities for criminals.

There are three kinds of subculture found in different areas:

- Criminal subculture – highly organised criminal gangs exist.
- Conflict subculture – no organised crime so they join gangs to fight each other.
- Retreatist subculture – they do neither of these so give up and turn to drugs or alcohol!

In all of these explanations crime is a response to the social situation, they emphasise social rather than individual causes of crime.

Check your understanding

Complete the sentences below:

a) Subcultures are small groups which have their own ••• and values.

b) Albert Cohen said that ••• invent their own subculture which turns society's values upside down.

c) Robert Merton thought that the goal of being successful was so strong that people ••• the rules to get there.

d) Cloward and Ohlin thought that the kind of criminal subculture depended on the ••• a person lived in.

e) Cloward and Ohlin thought that there were ••• different types of criminal subcultures.

f) Subcultural theories about crime are based on ••• rather than nature.

Exam practice

Youth crime in London

Youth subcultures based on battles between post codes and involving weapons have become part of London life.

Violent crime among the young has become very worrying for Londoners. The long-term trend for most types of crime recorded in London is going down. But the figures for serious violent offences by and against young Londoners are not going down. These have crept up over the past four years and many such incidents go unreported.

Youth subcultures based on **territorial identities** and vicious, sometimes fatal, feuds have spread and become part of London life. This **gang** culture is strong. '**Postcode violence**' is real and is very worrying for many young people.

a) Which types of crime against young people are going up, according to the item? (1)

b) Explain what the item means by gang culture. (2)

c) Outline two reasons why young people may belong to a gang subculture. (4)

d) A sociologist wants to research a criminal subculture, explain an ethical issue they would need to consider before starting research. (3)

Key terms

Subculture – the way of life of a small group within a society.

Strain theory – the idea that the pressure to succeed encourages people to turn to crime.

Territorial identities – when the area you live in is really important to who you are.

Gangs – organised groups of people who join together for profit or to defend territory.

Postcode violence – where gangs from different postal areas fight each other.

Stretch and challenge

- Give some possible reasons for the rise in violent crime described in the Exam practice.

- Think of possible solutions for the rise in gang subculture.

Find out about

Find out about gangs in the USA. How many are there? What norms, values, customs and traditions do they have?

Find out about youth subcultures: Teddy Boys, Mods, Skinheads, Rockers, Hippies, Suedeheads, Boot Boys, Punks, Goths and Emos should all prove good starting points. Were they deviant? Criminal? What were their norms and values?

Crime and deviance

Topic 11: How is social class linked to crime?

What am I going to learn?

- **To understand the links between social class and conviction and victimisation rates**

This topic links closely to life chances. Sociologists have been interested in the way that working-class people are more likely to be convicted of crime than others but are also more likely to be victims of crime. This section will explore reasons for this.

Grade boost

Make connections with the next two topics on gender and ethnicity in your answers about class: they are linked.

🔍 websites

For information about the police, justice system and how the public see the police go to: **www.statistics.gov.uk**

www.homeoffice.gov.uk has details of how the government is tackling crime.

To find out more about policing and crime in your local area go to **www.police.uk**

There is also information about how victims can find support at: **www.victimsupport.org.uk**

Conviction rates and social class

The evidence seems very clear cut. Official statistics repeatedly show that more working-class people than middle class are convicted of crime. To be more accurate you would have to say young working-class males. They are more likely to be prosecuted, convicted and sent to prison. Therefore, it seems that young working-class males are more likely to turn to crime.

Are most criminals young, male and working class?

Failures in education and feelings of low status have been put forward as reasons for this. **Cultural** and **material deprivation** of the poor are also linked to high **conviction rates** for the working class. However, conviction rates only include the people who get caught. Middle-class white collar criminals may not get caught or even be reported if they do. Corporate criminals may not even be thought of as criminals. **Self-report studies** suggest that crime is committed by members of all social classes.

Marxism, class and crime

Marxists suggest that the police are not fair in their approach to crime and are more likely to arrest working-class people. They are also more likely to put resources into policing working-class areas and into street crime, which is more likely to be working class. Marxists have the same view of the courts, which are middle-class institutions and may not favour working-class people. Laws themselves, Marxists argue, are made in favour of the rich upper classes and are about protecting property.

Victimisation, class and crime

As well as being more likely to be arrested, the poor are more likely to be victims of violent crime and burglary. The elderly may be particularly vulnerable. Fear of being a victim of crime is also very harmful to people's quality of life.

Check your understanding

Match the following terms with the definitions below:

Victimisation	Subculture	Cultural deprivation
Material deprivation	Conviction rates	Self-report study

a) What term is used to describe the way that some individuals are not able to afford the basics expected for a reasonable lifestyle?

b) What term means a confidential questionnaire where people admit to crimes they have committed?

c) What term means the way of life of smaller groups within a society?

d) What term means a lack of certain norms, attitudes and values that are taught through socialisation?

e) What term refers to how many people from certain groups are found guilty of crimes?

f) What term refers to the people who have crimes committed against them?

Exam practice

Is prison the answer?

Convicted offenders are mainly men from poor or working-class backgrounds. They will tend to be in their late teens or early 20s. A large percentage will have drug and alcohol problems. Many will be living with significant mental health problems. Many will not be able to read or have steady jobs. Most are white, but some will be black and a disproportionate number are from ethnic minority groups.

These groups of people are vulnerable to being convicted and sent to prison again. The courts and prisons are mainly there to deal with the problems caused by poor, young males.

Yet whether it is domestic violence or child abuse, middle-class white collar or corporate corruption, sexual abuse or the abuse of power, most crime never features in the official statistics on crime. Crime is far more common and committed by a wider range of social classes than the records of police, prisons and courts show.

Young men are one of the most vulnerable groups for criminal convictions

a) Using the item, identify two characteristics of convicted offenders. (2)

b) What does the item suggest that these groups are vulnerable to? (1)

c) Explain two features of patterns of victimisation. (4)

d) A sociologist wants to research the accurate rates of crime. Suggest one method they could use and suggest why it is a good reason. (3)

Key terms

Cultural deprivation – is when individuals lack the norms and values expected by society.

Material deprivation – is when individuals lack the basic necessities for a reasonable lifestyle.

Conviction rates – are about how many people from certain social groups are charged and found guilty of crimes.

Self-report studies – are when people are asked to say whether they have committed crimes in a questionnaire that is kept confidential.

Victimisation – is about who the victims of crime are.

Stretch and challenge

- If you wanted to arrest more middle-class and upper-class people, what new laws would you pass? What changes would you make to policing?

- Name ten things that prisons do which could be bad for society.

- Suggest the national impact if all prisons were closed and all prisoners released. What would you do with offenders instead?

Crime and deviance
Topic 12: How is gender linked to crime?

What am I going to learn?

● **To understand the links between gender and crime**

This topic will explore a range of issues around gender and crime. They are related to both conviction and victimisation. Also important are the different ways that men and women may be treated by the agents of social control.

Personal research idea

Carry out an observation at lunch time or break. Compare the behaviour of boys and girls. Are boys more aggressive than girls?

You will need to get permission to do this. You need to think through the ethical issues and plan what you will do if you see bullying or dangerous behaviour. You also need to operationalise the concept of aggressive behaviour. This means turning it into something you can easily measure. In other words, what will aggressive behaviour look like?

Across the generations

Ask older friends and relatives what they think about the idea of ladettes. Were there girls or women like this in the past?

Conviction rates by gender

In simple terms more males than women are convicted of crime. There are offences where women appear in larger numbers, such as shoplifting and offences related to prostitution. Only 5% of the prison population are female.

Socialisation

Norms of masculinity have been blamed for the higher rate of male convictions. Men are socialised to be aggressive and tough. However, many men manage to be masculine without getting into trouble with the law. Females are socialised to be more gentle, and stricter social control by parents may stop them getting into trouble. There is some suggestion that this is changing and more women are being convicted of violent offences, possibly due to **ladette culture**.

Chivalry factor

Some sociologists have argued that women are treated more gently by the forces of social control. This is called the **chivalry factor**. Chivalry was the code of honour of knights. The chivalry factor may start at school when teachers treat girls less harshly, and are likely not to shout at them, and punish them less severely. Males in positions of power, like police and judges, may see themselves like knights rescuing the poor girl. By comparison men may be treated worse so more men are convicted.

Demonisation of women

An interesting alternative to this is the idea that some women are treated particularly harshly by the agents of social control for some crimes. Where women are guilty of crimes that go against what is seen to be the caring nature of **women**, they may be **demonised**. For instance, women who are involved in hurting a child will be presented as evil by the media and may receive harsh treatment in the courts.

Victimisation

Patterns of victimisation vary according to the type of crime. Men are more likely to be victims of violent crime. Women are more commonly victims of sexual attacks and domestic abuse. However, men may be less likely to report domestic violence than women. Coronation Street ran a story on this with Tyrone in 2013. Non-reporting may affect figures.

Check your understanding

Complete the sentences below:

a) Men are convicted of ••• crimes than women.

b) ••• % of the prison population is male.

c) The ••• of masculinity have been blamed for higher conviction rates of males.

d) The chivalry factor is the idea that women may be treated ••• harshly by courts and police.

e) Women who commit crimes that hurt children or are cruel will be shown as ••• by the media.

f) ••• are more likely to be victims of violent crime.

Exam practice

Female violence on the up

Crime committed by women has soared since the late 1990s, it was revealed today. The number of women found guilty of murder, vicious assault and other attacks has risen by 81% since 1998.

The massive increase, revealed in the government's own data, means that women are now being convicted at the rate of more than 200 every week. Murders have more than doubled; life-threatening woundings are up by a fifth.

Police blame the rise on the 'ladette' culture, which they say has made female crime more violent. Changes in the law to allow 24-hour drinking, and cultural pressure on girls to act more like males has caused the problem. Some women are copying the worst male role models.

a) Using the item, what is the percentage increase in women convicted of violent crime since 1998? (1)

b) What does the item suggest are reasons for the increase in female violent crime? (3)

c) Explain what is meant by the term chivalry factor. (2)

d) Outline two reasons for differences in conviction rates for men and women. (4)

Key terms

Norms of masculinity – traditional ideas about how men should act including being tough and strong.

Ladette culture – a set of norms which encourages some girls to behave like men.

Chivalry factor – is the way that women are treated more favourably by police and courts.

Demonisation of women – is the way that women who commit certain crimes, which go against the caring nature of females, are presented as evil by the media.

Stretch and challenge

- Should women who have young children or are pregnant be sent to prison?

- Make a list of solutions to the amount of male crime.

- Compare male and female crime rates for:
  – violence
  – shoplifting
  – theft/burglary.

Extended writing

Describe how gender is linked to crime. (10)

Crime and deviance
Topic 13: How is ethnicity linked to crime?

What am I going to learn?

- **To understand the links between ethnicity and conviction and victimisation rates**

As with class and gender there is a tension between two ideas. On one hand, some ethnic minority groups are more likely to be convicted of crime. At the same time, ethnic minorities may suffer more as victims of crime and be discriminated against by police and courts.

Famous people

Stuart Hall

Stuart Hall moved from Jamaica to England in 1951. He realised that Britain's way of life was changing fast and helped set up the Centre for Cultural Studies in Birmingham in 1961.

In 1976 he wrote a book called *Policing the Crisis*. He noticed that the government was worried that it was losing control of the country. There were power cuts, strikes and inflation was out of control. He argued that the government used a moral panic about crime to justify a very tough approach to policing and controlling the streets. The crime of mugging was part of this and was associated with black people. Stuart Hall used Marxist ideas to try to explain what was going on.

Ethnicity and conviction rates

Ethnic minority groups are over-represented in the prison population, which has led many to think that ethnic minorities are more likely to be criminals than white people. However, things are rarely that simple in sociology or society. There are big differences between different ethnic groups and of course between men and women within ethnic groups.

Racism and conviction rates

The police have had troubled relationships with some ethnic communities since the 1970s. Racism may be one of the causes of the differences in conviction rates. Paul Gilroy argued that the police were racist and that ethnic minority people were not more criminal than other groups. Black and Asian people were victims of racism and so were in conflict with the police.

The Stephen Lawrence case highlighted the issue of police racism in the 1990s. The Macpherson Report which followed this found that the police were institutionally racist. The whole organisation was found by the report to be racist in its practices and thinking. The culture of the police was judged to be racist.

Stereotypes

Stereotypes may not have helped this and ethnic minorities may suffer from labelling by police and courts. Moral panics about ethnic minority crime are frequent and may not help this. **Immigration** itself has been a cause of moral panic in recent years.

Ethnicity and victimisation

As well as being more likely to go to prison, ethnic minority groups are more likely to be victims of crime. They are more likely to live in poorer areas, where there is poverty and more risk of crime. Racism may also mean that they are the victims of racially motivated attacks. So ethnic minorities suffer as victims and are unfairly blamed, according to Paul Gilroy.

Check your understanding

Match the following terms with the definitions below:

| Ethnicity | Racism | Stereotype |
| Discrimination | Labelling | Self-fulfilling prophecy |

a) What term is used to describe the idea that some races are not as good as others?

b) What term is used to mean an exaggerated view of a group of people?

c) What term is used to describe the effect a label can have when someone lives up to that label?

d) What term is used to describe the cultural group a person belongs to?

e) What term is used to mean the action of treating a person differently because of a part of their identity?

f) What term is used to mean attaching a word to someone which gives a fixed idea of what they are like?

Exam practice

Is racism still a problem in 2012 Britain?

Many improvements have happened for the black and Asian communities since the murder of Stephen Lawrence in 1993, but Britain still has a long way to go.

The statistics for ethnic minorities and crime are not encouraging: black men are 26 times more likely than a white man to be stopped and searched by police. Black and Asian defendants are still more likely to go to jail than white people when convicted of similar crimes.

The report, Statistics on Race and the Criminal Justice System, also found that ethnic minority defendants received longer **sentences** for almost every crime. For violence against the person, the average sentence was 16.8 months for whites, 20 months for blacks and almost two years for Asian defendants. The Ministry of Justice defended itself saying that this was not evidence of discrimination, but that every case was different.

a) Using the item, identify how much more likely a black man is to be stopped and searched compared with a white man. (1)

b) Suggest two ways that black and Asian people appear to be treated differently by the courts. (2)

c) Outline two possible sociological reasons for the differences between ethnic minorities and white people shown in the item. (4)

d) Explain, with reference to crime, what is meant by the term labelling. (3)

Key terms

Ethnic minorities – cultural groups that are small in number compared with the whole population.

Immigration – people moving to Britain from other countries.

Sentence – the punishment given by the court.

Stretch and challenge

- Would it help if all police officers had to study Sociology?

- Try to think of 10 things that could be done to reduce the rate of ethnic minority convictions.

- What could be done to improve ethnic minority relations with the police?

Grade boost

When writing about ethnicity and crime, try to show awareness that gender, age and class will also be important. An elderly black woman's experience of the police may be very different compared with young black males.

Crime and deviance
Topic 14: Is crime getting worse?

What am I going to learn?

● **To understand why sociologists treat official statistics on crime cautiously**

This topic is concerned with the wide range of issues that make the use of official statistics a problem for sociologists. These include practical problems with recording statistics and the many reasons that the public do not report crimes.

Stretch and challenge

- How would you measure the amount of crime in England and Wales?

- Research and design your own self-report questionnaire for crime.

- Research and design a victimisation survey for crime.

- How might the following affect official statistics on crime?
  - Institutional racism
  - Ageism
  - Chivalry factor
  - Moral panics
  - Labelling
  - Any other sociological ideas you can think of.

- What would the following theories say about official statistics on crime?
  - Functionalism
  - Marxism
  - Feminism
  - Interactionism.

Official statistics and crime

Police are expected to carry out the role of collecting official statistics on crime. The government need these to decide where to target police resources in future. The government want to show the public they are doing a good job in reducing crime. The media report on this, affecting future voting.

In recent years the trend has been to show crime rates falling overall. At the same time public feeling may be that crime is getting worse. This may be because tabloid newspapers tend to focus on the sensational.

Where do official statistics on crime come from?

The main source of official statistics is from **crimes** that are **reported** to the police. They also need to be **recorded** by the police to appear in official statistics. Sociologists argue that crime statistics are **socially constructed**.

Reasons why some crimes are not reported

Some crimes may not be seen as serious by the victim. They may feel that the police will not be able to do anything. Victims may be scared of telling the police, in case of repercussions. The criminal may be known, or related, to them. It could be a family member.

Sexual crimes may be too stressful or embarrassing to report. Crimes such as child abuse may not be reported for years.

Some crimes, such as underage drinking or use of illegal drugs, do not have a victim. On the other hand, crimes for which the victim has insurance are likely to be reported in order to make a claim.

Problems with the way that crime is recorded

Once a crime is reported the police have to record it if it is to be counted. There have been changes in the way that police record crime. Police forces are under pressure to hit targets for the reduction of crime and are judged on their clear-up or detection rate of crime. This has been an increasingly important part of police work since the 1990s.

Check your understanding

Complete the sentences below:

a) The main way that official statistics on crime are known is through crimes reported to the •••.

b) The government want to see official statistics on crime to show they are doing a ••• job.

c) Tabloid newspapers tend to report on ••• crimes.

d) The Home Office do a survey on crime in England and •••.

e) Crimes that are not ••• or recorded do not appear in official statistics.

f) Pressure on police to reduce crime may affect the way that crime is •••.

Exam practice

Crime statistics in England and Wales: a changing picture

Police – their main knowledge of crimes committed comes from the public.

Crimes recorded by the police in England and Wales fell by 8.4% between the years ending September 2011 and September 2012, according to the latest crime statistics; 8.9m crimes were reported in 2011/12. This was down from 9.6m the previous year, and was 29% lower than ten years ago, according to figures published by the Office for National Statistics (ONS).

The statistics showed a 41% drop in crime between 2002 and 2012 for police recorded crime figures. The Home Office crime surveys show only a 26% drop in the crime survey results over the same period.

Statisticians say one explanation for the difference may have been pressure on the police to record crimes as less serious ones. This helps them to hit performance targets. The study says the police figures may exaggerate the actual long-term fall in crime, especially since 2006–07.

a) What does the item suggest is the overall pattern for police recorded crime figures 2002–12? (1)

b) Using the item, by what percentage did recorded crime fall between 2011 and 2012? (1)

c) What is the percentage difference between police recorded crime and the Home Office crime surveys between 2002 and 2012? (1)

d) Suggest reasons for the difference between official police recorded statistics and the Home Office crime surveys. (3)

e) A sociologist wants to conduct research with victims of child abuse. Outline two problems they would have to consider when planning the research. (4)

Key terms

Reported crime – crime that the public tell the police about.

Victimisation survey – a questionnaire to find out if people have been victims of crime.

Self-report study – a questionnaire to find out which crimes people have committed.

Recorded crime – crime that the police add to their official records.

Socially constructed – the statistics are a result of the choices the public and police make.

Home Office – a department of the government that is in charge of immigration, security and law and order.

Extended writing

Discuss problems with the use of official statistics on crime. (20)

Find out about

How has modern technology affected crime? What new crimes have the Internet, mobiles and social networking made possible? How would these affect official statistics on crime?

Research methods

Topic 1: What is social research?

What am I going to learn?

● **To understand the main ideas of social research and its purpose**

This topic will consider the purpose of social research. It will also include some of the key issues about the kinds of data collected by sociologists and some of the first steps of research.

Why do sociologists do social research?

Sociologists do social research so that we have a better understanding of how society works. They hope to use their findings to influence how society is organised, but also to make people think differently about things. Sociologists work for universities, the government, private companies and other organisations such as charities.

Sociologists hope to influence the government when they are deciding on new policies. This is not always easy. Sociologists sometimes have to accept that their ideas will take time to be accepted and may only eventually influence the government.

What different sorts of data do sociologists use?

Data is the information that sociologists use in their research reports. **Primary data** is research information that sociologists collect themselves. This could include asking questions or observation.

The other kind of data sociologists use is called secondary data. **Secondary data** is information that has been put together by other people. This could include newspaper reports, diaries and novels, which are **qualitative data**. This means that the information is rich and has lots of detail.

Secondary data also includes official statistics collected by the government or other organisations. The **census** which is collected every ten years by the government is a good example of this. This type of data is **quantitative**.

If you study History make sure you realise that primary and secondary mean something different in sociology.

First steps

Before starting any research, a sociologist must decide what their research aim is and where they will gain a sample of people from (see next topic). Sociologists may be influenced by the place where they are getting their

Personal research idea

Use the Internet to look at crime rates for men and women.

Examine official statistics for crime in your local area. Try www.police.uk.

Famous people

Emile Durkheim

Emile Durkheim, one of the founding fathers of sociology, did a famous study called *Suicide*. He used secondary data in the form of official statistics. This was a cheap method as the data was already collected. However, official statistics were not easy to compare, as different places collected them in different ways.

Durkheim developed an idea that the better social connections a person had the less likely they were to commit suicide. He wanted to show how the most individual act (suicide) was still influenced by society.

funding from in deciding their aims. They may need to gain access to the people they wish to study and seek permission.

Once they have a research aim and a sample, sociologists may need to carry out a **pilot study**. A pilot study is a trial run to iron out any problems before starting the real thing.

Check your understanding

Match the term with the definition below:

| Primary data | Pilot study | Quantitative |
| Secondary data | Qualitative | Data |

a) What term is used to describe data that has been collected by someone else?

b) What term is used to describe information used by sociologists?

c) What term is used to describe information that has lots of statistics in it?

d) What term is used to describe information collected by sociologists themselves?

e) What term is used to describe data that has lots of detail?

f) What term is used to describe a test run for a piece of research?

Exam practice

Are men born to cheat on their partners?

A new sociological study suggests that men who don't cheat may feel trapped sexually.

Men who have affairs, however, give themselves the best of both worlds, according to sociologist Eric Anderson. In the study, most of them said they still want to stay with their partner, but hope they can get away with having extra sex with other people.

The American sociologist, who teaches at the University of Winchester, argues that being married stops men from doing what is natural. When men cheat it is purely for sex. Feminist sociologists would disagree with this and suggest that it is the way men are socialised that makes some men think like this.

Of those studied 78% said that they cheated, even though they said that they loved and wanted to stay with their partner. The sample was made up of 120 male university students, both gay and straight.

a) Using the item, identify what percentage of the men in the study cheated on their partners. (1)

b) According to the study, what has being married to one partner stopped men from doing? (1)

c) Explain two key findings of the study in the item. (2)

d) Suggest reasons why the men in the study may not have been truthful. (2)

e) Outline two sociological explanations of the findings about men's attitudes. (4)

Key terms

Data – information collected by research.

Primary data – research information that the researcher has collected themselves.

Secondary data – research information that has been collected for another purpose by someone else.

Qualitative data – is in words and has lots of detail.

Census – a questionnaire given to every household in Britain every ten years by the government.

Quantitative data – is in numbers and can be presented as graphs or percentages.

Pilot study – a trial run before the actual research.

Stretch and challenge

Suggest some problems that a sociologist might have when trying to study each of the following:

• Users of illegal drugs

• Nursery children

• Millionaires

• Homeless people

• Organised crime

What solutions could there be for the problems you came up with?

Think of ten disadvantages of using secondary data.

201

Research methods
Topic 2: What are samples?

What am I going to learn?

- To understand the main types of sample and why they are used

This topic is concerned with the reasons why sociologists use a particular type of sample. There are practical reasons for this, but the type of research method may also affect this.

Stretch and challenge

What type of sampling method would be best suited to studying the following? Give a reason for your choice.

- Students being bullied at a secondary school
- Homeless people
- People who use public transport
- Heroin addicts
- People who do graffiti

Over to you

Imagine that your headteacher wanted to do a survey of bullying. If they asked only Year 11 boys, this would not be a fair sample of a mixed 11–18 school. Therefore, it would not be representative. Work out for your school what would need to be included to make it a fair and representative sample.

Why do sociologists use samples?

Sociologists aim to study certain groups, which may mean everyone in Britain, but often they may target particular age, gender, social class, region or ethnic groups. The group they wish to study are the target population.

Samples are a way of finding out about the **target population**, by studying a small manageable number of the group.

What is representativeness?

Samples need to be fair in order to work. For it to be fair the sample should **represent** the whole target population. This means that the make-up of the sample should reflect the make-up of the population, for example the proportions of males and females.

What kinds of sample are there?

Getting access to a sample may require permission and some groups are hard to reach. A **sampling frame** is the list where your sample is selected from. The telephone directory or electoral (voting) register are examples of this. They are not perfect as some people will not be listed on these.

The ideal kind of sample is seen as a **random sample**. Random samples are selected by chance using names out of a hat or computer-generated lists. To be random every person in the target population must have an equal chance of being selected.

If a random sample is not possible, **systematic samples** are a good alternative. If your school was the target population, the school roll would be the sampling frame. Systematic sampling could mean taking every tenth name on the list, for example.

Quota sampling is when the researcher makes sure that they ask a certain number of different sorts of people. The researcher checks the person they are interviewing is the correct age, gender, etc.

Snowballing is very useful for outsider groups, such as criminals. The researcher uses one contact to introduce them to a second contact and so on.

Finally, even less random is the sampling method often used by students. An **opportunity** or **convenience sample** is used, which means anyone who is available and willing to take part.

Check your understanding

Match the term to the correct definition:

Sampling frame	Target population	Random sample
Snowballing	Opportunity sample	Systematic sample

a) What term means a sample chosen by chance?

b) What term means a sample where every tenth name is chosen?

c) What term means the people that the researcher is aiming to study?

d) What term means that the sample used were people who happened to be available?

e) What term means the place that the researcher gets their sample from?

f) What term means that a researcher uses one contact to find another slowly building up a sample?

Exam practice

Drug survey completed

The global drug survey will help understand drug-taking behaviour.

In just over 48 hours over 7,000 people completed the online global drug survey. The survey included people's views on taking drugs of all kinds from pain killers to alcohol and cocaine. The survey was completed online by volunteers.

The survey, designed by Global Drug Survey and Mixmag in partnership with *the Guardian*, is very large, and a very useful source of data about what drugs people use, how often they take them, and the effects of taking them.

The only other comparable survey is the British Crime Survey. The British Crime Survey, one of the largest in Europe, finds that roughly a third of its 27,000 respondents admits to taking drugs.

a) According to the item, how many people completed the Guardian/Mixmag Global Drug Survey in its first 48 hours? (1)

b) What does the item suggest is the only comparable source of data on drug use in the UK? (1)

c) Identify two things that the item suggests the survey will discover. (2)

d) Explain the meaning of the term random sample. (2)

e) Outline two weaknesses of the online voluntary sample of people that *the Guardian* survey uses. (4)

Key terms

Target population – the people the researcher aims to study.

Sample – a small group chosen from the target population.

Representative – the idea that the sample should have the same mix of people as the target population.

Sampling frame – the list where the sample is selected from.

Random sample – a group chosen by chance from the target population.

Systematic sample – uses a system, e.g. where every tenth name on a list is chosen.

Quota sample – where the researcher is looking for a certain number of particular groups.

Snowballing sample – using a connection with one person, which leads to other members of the group being studied.

Opportunity or convenience sample – when a researcher uses the people who just happen to be available.

Find out about

Widen your knowledge of methods used in the social sciences by using the library or Internet to find out about some of the following:

- Rosenhan experiment
- Milgram experiments into obedience
- Asch experiments into conformity
- Zimbardo – Stamford Prison experiment

203

Research methods
Topic 3: What are questionnaires?

What am I going to learn?

● **To understand the issues involved in the use of questionnaires**

This topic will look at the different types of questionnaire that sociologists use. Also important are the advantages and disadvantages of using questionnaires to collect data.

What is a questionnaire?

A **questionnaire** is a series of questions on paper or online, which a researcher uses to find out about a social issue. Questionnaires are probably the most widely used research tool in sociology and many other subjects. The term **survey** is also used sometimes to mean gathering quantitative data through questionnaires.

Why are questionnaires so popular?

Questionnaires are a popular research method as they are usually a fairly quick and cheap way of collecting data, compared with other methods. Because the **respondents** complete the questionnaire themselves there is no need for a team of interviewers, saving money. Lots of people can complete the same questionnaire at the same time making research quicker.

Questionnaires are very flexible as they can be completed with the researcher present, or they can be sent out through the post or online. Each of these ways of collecting the data has advantages and disadvantages.

The biggest advantage of questionnaires is the ability to repeat them in a different place and a different time, but being able to compare the results, as the data has all been collected in the same way. This quality makes them high in **reliability** (see Topic 7).

Disadvantages of questionnaires

Unless the researcher is present to distribute and collect the questionnaire there is the problem of a low **response rate**. This means that the questionnaires are not completed and returned. This will damage the size and, importantly, the representativeness of the sample. Many people will not bother to complete questionnaires; it is likely that those who do will have strong views on a topic. This would make the sample unrepresentative.

Questionnaires do not allow the respondent to explain their answers in detail. Respondents may lie on questionnaires. They may also misunderstand questions, try to give answers they think will please the researcher and rush their answers. These factors may make research **invalid** (see Topic 7).

Stretch and challenge

Design a questionnaire for use with primary schoolchildren to find out what they know about Christmas.

Where would you find a sample for this survey? Use the terms target population and sampling frame in your plan. Describe how you would obtain your sample.

What problems would you have to consider before starting this survey?

Famous people

Auguste Comte

Auguste Comte was the Frenchman who first coined the term sociology. It appeared in his book, *A Course in Positivist Philosophy.* He believed that sociology could become the science of society and produce facts like science.

Check your understanding

Complete the sentences below:

Quick	Response	Mail
Repeated	Returned	Questionnaires

a) Surveys involve collecting quantitative data and usually involve •••.

b) Questionnaires are useful because they are so ••• and cheap.

c) Some questionnaires may have the problem of a low ••• rate.

d) Questionnaires not being ••• may be a major problem.

e) Questionnaires can be sent by ••• or completed online.

f) Questionnaires can be ••• easily in another place.

Exam practice

Our Lord Simon Cowell

O come let us adore him! *Daily Mirror* survey in December 2011 finds that 22% of children believe Christmas is to celebrate the birth of Simon Cowell.

The survey asked 1,000 British children between the ages of five and seven about Christmas Day and 36% were unaware that it is to celebrate the birth of Jesus Christ.

They showed little knowledge of other Christmas traditions including the name of Santa's reindeer. Tulisa was the top wrong answer with 12%. Others were: Beckham (11%), Pippa (11%), Obama (9%), Dappy (9%), Fazer (7%), Tinie (5%), Cheryl (5%), Ronaldo (3%).

Simon Cowell – God?

The survey also found that 28% thought Lapland was a London nightclub. Some children in the survey thought that Gary Barlow, Mark Wright and Prince Charles are the Three Wise Men and some of those that did actually know the name Jesus, thought he was born in Brentford, Essex.

a) According to the item, how many children did not know that Christmas Day was to celebrate the birth of Jesus? (1)

b) Suggest a reason why the survey showed 36% of children did not know that Christmas Day was for Jesus Christ. (1)

c) Write a closed question that a researcher could use to find out how many children knew that Christmas was to celebrate Jesus' birth. (1)

d) Explain why questionnaires are a useful method for researchers. (3)

e) Outline two problems that researchers may have when using questionnaires. (4)

Key terms

Questionnaire – a list of questions on a piece of paper or online for use in research.

Survey – a general term used to describe a research project usually involving questionnaires.

Respondent – a person who completes a questionnaire.

Reliability – whether research can be repeated and results compared.

Response rate – the percentage of people who take part.

Validity – whether research actually gets close to the truth of what is happening.

Find out about

The Census – when does the census happen? How long has it been happening? What is it about? What has the most recent census discovered?

Interesting fact

The terms used in questionnaires can affect the answers given. A survey asked whether people were lower, middle or working class. When the term working class was used instead of lower class more people went for that category. People thought that lower class sounded very low status compared with working class.

Topic 4: What are the different types of interview?

What am I going to learn?

● **To understand about different types of interviews used by sociologists**

This topic is concerned with the advantages and disadvantages of different styles of interviews. The way that the topic chosen affects the style adopted will be discussed, as will the problems of recording results.

Stretch and challenge

● What alternatives are there to using unstructured interviews to study:

  – Criminals?

  – Victims of domestic violence?

● What are your personal characteristics? List them.

● How might your personal characteristics affect the interview if you interviewed a:

  – Disabled teenage boy?

  – Chinese elderly man?

  – Six-year-old girl?

  – Muslim woman aged 35?

● How might you be affected if you were interviewed by:

  – An attractive young person of the opposite sex?

  – A teacher?

  – An elderly person?

What is an interview?

In an interview the interviewer asks questions and the **respondent** replies. Answers have to be recorded, either in writing or by taping.

What are the different types of interviews?

There are two main types of interview. The first kind is a **structured interview**. There is a list of prepared questions. The questions are standardised so that they are all the same. Even if several different interviewers are carrying out the interviews, responses should be able to be compared.

Questions in structured interviews may be both open and closed. At one extreme the interview may be like a questionnaire. However, some may have complex questions which require in-depth answers. Interviewers need to be well trained and able to explain misunderstood questions. They may also need to interpret the respondents' answers and decide how to record their answers quickly.

Unstructured interviews

Some sociologists prefer a more flexible style of interview. **Unstructured interviews** are like conversations and do not have strictly pre-planned questions. The researcher adapts the questions as the interview develops. They can probe further if respondents say things that capture their interest. The respondents are able to explain things in their own words. This makes the researcher gain a more accurate picture of what is going on. If trust is built up, respondents may be more honest than in other sociological methods.

Sociologists still plan the interviews carefully and will have a list of topics for discussion. However, another plus is that respondents may say things they would never have expected, providing ideas for other questions.

Problems with interviews

Interviews are a popular research method, but do have drawbacks. Answers can be difficult to record. If the interviewer writes down answers whilst asking questions this may be off-putting. Tape recorders may be useful in unstructured interviews, but may discourage honesty.

A further problem is that of **interviewer bias**. Respondents may give different answers according to the interviewer's **personal characteristics**. For instance, a black respondent may give different answers to a white interviewer compared with a black one, especially if being interviewed about racism, which would affect the validity of the data.

Key terms

Respondent – person answering the questions.

Structured interviews – interviews where the interviewer has a pre-planned list of questions.

Unstructured interviews – Interviews that are more like a conversation.

Interviewer bias – the effect that the person interviewing has on the answers given by the respondent.

Personal characteristics – whether the person is young or old, rich or poor, black or white or any other part of their identity.

Rapport – means that the interviewer and respondent build trust with each other.

Check your understanding

Match the correct terms with the definitions below:

| Pilot study | Respondent | Unstructured interview |
| Interviewer bias | Structured interview | Methods |

a) What term describes the way that sociologists gather information?

b) What term describes an interview with pre-planned questions?

c) What term describes the effect that the personal characteristics of the interviewer have on the answers given?

d) What term describes an interview which is more like a conversation?

e) What term describes the person answering questions in an interview?

f) What term describes a test before the research is carried out?

Exam practice

Asking difficult questions

Unstructured interviews are a very useful method of research. Criminals and deviant groups may be more likely to speak honestly than other methods. They are also useful for finding out about sensitive issues, such as victims of domestic violence or emotional issues. Good interviewers are really skilful and able to build **rapport** with the person they are interviewing.

Unstructured interviewers need to be very careful about sensitive issues because they could cause upset. Very intense interviews may require a debrief. This is an after the interview discussion to check that the person interviewed is feeling OK.

a) Using the item, explain what is meant by a debrief. (1)

b) Suggest one area of social life that unstructured interviews may be useful for studying. (1)

c) Explain two advantages of using unstructured interviews. (4)

d) Outline two problems with using unstructured interviews. (4)

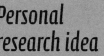

Personal research idea

Work with a learning partner:

One of you – design a questionnaire to find out about people's music taste. Ask at least ten people.

The other – carry out a small number (two or three) of unstructured interviews to find out about their music taste.

Compare your results. Who got the best information? Why do you think this?

Research methods

Topic 5: What are the different types of observation?

What am I going to learn?

- To understand how sociologists use the different types of observation and the strengths and weaknesses of each

This topic will explore different types of observation. It will examine the difficulties involved in studying human social behaviour first-hand.

Interesting fact

Some participant observers use a gatekeeper to gain access to the group they want to study. A gatekeeper is a person who allows them into the group they are studying. James Patrick, a young sociologist, was introduced to a gang in Glasgow through a member of the group that he met. This allowed him to carry out a participant observation of the group over time. Patrick found himself in some dangerous situations.

Famous people

Laud Humphreys

Laud Humphreys carried out a study called *Tearoom Trade: Impersonal sex in public places*. This was a study of homosexual activity carried out in men's toilets. He did not actually take part but acted as a lookout. Later, he asked the men involved for an interview to explain themselves. He was surprised how many of them were prepared to do so and how many of them lived respectable lives.

His research is well known and has raised issues about whether what he did is acceptable.

What is observation?

Observation means observing social life as it happens in its natural (usual) setting. This could mean a classroom, workplace, street or playground. It is seen as naturalistic because humans are in real-life settings.

Different types of observation

When observing social life the observer must decide whether they will tell the people being observed that it is happening. If the observer tells them then this is **overt observation**. The problem with this is that people will change their behaviour when they know they are being observed. Watch how your classroom teacher behaves differently when the headteacher comes into the room.

Therefore, some sociologists prefer to do **covert observation**. This means the observation is kept secret in the hope that people will behave naturally. Of course, the observer's presence may still affect behaviour.

The other decision an observer must make is whether to join in with the group they are observing. Joining in with the group is called **participant observation**. When they just observe this is called **non-participant observation**.

The observer needs to consider how to collect and record information. Observation could involve collecting quantitative data through the use of tally charts. Participant observers tend to collect qualitative data and describe the groups they are observing.

Is observation useful?

The strength of observation is that it gets closer to real life than other methods. This gives the research great validity. Observation, especially covert, is very useful for finding out about **outsider groups**, such as criminals.

The problems are that observations are open to being one-sided or biased. The observer can affect the behaviour they are studying.

Check your understanding

Complete the sentences below:

a) ••• observation is when the observer tells the group they are observing them.

b) ••• observation is when the observer is secretly observing a group of people.

c) ••• observation is when the observer joins in with the group they are observing.

d) One problem with overt observation is that people may ••• their behaviour.

e) Even when observation is covert the observer may ••• the behaviour of the people they are observing.

f) Observation gets close to real life so is high in •••.

Exam practice

Tally's Corner

The researcher needs to get permission to study the group if they are overt. For covert research the researcher needs to find a way of being accepted by the group. They may have to dress or act differently to stand a chance of being accepted.

The covert observer is also deceiving the people they are observing. The researcher has to consider whether this can be justified.

One famous study is Elliot Liebow's *Tally's corner* which was a study of black American men who were mainly unemployed. Liebow was white but still managed to gain access to the world of the street corner these black men spent time on. His research was highly praised and he gained understanding of the men and their lives treating them with respect. All the names he used were made up. However, he admitted that they may not have shown him everything about their lives because he was white.

a) Using the item, why may the researcher need to dress or act differently? (1)

b) Suggest a reason why the names in the research Liebow did were made up. (1)

c) Explain what is meant by the term participant observation. (4)

d) Outline two reasons why Elliot Liebow may have chosen to do participant observation for his research. (4)

Key terms

Overt observation – when the researcher is openly observing the group.

Covert observation – when the researcher is secretly observing a group.

Participant observation – when the observer joins in with the group they are observing.

Non-participant observation – when the observer is just watching the group and not joining in.

Outsider groups – those people who live lifestyles on the edge of society.

Stretch and challenge

Imagine you were doing research as a covert participant observer amongst criminals.

What should an observer do if they see someone breaking the law in their observation? Should they break the law themselves if they are participant observers? Should they put themselves in danger?

Do you think it is OK to make friends with people just so that you can research them? How do you think they will feel when the research ends and you disappear?

Design a list of guidelines for researchers doing observation.

Topic 6: How do sociologists choose a method?

What am I going to learn?

- **To understand the range of issues involved in choosing a method of research**

This topic will consider the practical issues affecting the choice of topic. However, sociologists are also influenced by their ideas about what makes good research.

Interesting facts

Content analysis is one method of using secondary data. Researchers may use a tally chart to record how many times certain types of words are used. Research into violence in television programmes might record acts of violence on a tally chart.

The Glasgow Media Group have carried out research, using content analysis, into the way news is presented, and questioned whether it is unbiased in their books *Bad news* (1976), *More bad news* (1980) and *Really bad news* (1982). The group have done research on the media for over 30 years and have their own Facebook page.

Positivists

Positivist sociologists believe that sociology should be like a science and prefer methods that give facts and statistics. Questionnaires and structured interviews are the best for this.

Anti-positivists believe that it is more important to find out the meanings of social life. They prefer methods that give lots of detail like observation and unstructured interviews.

What are the choices of method?

First, researchers have the choice of collecting primary data themselves or using secondary data that is already available. Using secondary data may save time and money. However, the information may not be in exactly the form the researcher wants; it may also be out of date.

Collecting primary data

There are several main methods used by researchers. These include questionnaires, interviews, observation and experiments. Experiments are not used as often by sociologists as psychologists, but there are some interesting studies.

What sort of data does the researcher want?

Some research data will be in the form of short answers or notes that are easy to quantify. This type of data is called quantitative and is useful for turning into graphs, tables and percentages. This may be the type of data that the researcher wants. If so, they are likely to use **closed questions** in a questionnaire or interview. They could use observation with a **tally chart**. Tally charts are a way of counting how often something happens through ticking a box or column.

The other form of data is qualitative. This data is more descriptive and detailed. Qualitative data is very useful for describing and understanding what a different culture or subculture is like. This type of research is useful for finding out the meaning of people's behaviour. Researchers are likely to use **open questions** in questionnaires, interviews or observation if this is their aim.

Therefore, the sort of data required will affect the choice of method.

Access

The topic chosen and the type of sample available will affect the method chosen. For instance, criminals are unlikely to wish to complete a questionnaire. Researchers would have to either observe them or build up enough trust to do a **confidential** interview.

Check your understanding

Complete the sentences below:

a) Sociologists need to decide whether to collect their own ••• data.

b) Some sociologists use ••• data that has been collected for another purpose.

c) ••• data is useful for making graphs and percentages.

d) ••• data is preferred by some sociologists who want to really understand the meaning of social life.

e) Open questions allow people to explain their •••.

f) Closed questions only allow fixed •••.

Exam practice

How the Reading the Riots project was carried out

After the riots: London.

The researchers collected and analysed 1.3 million words of rioters' first-person accounts.

Reading the Riots is the only research study into the summer riots involving interviews with large numbers of people who were closely involved in the riots. The project run by *the Guardian* and the London School of Economics (LSE), used sociological methods to try to understand why the riots happened.

The research was inspired by a study of the Detroit riots in the USA in 1967. The Detroit study used closed-ended questions to collect quantitative data. However, this study used a qualitative approach. This meant using unstructured interviews that flowed freely like conversations.

The first phase of Reading the Riots was completed in three months. The confidential interviews were carried out with hundreds of people directly involved in the riots in six cities. The researchers also studied 2.5 million tweets that were on Twitter connected with the riots.

The second phase will involve interviews with police, court officials and judges.

a) Using the item, identify how many of the rioters' words were studied. (1)

b) Write an open question to ask a person involved in the riots why they took part. (1)

c) Write a closed question to ask a shop owner whose property was damaged in the riots. (1)

d) Explain what is meant by the term sample. (2)

e) Suggest reasons why the researchers studied six cities in England. (3)

f) Explain how the Reading the Riots study was different from the study of riots in Detroit. (2)

Key terms

Closed questions – only allow fixed answers, such as yes or no.

Tally chart – a grid that allows the researcher to keep a record of how many times they observe something.

Open questions – allow the respondent to answer in detail and as fully as they wish.

Confidential – means that who took part and what they said is kept secret.

Content analysis – a method for studying closely what is in secondary data, such as the media.

Stretch and challenge

Do you think that the study of tweets on Twitter is a good method of studying the riots?

Suggest other ways in which the riots could be studied.

Design a series of closed ended questions for use with:

– Rioters

– The police

– Members of the public not involved.

Grade boost

Create a mind map or spider diagram of all the different possible reasons for choosing a research method.

Topic 7: How do sociologists evaluate research?

What am I going to learn?

- **To understand how to make a judgement about how useful a piece of research is**

This topic will consider the key terms that are associated with judging a piece of research. It will explain them and help students to use them.

Interesting fact

The reputation of sociology

The International Sociological Association has published a code of ethics for all sociologists to follow. All sociologists are expected to follow these guidelines. Sociologists should not do anything which damages the reputation of sociology. Sociologists must choose their research carefully and aim to improve the quality of human life. They must present their findings accurately and honestly, whatever the wishes of the people who may be funding the research.

Grade boost

When writing about problems in research, please avoid stating that a method has reliability and validity in the same sentence. This suggests that you do not understand either, as it would be very unusual for a piece of research to show both these qualities at the same time.

What are reliability and validity?

All research should be evaluated in terms of these two ideas.

Reliability means that the research should be able to be repeated in a different time or place and similar results gained. Any differences should be because of real differences between the people studied, not just because it happens to be a different researcher. Questionnaires and structured interviews tend to have the highest reliability as long as the sample used is representative. An unrepresentative sample will make research less useful.

Validity is concerned with whether the research has uncovered the truth about social life. Participant observation and unstructured interviews tend to have the highest levels of validity, providing the researcher is highly skilled. If subjects are not truthful, validity will be lowered. Questionnaires and closed questions can also lower validity, as people cannot say what they really mean.

Ethics in research

Ethics are to do with whether a piece of research is morally right or wrong. This could be to do with the area of research or the way that the research has been carried out.

All people who are **subjects** of research should have given their **informed consent** when they are taking part in research. Covert research should only happen when there is no other way. Once the research has begun, the subjects have the **right of withdrawal**. They can end their involvement at any time.

Subjects should be anonymous and what they say or do should be confidential and private. Names and details should be changed so that subjects cannot be identified.

Physical and psychological harm

Participants in research should not be put at risk of **physical** or **psychological harm**. This means that they should be safe and not upset, stressed or unbalanced by the process. The participants should not feel bad about themselves because of anything they did or said during the research. There should be a debrief process after the research finishes.

Check your understanding

Match the terms below with the correct definition:

Reliability		Validity
Ethics		
Psychological harm	Anonymity	Confidentiality

a) What term is used to describe keeping people's names secret?
b) What term is used to describe the extent to which research can be repeated and results compared?
c) What term means that people's answers need to be kept secret?
d) What term is about how close to the truth a researcher is?
e) What term is to do with whether research is acceptable?
f) What term means damage to a person's state of mind?

Exam practice

A useful way to think about validity and reliability is like a see-saw. As one side goes up, the other comes down. Researchers find it difficult to have high levels of both unless they use more than one method. This is called methodological **triangulation**.

Sociologists often do this as a way of supporting their results. It means they can combine qualitative and quantitative methods in the same piece of research. For instance, they can do unstructured interviews to find out about an area of research and then use this to decide on questions for a questionnaire.

Some researchers also check results by using different interviewers or carrying out the research at different times. This is a different kind of triangulation but is another way of checking that results are accurate. An example of the need for this is featured below.

University College London researchers compared alcohol sales figures with surveys of what people said they drank. They discovered that the amount people said that they drank was almost half of alcohol sales. Therefore, almost half of the alcohol drank was not being included in the respondents' answers.

a) Using the item, identify one reason why researchers may use more than one method. (1)
b) Suggest one possible reason for the difference in alcohol sales and what people said they drank. (1)
c) Explain what is meant by the term validity. (2)
d) A researcher wishes to study people who have grown up in families with domestic violence. Outline two problems that they may have in carrying out the research. (6)

Key terms

Ethics – whether research is morally right or wrong.

Subjects – the people who are being studied.

Informed consent – subjects of research should know what the research is about and have agreed to take part.

Right of withdrawal – subjects should be able to end their involvement at any stage if they wish to.

Participants – people who are taking part in research.

Physical harm – injuries to a person.

Psychological harm – harm to how a person feels including stress, fear, upset or worry.

Triangulation – using more than one method to support results.

Stretch and challenge

You are leading a team of sociological researchers and have been asked to carry out research into the following areas:

- Effects of divorce on children
- Victims of racist abuse
- Effects of unemployment on men
- Young people who self-harm.

Explain what ethical problems there are with each, and how you would overcome them.

Sociological theories
Topic 1: Marxism

What am I going to learn?

- **Marxism is a theory that explains human society in terms of inequality between rich people and poor people. It says rich people exploit poor people**

This theory is based on the writing of Karl Marx (1818–83) and is still influential today. It claims that wealthy people have more power than poor people because they own the things needed to make products, and they control the institutions of society such as the law and religion. They control the police and army. Poor people tolerate and live with this unequal situation because rich people teach them it is correct and how society should be.

Over to you

Have a look at magazines that are devoted to the lives of celebrities and rich people. What image do they show of such people? Are they seen as greedy and selfish because they have so much money when others are poor, or are they seen as people to admire because they can spend so much on themselves?

Karl Marx

Karl Marx (1818–83) was a philosopher, writer and economist. He was born in Germany but lived most of his life, and is buried, in London. His political views were very unpopular in Germany and France, so he came to live in England. He spent much time in the British Museum writing about economics and philosophy. Even some people who do not agree with communism have said that his understanding of how society works is very accurate.

Famous people

🔍 websites

Find out more about Marxism and communism by looking at 'How Communism Works' at this weblink: **tinyurl.com/9qdljr2**

The gravestone of Karl Marx in Highgate Cemetery, London. He was one of the most influential thinkers of all time.

What is Marxism?
Social class and capitalism

Marxism is a view of the social world that sees rich people (the **bourgeoisie**) as controlling the whole of society for their own benefit. Poorer people (the **proletariat**) work for rich people because they have no choices; they have few opportunities as individuals to make things better for themselves. Rich people have a very good life, with opportunities, comfort and all that they need. Poor people fight to survive because their lives are hard.

Capitalism

According to Marx, the whole social system is based on the need for profit. Workers take **raw materials** and make items that can be sold. Their work adds value to the item, but the workers do not keep the added value; that goes to the capitalists. For example, a tee shirt may cost £5 to make, but be sold for £30. The owners (bourgeoisie) keep the extra money themselves. They get richer but poor people stay poor.

Control and ideology

Poor people put up with this situation for two basic reasons. The first is that rich people control politics, government, the army and the police. If poor people complain or unite, they are put in prison. The second way people are controlled is through **ideology**. An ideology is a system of beliefs about the world. They are taught in schools, in work, through the media and by religion that it is acceptable for some people to be rich 'because they earned it', whereas other people can work all their lives and stay poor.

Revolution

Marx said that when poor people finally realised what was happening in the world, they would band together and overthrow rich people in a **revolution**. He thought this would happen in his own lifetime in Britain. Many countries have had revolutions and overthrown rich people, for example Russia in 1917, Cuba in 1958, where the Communist Party took over. However, in some of these countries, the new social systems did not always benefit everyone equally and some have since returned to capitalism.

Check your understanding

Mix and match the following Marxist terms and their meanings:

a) Exploit   a system of ideas and beliefs about how the world should be

b) Bourgeoisie   poorer people and the working class

c) Proletariat   to use someone else for your own selfish purpose

d) Raw materials   a belief that everybody should share equally in society

e) Ideology   basic material from which a product is made

f) Revolution   a sense of not belonging to society

g) Communism   over-throwing a government

h) Alienation   very wealthy people who own a great deal

Exam practice

Communism is a political philosophy which argues that all people should have equal rights to wealth. Marxism is a way of understanding and analysing the organisation and structure of society. It is also a way of understanding how societies develop and change. If a product that someone buys is sold for a big profit, Marx believed that the purchaser is being exploited by the producer of that product. The workers are also exploited as they gain no pleasure and little pay for making that product. Workers (and purchasers) feel **alienation** as they are not part of society. Profit, Marx believed, leads to a divided society between the 'haves' and 'have nots'. He identified the rich as being the 'haves' and the poor as being the 'have nots'.

a) Using the item, identify and explain the meaning of communism in your own words. (2)

b) Which writer originated the ideas of Marxism? (1)

c) Using examples, explain one way in which poor people are exploited by rich people. (3)

d) Explain the meaning of the term proletarian, using an example. (2)

e) Explain the meaning of the term bourgeoisie, using an example. (2)

Key terms

Exploit – to use someone else for your own selfish purpose.

Bourgeoisie – very wealthy people who own a great deal.

Proletariat – poorer people and the working class.

Raw materials – basic material from which a product is made.

Ideology – a system of ideas and beliefs about how the world should be.

Revolution – over-throwing a government.

Communism – a belief that everybody should share equally in society.

Alienation – a sense of not belonging to society.

Stretch and challenge

Should everyone in the UK earn exactly the same pay, no matter what job they do, because they are all equally important to society?

Grade boost

You are not likely to get a question that involves theory directly, but if you can mention it with understanding when you are writing extended answers, then you are likely to be in the top mark bands. Don't use it unless it is actually relevant to what you want to say.

Sociological theories
Topic 2: Functionalism

What am I going to learn?

- That another set of sociologists, functionalists, believe society to be very good the way it is. They think everybody has an equal chance to do well and change is not always healthy for society

Functionalism is an American theory based on the work of a French sociologist, Emile Durkheim. Talcott Parsons developed Durkheim's ideas. They believed that society is like a living thing, each part is connected to the other parts and they all work together to create something that is more important than any single individual.

Classic functionalism

Societies work together so that people know what to do and how to behave. Each part of society has a **function**. The job of the sociologist is to work out how society works, how it fits together and what jobs the various organisations in society do. This is known as **functionalism**. This type of thinking was important in the 1940s and 1950s in America but is less popular with sociologists now. It is more important because it has influenced the way that people in government think about the world.

Social order

According to functionalists, in order to create a successful society, people must share values and norms. They then work together in social organisations, such as education or the family, to make life better for all people. These organisations become a social system. If one part of the system does not work well, then other parts also fail. Thus, people who are deviant are a serious problem because society will be threatened.

Institutions in society

Each institution in society does a specific job, or function. For example, families create emotional security for people and help train children to be good citizens. The education system passes on social norms and values. The legal system keeps people in order so they do not break rules.

The New Right

This type of theory is based on functionalism. It suggests that society does not need to change, and that it can work very well if it is left alone by governments to sort itself out. It was really popular with Conservative politicians in the 1980s and 1990s, and is still popular with Conservatives now. They believe that some problems in society are caused by the government taking on too much responsibility, instead of leaving individuals to sort themselves out.

Over to you

To what extent do you agree with functionalists that our society is basically fair and equal to everyone, so only the best succeed?

Famous people

Emile Durkheim

Emile Durkheim (1858–1917) is said by many writers to be the first real sociologist. Durkheim invented a scientific method for studying society and used statistics to provide evidence for his theory regarding the causes of suicide. He struggled in his lifetime to get people in France to recognise that sociology was a new way of understanding the world but his books are still read by people today.

Functionalists and New Right thinkers claim society offers a ladder of opportunity for those who are prepared to work hard and do their best to get on in life. This is known as meritocracy. Do you agree this is true?

The **New Right** believed that competition between institutions in society makes them work more efficiently, so the role of government is to look after defence, the law, and to help citizens get jobs. It also believes that welfare benefit payments are bad for people and stop them working.

Check your understanding

Create two columns headed Marxism and Functionalism and copy the statements into the correct column.

Society is run for the benefit of the rich	Society is run for the benefit of everyone
Sees different groups in society as being in competition for the best things in life	Sees different groups in society as working together for the good of everyone
Social change is usually dangerous for society	Social change is generally a good thing
There are many groups in society but they all work together for the good of all of us	There are two separate groups in society, they are the rich and the poor
Is associated with the work of Karl Marx	Is associated with the work of Emile Durkheim and Talcott Parsons
Sees education as a way of passing on social values so children become good members of society.	Sees education as a way of controlling the minds of young people so they cannot think for themselves

Exam practice

Emile Durkheim said that every society had crime and rule breaking. Thus, if crime is a cultural universal, then perhaps it is necessary to have crime for society to work (function) well. So, Durkheim believed that crime was good for society. He thought that we need some people to be criminal so that everyone knows and understands the rules. If we judge the law breaker as bad, then everyone else recognises that law breaking is wrong. Also, if there was no crime, then lawyers and policemen would have no jobs. There would be higher unemployment. Crime is therefore good for society as long as there is not too much crime happening.

a) Name the original father of sociology who developed sociological methods. (1)

b) When was functionalism a very popular theory? (1)

c) Explain the meaning of the term functionalism. (2)

d) With an example, explain one reason why Durkheim thought that some crime was good for society. (3)

e) Explain one idea held by the New Right, from any area of sociology that you have studied. (3)

Key terms

Function – the purpose of a person, or an organisation in society.

Functionalism – the study of the purposes of organisations in society.

New Right – a set of political beliefs based on functionalism and popular in the 1980s.

Stretch and challenge

What do you think are the important differences between Marxism and functionalism? Can you think of any ways in which they are similar? Use books and the Internet to help.

Grade boost

Speed writing is an important skill and you should be practising writing for at least ten minutes a day to make sure you can get all of your ideas down on paper in the examination.

Over to you

To what extent do you agree with functionalists that those who work hardest have the best life chances?

217

Sociological theories
Topic 3: Feminism

What am I going to learn?

- **Feminism is a set of theories which suggest that women are not considered equal to men in society. Feminists want to fight for better rights for women and men**

Although women have been fighting for the same social rights as men for very many years, it was in the 1960s and 1970s that feminism became very popular. Large numbers of women began to point out that women were overlooked in society. It was legal to pay them less for the same work and they required permission from their husbands to sign legal documents. Although feminist theories tend to look at the role of women in society, they have also said that men are harmed by sexism, too.

Over to you

Look in a newspaper such as the *Sun*, or look in a magazine designed for men. What images of women do you see? Are they shown in a positive way in your view? You could make a collage of positive and negative images of women. Avoid very sexualised images if you intend to put the work up in a classroom.

Famous people

In the 1990s, a girl band known as the Spice Girls promoted the idea of Girl Power, and became one of the most influential music groups of the time. They produced commercial pop music that celebrated the idea that girls could be both sexy and high achieving in the world. They emphasised the idea of strong female relationships and friendships. The band has since split but has come together for concerts and a musical based on their songs.

What is patriarchy?

Feminist theories of society tend to be concerned with fighting for equal rights for women. Feminists claim that women are generally ignored by researchers, so the role of feminist research is to find out about the lives and activities of women in society.

Patriarchy

In many societies, men have taken a dominant role. This control is known as **patriarchy**. It can be seen in religion where God is often seen as a male. Women are usually associated with the home and children, while men have dominated the world outside the home. In our society, men were very much in charge, so women did not have the right to vote on the same terms as men until 1928. They did not have the right to equal pay until the 1970s. Even today, in many countries of the world, women have few rights.

Sexism

Feminists point out that women are still not equal with men in public life. They tend to earn less, they are less likely to make it to top positions in government and work. They are criticised if they do not have perfect bodies and older **women** become '**invisible**' so we rarely see them in the media.

Areas of concern

Feminists are interested in issues such as workplace equality, but campaign on more personal concerns, too. Sexual violence, forced marriage, domestic abuse and the sex worker trade are seen as feminist issues too. They point out that women are often seen in terms of their bodies so that they are shown as sex objects rather than as people in the media.

Do women still have to fight for their rights in British society? How about in other countries, are men and women equal?

Men's liberation

Some men have been very threatened by **feminism**, so stereotypes of feminists are often negative. Feminists point out that men are harmed by traditional male roles, as they are not allowed to express their gentler side. In addition, although women are disadvantaged in the workplace, men may be disadvantaged in domestic disputes involving children.

Check your understanding

True or false?

a) All feminists hate men.

b) Feminists often believe that men are harmed by patriarchy.

c) On average women are more likely to be poor than men.

d) Feminism has died out in the UK.

e) Many women are expected to do more in the home.

f) Women are concentrated in lower paid jobs.

g) Stereotypes of feminists in the media are often negative.

Exam practice

Feminism is a set of theories concerning the role of women in society. There are a number of key issues that feminists are concerned with. The dominance of men in society is known as patriarchy, but other issues include gender stereotyping which shows women as inferior or stupid, for example blonde jokes. Women earn less and are often dependent financially on their partners. They may be discriminated against in law or they may be less likely to be promoted. It has been pointed out that women are expected to take on a triple shift in relationships: domestic labour, paid work outside the home and emotional work with the family.

a) Fully explain the meaning of the term feminism. (2)

b) What term is used to mean male dominance in society? (1)

c) Using the item, fully explain one reason why many people feel feminism is still important in the modern world. (3)

d) Explain one way in which men may be discriminated against in our society. (3)

e) What three roles make up the triple shift that many women take on in families? (1)

Key terms

Patriarchy – the domination of women by men.

Invisible women – women over a certain age are rarely seen in the media.

Feminism – the belief that men and women should be more equal.

Sexism – discrimination against women.

Stretch and challenge

Feminism is no longer needed in our society. Make points for and against the viewpoint.

Over to you

Curiously, while many men and women have feminist views, they often dislike or reject the label of feminism itself. You might be interested in considering who benefits if men and women think that feminism is a bad thing.

Across the generations

Speak to older men and women who lived through the 1970s, people who are over 50. Ask them for their memories of feminism and feminists at the time.

Sociological theories
Topic 4: Interactionism

What am I going to learn?

- **Interactionism is completely different from the other three theories considered in this section because it looks at how people interact together on a daily basis**

Interactionism is a theory that became influential in the 1920s in the USA. It argues that people's daily behaviour depends on what they believe about the world. Each person creates a view of the world and then behaves as though that view is actually true. Interactionism is not interested in the big picture, but looks at the very small-scale view of how people behave.

Over to you

Do teachers react in the same way to uniform infringements in your school or do some people get picked out more often than others? What is the possible cause of this?

Famous people

Howard Becker

One famous interactionist sociologist is Howard Becker (b. 1928). He became famous for a study known as *Outsiders* (1973) where he studied drug users and musicians. He said that gaining a negative label made it harder for people, but that they had some choice as to whether they accepted the label or how they reacted to it.

Over to you

Create a cartoon storyboard illustrating the life of someone who has done badly in school and who has been labelled by teachers. What happened?

What is interactionism?

What is the theory?

The **interactionists** believe that all our behaviour is based on what we think about others and what we think they think about us. When we see someone, we make judgements based on their behaviour, clothes, style, looks, age and appearance. Sometimes these judgements are positive, sometimes negative. We assume that the judgements we make are accurate and base our actions on these judgements. Those people will respond to how we act, and can either accept our view of them or fight it.

We also aim to manage and control how other people see us. So, we wear special clothes to make an impression, or act in a certain way. How other people respond to the messages we pass on to them, influences how we act. All social life is a **negotiation** between individuals or groups of people.

What social images about himself is this man attempting to pass on through his clothing and behaviour? Have a look at your friends' answers, do you agree?

The role of response

If people receive a negative **response** from others, they might accept that the other person's view of them is true. They will then come to believe that they are unattractive or stupid and continue to act in that way. If they have a positive response, they may then believe they should repeat the actions to gain more rewards. In this way, people can be directly influenced by the reactions of others. **Labelling** is the process of making a judgement, and **self-fulfilling prophecy** is the way that the judgement can become true in that situation.

For example, if a police officer keeps seeing teenagers in a public place, he may label them as difficult. He may stop them whenever he sees them. They will react badly to him. He will come to believe that they are trouble-makers and act accordingly. He may be aggressive and then get a bad reaction from them. This may lead to them being aggressive to all police officers

Check your understanding

Fill in the missing words:

a) Interactionism is a ●●● which explains how people relate to each other in real life.

b) Labelling theory suggests that people ●●● each other on the basis of appearance.

c) People can manage the impressions that ●●● have of them by changing their clothes and hairstyles.

d) Self-fulfilling ●●● says that people come to act like the labels others have given.

e) If people receive a ●●● response from others, they may come to believe that they are unattractive or stupid.

f) People can be directly ●●● by the reactions of others.

Exam practice

In 2010, the Equality and Human Rights Commission (EHRC) published a study which said that black people were more than six times more likely to be stopped and searched by the police than white people. In addition, Asian people were four times more likely to be stopped. According to the study, the reasons for the frequent stops and searches were stereotyping and discrimination. This could be supported by the way that some areas of the country had a worse record for stopping and searching people than others. The worst areas seem to be Dorset, Hampshire and Leicestershire. About 20% of black Londoners were stopped and searched in 2007 according to the study.

a) According to the item, who conducted the study? (1)

b) According to the item, which social group was stopped and searched most frequently? (1)

c) What did the EHRC think was the cause of the differences in stop and search records of the various police forces? (1)

d) Fully explain the meaning of the term labelling theory. (3)

e) Using labelling theory, suggest and explain the effect of the police stop and search habit on black people in London. (4)

Key terms

Interactionism – the idea that we should study how people act and behave together in the everyday world.

Negotiation – trying to reach an agreement or understanding with other people.

Response – reaction from someone.

Labelling – the process of making a judgement about someone.

Self-fulfilling prophecy – the way that a personal judgement can become true.

Stretch and challenge

Which is easier to get from others, a negative label or a positive label? Why?

Over to you

Is the idea of 'naming and shaming' criminals likely to work in your view? Give reasons for your opinion.

🔍 websites

tinyurl.com/3lnuftx

Have a look at this *Guardian* newspaper story about a school which colour codes its pupils according to their ability. The best pupils wear purple ties. What would be the effect of this on clever students and on those who do not get to wear purple ties?

Examination practice and technique
Examination guidance

It is not enough to know a lot about sociology to do as well as you can in the examination; it helps if you understand how the examination system works so you can get the most from your knowledge and maximise your marks.

Assessment process

There are two papers for the full GCSE. Each lasts for 90 minutes. Each is marked out of 100, but the actual pass mark for a C and an A grade will change each year. The two papers are:

Soc1 Understanding Social Processes; the compulsory core and options on families and education

Soc2 Understanding Social Structures; the compulsory core and options on work and crime

These two papers will look very similar. There is a compulsory core worth 60 marks with short mark questions of between 1 and 6 marks based on items. You should answer all of the questions on the lines provided in the booklet.

There is a choice of four extended writing topics. You must choose one to answer, and having chosen your topic, you answer all three questions in your booklet. The questions will always have the same command words:

- Describe ... (10 marks)
- Explain ... (10 marks)
- Discuss ... (20 marks)

Sociology skills

You are being tested in three skill areas for sociology:

Assessment objective	What it says on the specification	What this means in practice
AO1	Recall, select and communicate knowledge and understanding of social structures, processes and issues	You will be able to remember, choose examples and describe what is happening in the social world
AO2	Apply knowledge and understanding in a range of contexts both familiar and unfamiliar	You will be able to explain what is happening, using sociological ideas, in order to answer questions about a range of different situations
AO3	Select, interpret, analyse and evaluate information from different sources	You will be able to read and understand writing, graphs, pictures and ideas from different sources of information about society.

What are Sociology examiners looking for at GCSE?

Markers are taught to mark positively, this means that they will look for marks and do not take marks off for mistakes. They will ask themselves whether you have shown evidence of the following skills:

- Do you understand the meaning of the question?
- Do you refer to examples and evidence?
- Do you use sociological language and ideas?
- Do you describe our culture and society accurately?
- Is everything in the response related directly to the question?
- Are there relevant comments explaining the issue under discussion?
- Is the writing organised and structured throughout?
- Can you apply sociological ideas to a new situation?
- Is the answer well written, legible and of appropriate length?

How do you improve your performance in the examination?

Here is a simple checklist of things that you should be doing to achieve your best under examination conditions:

1. Revise and understand your class notes. Examiners are looking for evidence of sociological knowledge such as key terms or facts about British society.
2. Look at the specification, which is on the WJEC website. Anything on the specification can form the basis of a question.
3. Read around the subject. The more you know, the easier it is to develop further understanding. Do not rely just on your teacher notes.
4. Do not be frightened by examinations. It is wise to learn relaxation techniques so that your approach to the paper is calm and collected.
5. Look at past papers, mock papers, mark schemes and candidate essays. You will have a clear idea of the standard expected and how you can achieve it.
6. Write good English and use sociological language. If your writing is hard to read, ask for help from someone to sort this out.
7. Plan your time in the examination. You need to spend about 45 minutes on Section A and leave yourself 45 minutes for Section B.
8. Answer the question. The question should tell you exactly what to do! If you do not answer the question, then no matter how good your writing, or how much you write, you cannot get the mark.

Command words

Not all marks are equally easy to gain on an examination paper. Sometimes you will need to work hard for a one-mark question, but other one-mark questions are very straightforward to answer. The trick is to look at the question carefully and work out what is needed. You can find model answers in the mark schemes.

Key terms

Specification – the information put out by the examining board for teachers and candidates about the content of the examination.

Mark schemes – the guide for markers to explain how to reward answers to questions.

Assessment objectives (AO1, AO2, AO3) – what examiners are looking for in answers.

Item (stimulus) – piece of writing, picture or graph with each question.

Exam boost

Teachers will have taught you how to answer questions and plan your essays. Take careful note of what you are told. If you are unsure of anything, then speak to someone and get help.

Grade boost

It is important to plan your time; leave about 45 minutes for each section if you are aiming for an A* grade. If you will be happy with a C, spend more time on Section A and perhaps just answer section B, questions a and b carefully.

Examination practice and technique

Section A

Generally, you should expect to see an item that will get you thinking about the topic and then some questions will follow. Care is required in reading the stimulus pieces; they are there to help you.

Dealing with the item

If you are told to look at the item in a question, then only the answer in the item is accepted, even if what you say is correct.

Read graphs with particular care, they can sometimes be misleading if you do not read the small print or the labels with care. For example, are the numbers in thousands, percentages or are they actual figures?

The possible questions

The only clue as to how much to write should come from the command words to the question and the marks available. Write enough to get the marks, but do not overwrite as you will leave yourself short of time for extended writing.

The typical commands are:

Identify... either name something such as a social process or find the answer in the item.

Using an example, explain ... one mark is for the example, and one for the explanation.

Fully explain ... give a reason and then develop it with an example or specific sociological language. If three marks are available then you will need an example and some language.

Suggest one (or two) reasons why ... you will only be marked for one (or two) reasons. Anything more will be ignored, so don't say 'also' in your answer.

Briefly explain... make a simple point, if there are two marks available, write another sentence that is an example or some development using sociological language.

Research questions

You will be asked about research methods; this may take the form of identifying problems with a research design or a method. Marks are allocated for knowing and using the language of research in such a way that it is obvious you know the meaning of the term, linking the term to the context of the question and explaining it.

How and why

Many candidates struggle with 'how' and 'why' questions.

'How' – this command is asking you to describe what actually happens. It is descriptive because you should say what actually happens in the social world.

'Why' – this command is slightly more complex, because you are being asked for a reason. You should explain a cause of something in society.

For example:

'Explain **how** women's lives have changed' requires a list of changes.

'Explain **why** women's lives have changed' requires a list of reasons for those changes.

Section B

There is a choice of four options on each paper. Choose one option only and answer all three questions.

This part of the paper tests extended writing and so bullet points are not accepted and should not be used unless you are very short of time. Write good clear paragraphs that follow the basic plan of:

a) Make a statement about society.

b) Explain the point and develop it using sociological language.

c) Use a sociological example to show understanding.

You will not make the top mark bands unless there is specific sociological content such as key language, theories, news events, statistical facts about British and Welsh culture, reference to researchers and theories that are relevant.

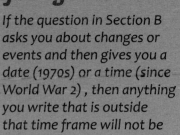

Improve your grade

If the question in Section B asks you about changes or events and then gives you a date (1970s) or a time (since World War 2) , then anything you write that is outside that time frame will not be credited.

Describe ... (10 marks)

Give facts about whatever it is you are asked about. Aim to write about 150–200 words. Make at least five or six points, unless the question specifies a number of points, in which case, stick to the question. Do not repeat yourself, and plan your answer. You will gain marks for knowledge and examples.

Explain ... (10 marks)

Give reasons for something (usually how or why). See the notes about this in Section A. This requires more depth of understanding, so perhaps three or four points made well is enough. Stick to the question, and keep referring back to what it is that you are explaining. You will gain marks for offering clear reasons for whatever it is that you are asked to explain.

Discuss ... (20 marks)

This question tests a high level of thinking and requires you to look at something from more than one point of view. Try and write about 300 words, and aim to provide a brief introduction, four or five paragraphs and a short summative conclusion. This may be where theory and research can be used effectively.

Revision tips

Focus

Many of the questions on the paper will ask you to explain the meaning of words. You should have a good definition and an example for every term on the specification in your notes. Use the language in your writing and thinking. After that, you might want to describe changes and events in society. When you are comfortable with that, then look at reasons to explain why things are as they are, using the terms and concepts.

Tactics

People have different ways of learning and you will know what works for you. Use your school's advice. The only thing that you might like to consider is that research shows that a last minute cram is less effective than steady repetition throughout the whole course. Revisit notes and ideas on a regular basis.

Good luck with your studies.

Examination answers analysed

Whenever your teacher marks a piece of work, look very carefully at what has been said and the mark you were given. Look at what others were given for the same questions. Why did they do better or worse? You can then learn how to improve your answers.

Section A

One-mark answers

One-mark answers are usually right or wrong. They are usually based on the item. You are not required to write a great deal to gain the mark.

> Write a closed question that a sociologist could use in a questionnaire to find out what people think of the police. (1)

Ceri
Do you like the police?   Yes   Don't know   Maybe   (1/1)

Writes a clear and concise answer. One mark awarded.

Reese
Do you think the police do a good job in society, and are they useful to us?   Yes   No   (0/1)

This is more than one closed question and as such is not one that could be used in a questionnaire. No marks.

Two-mark questions

Sometimes two-mark questions will command you to 'identify and explain…', but sometimes they will just ask you to 'fully explain…'. Whatever the command, you should make a statement and then develop it with a sociological example or some sociological knowledge.

> Fully explain the meaning of the term questionnaire. (2)

Ceri
A questionnaire is questions and people are asked questions to fill in the questionnaire.   (0/2)

It is difficult to tell from this if Ceri knows the answer or not. Other methods also use questions. No mark awarded.

Reese
Questionnaires are a list of questions on a piece of paper or a website. People usually fill them in themselves, and an example is the Census.   (2/2)

This has probably done more than is needed because there is knowledge and an example. Two marks.

> Fully explain the meaning of the term ethnicity (2)

Ceri
Ethnicity is what ethnicity you are; for example, there are many ethnic groups such as African-Caribbean and English and Welsh and other people who are from other places.   (1/2)

Ceri has given examples, but the definition has not been accepted because it simply repeats the term. One mark awarded.

Reese
Ethnicity refers to your cultural background; for example, Welsh or Scottish or Irish.   (2/2)

Reese has written fewer words but it is clear the key term is understood and there are three examples. Two marks awarded.

Three-mark questions

Three-mark questions require a statement, an example and development using sociological language or a key term. Some six-mark questions have two parts, each of which is worth three marks, so practising these is a useful skill. Three-mark questions are used to test understanding of research methods. Here, it is important to identify a key term and explain it as well as to understand how it applies in research work.

> Identify and fully explain one sociological reason why some people are sexist. (3)

Ceri
Many people are brought up to be sexist or have sexist views. Sexism is when people are prejudiced against people on the basis of gender, so they expect women to be inferior and do not promote them in work. (3/3)

Ceri has made a point, explained a term and then shown understanding of how the belief affects the behaviour. Three marks awarded.

Reese
Some people are sexist because they have been brought up around sexism from a very young age and they heard their parents being sexist so they grow up to believe it is acceptable to be sexist. (2/3)

This shows understanding of the reason why some people are sexist but it is not clear that Reese knows quite what sexism is. Two marks awarded.

> Identify and explain one problem that a researcher may have when researching children's television viewing habits. (3)

Ceri
They might not tell the truth because they are ashamed of what they watch and this is not reliable. (2/3)

This is not clear. Who are the 'they' referred to in the answer? Assuming it is children – then there are two points, they lie and a reason. This is not an issue of reliability but validity. Two marks awarded.

Reese
It is unethical to study children without informed consent from their parents. The researcher will need to get permission to carry out the study so as to protect the children. (3/3)

A key term is used in such a way that it is clear that it is understood. The point is made with reference to the question. Three marks awarded.

Four-, five- and six-mark questions

These extended writing questions require a statement, an example and development using sociological language and for key terms to be used. Additional factual knowledge should be used.

> Identify and explain the difference between formal and informal socialisation. (5)

Ceri
Formal socialisation is when people deliberately try to change your behaviour, such as in work or in school where you learn how to behave. Informal socialisation happens more by accident, when you are taught by your family or pick up norms from the media. The difference is that informal socialisation is not structured or deliberate. (5/5)

Each point is explained and an example given. There is a clear statement of difference. Five marks awarded.

Reese
Informal socialisation happens in the home and when your parents teach you norms and values and you learn how to act without being aware of it. However, formal socialisation happens in school when you are taught things about how to behave, so they are different. (3/5)

Informal socialisation is explained, though with inaccuracy. Credit given. Formal socialisation is not explained though the reference to being taught behaviour is useful. There is no statement of difference. Three marks awarded.

Section B

In this section, there is no link between how much you write and your final mark. Examiners prefer answers where the marks are easy to see and the arguments are simple to follow. Make your point, explain it with a key term or example and move on quickly.

'Describe ...' questions

These require facts and sociological information to be given. To make the top mark bands (6 marks and above) there will need to be explicit use of key terms.

> Describe traditional gender roles in the family in the UK. (10)

Paragraph 1 – Female roles are described clearly and there is reference to a sociologist. There is a focus on the question and plenty of key terms and facts.

Paragraph 2 – Male roles are explained clearly. Equal amounts of time and writing are spent on both men and women. The points are accurate and there is evidence that key sociological terms and ideas are understood.

Ceri

Traditionally in the UK, the woman of the household would be domesticated, unemployed and obedient to her husband's wishes. She would be socialised early in life to be sweet, caring and motherly. She would look after the children, keep the house in order and bear children for her husband. Feminist, Anne Oakley, described this as stopping women from developing themselves. Even today, many women take on this traditional role of looking after the home, even if they work.

On the other hand, a man was expected to be manly and had been socialised through canalisation to like football and be employed supporting his wife. Such behaviour was encouraged by functionalists who suggested that people had their own roles to play in the family. Men were breadwinners and did not do housework or child care, apart from discipline as they were seen, as the head of the house.

(10/10)

> Describe the meanings of the terms crime and deviance. (10)

Paragraph 1 – The definition is clear and the examples are also fair. There is some understanding of sanction.

Paragraph 2 – This is very confused and factually incorrect; many crimes are deviant. However, there is reference to unwritten rules and informal sanctions (people will dislike you).

Reese

A crime is the breaking of a written law, and to commit a crime may leave you with a jail sentence, a fine or a criminal record. Examples of a crime include murder (where you kill people) or a breach of the peace (acting disorderly and unacceptably in a public place) or shoplifting, which is theft from a shop, or maybe stealing cars. It is when crimes are committed and written laws are broken and people can be put in prison.

A person is deviant when they break their society's unwritten rules but not the law. A deviant act is when you get a sanction such as a detention. An example is stealing the school's pens and paper and a deviant act will not give you a criminal record but some members of society will dislike you.

(5/10)

'Explain …' questions

These require reasons for sociological phenomena to be given. To make the top mark bands (6 marks and above) there will need to be explicit use of key terms, writers or reference to social facts. You will also need to use the word 'because' a lot.

> Explain why people work. (10)

Ceri

People work for many reasons. The most important of these is money. This is known as an instrumental reason for working and if you do not have a job in our society, you risk being poor because you will have to have benefits to live off. People work to buy nice things and have a good standard of living, for example, doctors are well paid and footballers.

Another reason why people work is because they are following their dreams and their interests so they become actors or healthcare workers or marine biologists because they are really interested in that thing and want to spend their lives doing it. This is a vocation.

Other people work to get status and power, like lawyers and politicians and footballers who are really looked up to and can do what they like. This is because some jobs are really important. An example is Obama.

Other people like jobs to get company and get them out of the house so my Nan has a job in a charity shop because it is important to her and she meets people. This is a social reason for working and is part of why people have jobs outside the home and she does things that are useful even though she does not get money. It is volunteering.

Some people work for satisfaction (intrinsic and extrinsic) where the person has an interest but works for low pay, like a youth worker because they like the job.

(10/10)

Four reasons are explained with examples and ideas from the real world (Obama and Ceri's Nan). There are key terms such as status and vocation. Because Ceri had spread her writing out in paragraphs, she was able to add ideas after checking her work, just to be sure of the marks.

'Discuss …' questions

These questions expect you to put forward a point of view, or to be aware that there is more than one point of view that you can consider. You should be using evaluative language and connectives to gain the marks. Add social facts, writers or theory. Don't forget to look and see whether you are being asked 'how' or 'why', because it should make a big difference to your answer.

> Discuss reasons why material deprivation can affect how children do in school. (20)

Paragraph 1 – The definition is clear. Ceri knows what material deprivation is and why it is important.

Paragraph 2 – A key term is used. The discussion comes from mentioning richer children, so there is a contrast being made.

Paragraph 3 – Knowledge of the law about education is shown and a different reason is considered. Again there is some discussion because rich children are mentioned.

Paragraph 4 – Facts about the British education system are mentioned and there is evaluative language.

Paragraph 5 – This is underdeveloped but it shows theoretical understanding and awareness of two points of view.

Paragraph 6 – The conclusion is relevant and refers to the question.

Summative commentary

There are lots of ideas; Ceri has shown knowledge of British society. There is evidence of theory, knowledge of language and some evaluations made. Every paragraph is relevant to the question.

Ceri

Material deprivation is when people do not have enough money and poor children do not do well in school because there is not enough money in the family. They lack things they need to do well.

Children who are poor (FSM – Free School Meals) may be clever but they do not have the financial support in their family so they may not get enough to eat or they may have to do without books or computers. Richer children may have good bedrooms and nice places to study but poorer children may have to do without these things. They cannot go on trips or expensive holidays. According to official statistics, many children on free school meals do not achieve good literacy skills at age eleven.

In addition, children may not have good food to eat. Good food is expensive compared with cheap fatty food. Being poor can affect nutrition, so there are a lot of health problems for poorer children, and they are more likely to have asthma or be obese. If they do not get good food they will be bullied or have time off so they miss lessons. If they miss lessons they will not do well in school because it will affect their learning. They may be bullied if they are obese and stay away from school, which makes the problem worse for them. Parents can get sent to prison if children do not go to school. Rich children do not have this problem.

Because many schools in poor areas get poor examination results, children who go to them may not be doing as well as those in other schools. Sometimes parents move to go to good schools so poorer children do not know how good the good children are. Some of these poor schools have been turned into Academies and they can choose pupils, so they may not want poor children as they don't get the results. This is a really important reason as it shows that material deprivation can affect your chances.

Marxist writers about education say that the education system benefits the rich because they run the system. This means that poor children do not get the same chances. Functionalists say the education system is meritocratic and people can do well if they try. People have different points of view on material deprivation.

There is a digital divide and children do not have access to the internet and to knowledge if they have material deprivation. This shows that there are a lot of reasons why material deprivation can cause school failure for poor children but the most important is lack of the things that they need.

(20/20)

Check your understanding answers

1: Compulsory core

Topic 1: What do sociologists do?

a) sociology
b) research
c) teaching, social work, business, management, medicine, law, crime, government and politics
d) strange things about the world
e) the reasons for the change that takes place
f) inequality, racism and sexism
g) understand

Topic 2: What is culture?

a) Culture
b) Cultural diversity
c) Cultural relativity
d) Cultural universal

Topic 3: What are social rules?

a) Deviant – a person who breaks a social rule
b) Criminal – a person who breaks a law
c) Norms – the unwritten rules of expected behaviour
d) Values – beliefs that people in a society share
e) Mores – beliefs about what is good or bad behaviour
f) Culture – a way of life of a group of people
g) Society – a group of people who share a way of life; a formal group such as people who live in a particular country
h) Laws – written rules for everyone in a country to follow

Topic 4: What is social control?

a) A system of making people follow social rules
b) Breaking a social rule
c) A punishment
d) An unwritten punishment for breaking a social rule
e) A group in society that teaches or encourages us to follow social rules
f) A difference that marks people out from others in society

Topic 5: What is cultural diversity?

a) norms
b) cultural diversity
c) anthropology
d) Margaret Mead
e) New Guinea
f) Arapesh
g) subcultures

Topic 6: What is the nature/nurture debate?

a) A formal argument about an idea or a theory
b) The idea that people are born to act as they do
c) The idea that people are taught to act as they do
d) Boys are born aggressive
e) Boys are taught to be aggressive through toys and computer games
f) People's behaviour changes over time
g) People's behaviour changes from culture to culture

Topic 7: What is socialisation?

a) socialisation
b) primary socialisation
c) secondary socialisation
d) informal socialisation
e) formal socialisation
f) new

Topic 8: What are agencies of socialisation?

a) Agency of socialisation
b) Mass media
c) Norms
d) Primary socialisation
e) Values
f) Socialisation

Topic 9: What is social identity?

Tom has high status in work … because he is a Headteacher and people respect him.

Tom has a role as a husband and father, … so he looks out for his family.

Because Tom lives in Cardiff, the capital of Wales, he has an identity … as a Welshman.

One stereotype of Welsh people … is that they all like the rugby.

Tom's identity is a … teacher, father, husband, rugby fan and Welshman.

Topic 10: What are the processes of socialisation?

a) process
b) imitate
c) media
d) channelled
e) feminist
f) encourage
g) role models
h) language
i) pink
j) toys

Topic 11: How do children learn gender identity?

a) Mass media
b) Sex
c) Gender
d) Gender role socialisation
e) Domestic
f) Imitation

Topic 12: How do children learn their ethnic identity?

a) Nationality
b) Ethnicity
c) Ethnic minority
d) Negative image
e) Eisteddfod

Topic 13: How do the family act as an agency of primary socialisation?

a) Family
b) Sanction
c) Approval
d) Expectation
e) Canalisation
f) Gender

Topic 14: How do the media act as an agency of socialisation?

a) informal/secondary
b) any relevant answers accepted
c) time
d) fact
e) business
f) buy
g) stereotype
h) Representation

Topic 15: How do schools act as an agency of socialisation?

a) formal socialisation
b) the National Curriculum
c) code of conduct, rules
d) hidden curriculum
e) detention and exclusion
f) formal curriculum

Topic 16: How does sport act as an agency of socialisation?

a) Sports are usually defined as activities that are physical, often involving competition and teams.
b) People enjoy watching sport because of the high levels of skill involved.
c) Parents often encourage children to participate in sporting activities.
d) Sports personalities can be positive role models for children.
e) Many boys see sport as an important part of being masculine.
f) Many sports personalities go on to have careers in other areas.
g) Some sports are gendered activities so football can be seen as masculine even though many girls enjoy the game.
h) Sport actively encourages many positive values such as competition, team work, and health and fitness.

Topic 17: How is work an agency of socialisation?
a) socialisation
b) workplace culture
c) uniforms
d) 'have a nice day!' Or 'would you like fries with that?'
e) code of conduct
f) profession
g) resocialisation

Topic 18: How do your peer group work as an agency of socialisation?
a) A peer group is a group of people of similar age and culture to us.
b) Peer groups are an important part of secondary socialisation.
c) Small children are taught to fit in with their peer groups by being taken to playgroups and schools.
d) Peer pressure is when people feel a need to fit in with others like themselves.
e) Positive peer pressure helps people to do well and makes people feel very good.
f) Negative peer pressure can encourage people to do risky or dangerous things.
g) A subculture is a group of people with similar attitudes and ideas that are different from most people in society.
h) People turn to peer groups as a normal part of growing up and away from their families.

Topic 19: What happens to unsocialised children?
a) Socialisation
b) Feral child
c) Genie
d) Speech
e) Nature Theory
f) Nurture Theory

2: Families

Topic 1: What is a family?
a) Cultural universals – social behaviours that can be found in all cultures
b) Family structure – how people organise themselves as family
c) Kinship – sense of duty and feelings to family members
d) Family ideology – ideas of what a 'proper' family should be like
e) Norm – normal and expected way to behave
f) Socialisation – the process of learning the rules of a culture
g) Primary socialisation – being taught how to behave by your family
h) Canalisation – children are channelled into certain behaviours and activities by parents and other adults
i) Family – a group of people related by blood, marriage or adoption
j) Culture – the way of life of a group of people

Topic 2: What cultural variations exist in families?
a) Polygamy
b) Monogamy
c) Patriarchy
d) Collectivist cultures
e) Arranged marriage

Topic 3: What is a nuclear family?
a) A nuclear family consists of a married couple and their children.
b) An extended family consists of a nuclear family and other relatives who live close by or with the nuclear family.
c) George Murdock said that all societies have nuclear families.
d) Some people believe nuclear families are the best kind of family because it is better for children.
e) Talcott Parsons said that a nuclear family is essential for the proper socialisation of children and of parents.
f) Feminists and other sociologists say it doesn't matter about family structure if there is love and care for children.
g) Many politicians such as David Cameron support nuclear families.

Topic 4: How have families changed since the 1950s?
a) typical family
b) live together
c) same sex
d) falling
e) divorce
f) choices

Topic 5: Why have families changed since the 1950s?
a) There are many reasons for changes that have taken place in family structure.
b) One reason for family change is secularisation which is where organised religion is less important in people's lives.
c) In the 1970s, many feminists began to challenge the idea that men should be in control of society.
d) As contraception became easier for women to use, so family size began to fall.
e) One norm that has changed in British society is the idea that people should not have sexual relationships before marriage.
f) In modern society, men and women expect to be more equal in families.

Topic 6: What types of family and household structure are developing in modern Britain?
a) Cohabitation – people live together
b) Apart/together – people live in separate homes and children move between them
c) Singlehood – people choose to remain without a partner
d) Lone parenthood – people bring up children alone
e) Blended family – there are two parents but children from more than one relationship
f) Gay family – both parents are of the same biological sex

Topic 7: Is single parenthood a problem for society?
a) False, they are more often over 30.
b) False, many were in relationships that broke down.
c) False, some do, but many go on to successful happy lives.
d) True, about 60% in the UK have jobs.
e) False, most children are registered to two people.

Topic 8: Why are there changing attitudes towards divorce?
a) Divorce is more common now than it was in the 1950s.
b) The laws controlling divorce have been relaxed to make it easier.
c) Divorce is a distressing and stressful experience for most people.
d) Attitudes towards divorce have changed as it is no longer seen as a matter of family shame.
e) The divorce rate is highest among people aged 40 and over.
f) Divorce rates appear to be falling because fewer people are getting married.

Topic 9: Is the family under threat from social change?
a) Gay marriage – same sex couples live together as partners and have gone through a civil partnership ceremony.
b) Families of choice – people choose who they consider as family.
c) Feminist sociologists – argue that women and men should be more equal in society.
d) Singlehood – people choose to remain unmarried.
e) Fatherhood – men take an active role in the lives of their children.
f) Post-familial society – worldwide trend where people are choosing not to form traditional family structures.

Topic 10: How are the roles of children in the family changing?

Typical 1950s childhood	Modern childhood
Children lived in large families and had many brothers and sisters	Children often live in small families with few brothers and sisters
Children left school at 15 and began work to support the family	Children stay on in school and college for much longer as there is little work for young people
Children played outside in the street with each other because there were few cars	Children tend to stay indoors and play computer games or they go to organised activities and clubs
Children usually had two parents, a working father and a housewife mother	Children live in a variety of family arrangements and may have parents who live separately
Children would experience harsh discipline in the home and hitting was very common	Children are protected by law from violence in the home and many parents disagree with smacking children

Topic 11: How have the lives of old people in families changed?

a) 80
b) support or care
c) sandwich
d) boomerang generation
e) job
f) households

Topic 12: What is the role of men in the family?

Typical 1950s family role for men	Modern men in families
Most men did not do housework or cook as these were seen as women's roles	Men are willing to help in the home and many enjoy cooking
Men disciplined children and some would hit them if they were naughty	Men are more caring fathers and involved in their children's lives
Men worked long hours outside the home and went to pubs in their leisure time	Men are happier to stay at home with their families and share in family life
Men lived in family homes with their wives and children	Men and women do not necessarily live with each other but share responsibility for parenting
Men would hide the fact they were gay because it was against the law; they would often marry women and hide their sexuality	Gay men can set up civil partnerships with other men and bring up children together without it seeming unusual or wrong to most people

Topic 13: What is the role of women in the family?

Typical 1950s family role for women	Modern women in families
Women worked in the home, cooking, cleaning and shopping	Women expect men to help and have appliances to make life easier
Women had larger families, so they were unable to work because of regular pregnancy and childbirth	Women have access to contraception, so they have smaller families and more time to do other things
Women might have had jobs, but the husband might not like it, because it would seem he could not earn enough to support a family	Women have careers and can support the family on their own without a man if they need to
If husbands were abusive and dominant, women had to put up with it. It was seen as her problem for provoking him	Women have the option of leaving a violent partner if they can. It is seen as a failure of a man if he hits his wife
Women were not often in charge of the family money. Husbands would give women housekeeping money and spend the rest on themselves	If both men and women earn pay, they can choose how to spend their money together. Women have more power to make decisions

3: Education

Topic: 1 What is the purpose of education?

a) Formal education consists of being taught skills by teachers who are paid to teach children.
b) Informal education is when people learn things they need to know for their own pleasure or needs.
c) Formal education is usually tested by assessments and examinations.
d) In Britain all children must receive a formal education whether at school or in the home.
e) People who have a good education tend to earn more than people who do not have qualifications.
f) Wherever you go in the world, the school system is different for each country.

Topic 2: Why do we have an education system?

a) Norm – normal and expected way to behave
b) Socialisation – the process of learning the rules of a culture
c) Secondary socialisation – being taught how to behave by people in the wider world
d) Informal socialisation – learning how to behave as you live your life
e) Formal socialisation – when people deliberately set out to change how you act
f) Agencies of socialisation – groups in society that teach or encourage people to follow social rules
g) Social control – a system of making people follow social rules
h) Compulsory education – the law states that children must have an education

Topic 3: What is the education system of England and Wales?

a) Comprehensive school – all children can attend regardless of ability
b) Grammar school – teaches traditional academic subjects
c) Faith schools – teach about their own religion as well as normal subjects
d) Specialist schools – specialise in a particular part of the curriculum such as art or sports
e) Academies – set up in areas where schools need to improve and are funded by business or faith groups; they can select their pupils
f) City Technology colleges – are owned and funded by businesses and focus on sciences

Topic 4: What changes have taken place within schools since the 1970s?

Typical 1970s education	Modern education
Violence in schools was common and many children were hit or caned	Teachers may not touch children
Teachers used chalkboards and chalk	There is computer technology in schools and teachers use PowerPoint and other lessons
Lessons often involved copying from a blackboard or a textbook	Pupils learn through group work, discussion and games
Girls and boys had different lessons and boys were believed to be more clever	Girls and boys study the same lessons and girls tend to do better
Few children sat examinations	Most children sit examinations all through their school experience
Teachers taught what they wanted	Teachers must follow the National Curriculum

Topic 5: Is the education system meritocratic?

a) meritocracy
b) boys
c) Chinese
d) free
e) university
f) practical skills

Topic 6: What is the cause of some children doing less well than they should?

a) False, some groups do not have equal chances
b) False, there is no evidence to support this view
c) True, the evidence seems to suggest that richer people do encourage reading
d) True, evidence from David Egan supports this
e) True, there is little or no evidence that suggests differently

Topic 7: What are the reasons for gender inequality in education?

a) Girls tend to outperform boys at all levels of the education system.
b) Feminists suggest that boys are over-confident because we live in a patriarchal society.
c) The crisis of masculinity suggests that boys no longer know what it is to be a man and lack confidence as a result.
d) Home-based theories of male failure say that men do not spend enough time reading to male children.
e) School-based theories of male failure suggest that schools are feminised places as there are too many female teachers.
f) Some sociologists say that peer groups are an influence as boys adopt laddish behaviour to gain respect from their mates.

Topic 8: What are the reasons for ethnic inequality in educational attainment?

a) cultural
b) Chinese and Indian
c) African Caribbean
d) excluded
e) racist
f) multi-cultural

Topic 9: What are the reasons for social class inequality in schools?

a) Cultural capital – knowledge of how the education system works
b) Selection – schools choose the pupils that they want and reject ones that are difficult
c) Multi-factor – more than one reason acting together
d) Cultural disadvantage – the idea that some cultures are not as 'good' as others

e) Digital divide – the difference in access to the Internet between rich and poor
f) Material disadvantage – people do not have the things they need for success
g) Working class – having a job which depends on skill with your hands
h) Deprivation – being without things that are essential for living in your culture

Topic 10: What processes in schools may cause some children to fail?

a) hidden
b) Anti-school
c) prophecy
d) stereotype
e) label
f) bands or streams

Topic 11: What are anti-school subcultures?

a) Ladette
b) Anti-school subculture
c) Lads
d) Working class
e) Online survey
f) Labelling theory

Topic 12: How does material deprivation affect children's education?

a) Poverty
b) Material deprivation
c) Longitudinal
d) FSM
e) Cultural capital
f) Digital divide

Topic 13: How may cultural deprivation affect children's education?

a) Cultural deprivation – working-class children have a culture that leads to failure in school
b) Material deprivation – working-class children fail because they lack possessions and money
c) Immediate gratification – looking for pleasure in the present rather than putting it off
d) Vocabulary – language and words
e) Badly socialised – lacking training in the skills for success in life
f) FSM – a category of children who qualify for free school meals
g) Cultural capital – middle-class people know how to work the system to benefit their own children

Topic 14: What happens in Further Education and Higher Education to cause inequality?

a) False, anyone can go if they qualify
b) False, lots of people struggle to gain a career later
c) True
d) True
e) True
f) True, some famous people have not
g) True

4: Compulsory core

Topic 1: What is inequality?

Sociologists are interested in finding out about the **inequalities** between different groups. Poor people tend to have a different lifestyle compared with **rich** people. The poor are likely to have lower wages, worse **health** and live in poorer housing. Rich people are likely to have better **opportunities** than poor people. Sociologists try to understand the **reasons** for these differences.

Topic 2: What are the causes of inequality?

a) Sample
b) Racism
c) Life chances
d) Ageism
e) Questionnaire
f) Sexism

Topic 3: What are prejudice and discrimination?

a) Ageism	d) Prejudice
b) Inequality	e) Racism
c) Sexism	f) Discrimination

Topic 4: What are the reasons for prejudice and discrimination?

a) culture	d) stereotyped
b) socialised	e) problems
c) teaching	

Topic 5: What are status and prestige?

a) prestige	d) status
b) ascribed	e) achleve
c) achieved	

Topic 6: What is wealth?

Wages	Income
Interest on your savings	Income
A holiday home	Wealth
Pension	Income
Jewellery	Wealth
Stocks and shares	Wealth but may provide income when dividends are paid
Benefits	Income

Topic 7: Who are the elites? What power and privilege do they have?

a) elite	d) aristocracy
b) Marxists	e) male
c) privilege	f) power

Topic 8: What are life chances?

a) life	d) together
b) lifestyle	e) improve
c) quality	

Topic 9: What does social exclusion mean?

a) crime	d) ethnic
b) lifestyle	e) opportunities
c) out	

Topic 10: What is poverty?

a) Food, water, shelter, clothing, warmth
b) TV, internet, mobile phone, car, games console, dishwasher, DVD, iPod, holiday, nights out

Topic 11: What is social class?

a) Upper class
b) Women's place, wealthy who don't work, unemployed
c) Registrar General scale
d) 2001

Topic 12: What is ageism?

a) childhood	d) ageism
b) small	e) stereotyping
c) Victorian	f) media

Topic 13: How does gender affect women's life chances?

Three ways in which women made progress in the 20th century were gaining the vote, earning equal pay and the act which made sexual discrimination against the law. Feminism has helped women to achieve this. However, some feminists believe that women still do not have full equality and are still disadvantaged compared with men. Two reasons they believe this are due to the glass ceiling and the double burden.

Topic 14: How have changes in gender roles affected men?

a) independent	d) husbands
b) shipbuilding	e) crisis
c) new	

Topic 15: How have norms about sexuality changed in the last 50 years?

a) 1967	d) homophobia
b) 2001	e) transgender
c) sexuality	

Topic 16: What is racism?

a) belongs	d) blamed
b) history	e) institutional
c) laws	f) Macpherson

Topic 17: How does disability affect life chances?

a) Disability does not simply mean people in wheelchairs. It also includes people with a range of physical and mental conditions. They may have been born with them or have become that way due to illness.
b) Disabled people may suffer worse life chances because of prejudice and discrimination.
c) Some people assume that disabled people are not intelligent and are not independent.
d) People need to be better educated about disability.

Topic 18: Why is there an underclass?

a) underclass	d) competitive
b) government	e) rich
c) poor	f) deprivation

Topic 19: How do class, age, gender, ethnicity and disability affect people in the world of work?

a) Discrimination	d) Ethics
b) Gender	e) Race
c) Exploitation	f) Ethnicity

Topic 20: How do class, age, gender, ethnicity and disability affect health life chances?

a) The nation has overall become healthier in the last few decades. However, some groups are still not eating a healthy diet. The government have tried hard to convince people through campaigns, such as the five a day fruit and vegetables.
b) Smoking is not as popular as it was, but poorer people are still risking their health through this. The government are concerned about the huge cost of providing healthcare for people not looking after themselves.
c) As well as this there are other concerns that vulnerable groups, such as the elderly and disabled may not get the same treatment as other groups. This is an example of discrimination. Children in today's society are suffering many mental health problems. Social characteristics can play a strong part in deciding a person's health life chances.

Topic 21: What do the major sociological theories say about inequality?

a) Marxism	c) Functionalism
b) New Right	d) Feminism

Topic 22: Is Britain an equal society?

a) Meritocracy is the idea that success should come to those who are most able and who work hard. There is a lot of concern from many people that Britain is not a very fair society.
b) Prejudice and discrimination may stop many talented and hardworking people from being successful. This is bad for our

235

society as we are wasting the best **talent**.

c) Life chances vary considerably based on your class, age, **gender**, ethnicity and whether you are disabled. It is important to remember that we all belong to more than one of these groups. The life chances of an upper class woman are very different from those of a black **working**-class woman.

5: Work

Topic 1: Why do people work?
a) paid
b) money
c) extrinsic
d) intrinsic
e) community
f) identity

Topic 2: What is leisure?
a) Identity
b) Non-work
c) Validity
d) Income
e) Work
f) Leisure

Topic 3: What are the different types of work?
a) primary
b) tertiary
c) secondary
d) tertiary
e) primary
f) secondary

Topic 4: What other changes have there been to the economy?
a) Ethics
b) Employment
c) Globalisation
d) Multinationals
e) Technology
f) Participant observation

Topic 5: How has work changed in the UK?
a) False
b) False
c) True
d) True
e) False
f) True

Topic 6: How has the experience of work changed?
a) Luddites
b) deskilling
c) Mechanisation
d) line
e) automation
f) efficient

Topic 7: What is the experience of work like for workers?
a) Employment
b) Automation
c) Alienation
d) Deskilling
e) Mcdonaldization
f) Globalisation

Topic 8: What are the effects of unemployment?
a) methods
b) age
c) ended
d) poverty
e) depression
f) underclass

Topic 9: How has work changed for women?
a) home
b) jobs
c) nuclear
d) work
e) pill
f) discrimination

Topic 10: How has work changed for men?
a) Respondent
b) Feminisation
c) Masculine
d) Breadwinner
e) Gendered work
f) Alienation

Topic 11: What is work like for different ethnic groups?
a) ethnic
b) Empire
c) advertising
d) illegal
e) Britain
f) racist

Topic 12: How are different age groups treated at work?
a) Ethics
b) Discrimination
c) Pilot study
d) Ageism
e) Exploitation
f) Stereotyping

Topic 13: Are workers exploited?
a) Income
b) Sweatshop
c) Minimum wage
d) Unstructured interview
e) Piecework
f) Alienation

Topic 14: What are trade unions?
a) illegal
b) prison
c) advice
d) pay
e) strike
f) laws

6: Crime and deviance

Topic 1: What are crime and deviance?
a) False
b) True
c) True
d) False
e) False
f) True

Topic 2: What is informal social control?
a) norms
b) sanctions
c) informal
d) communities
e) family
f) punishing (or sanctioning)

Topic 3: What is formal social control? – The police

The police are an important agent of social **control**. They have many practical roles in society, but are seen as there to **protect** and serve the public. There are different ideas about what **style** the police should use to carry out their role. One of these is called **community** policing which means making strong links with local people. At the other extreme, a harder style of policing is called **zero** tolerance. Functionalists see the police as a positive force, whereas Marxists think the police help the **ruling** class stay in control.

Topic 4: What is formal social control? – The judiciary
a) judiciary
b) Youth
c) Magistrates'
d) Crown
e) jury
f) rich

Topic 5: How is social control kept by the media?
a) Deviance
b) Folk devils
c) Deviancy amplification
d) Media
e) Sanctions
f) Moral panic

Topic 6: What is white collar crime?
a) False
b) False
c) False
d) True
e) False
f) True

Topic 7: What is corporate crime?
a) businesses
b) collar
c) company
d) pregnant
e) public
f) same

Topic 8: What does sociology tell us about Youth Crime and Street Crime?
a) White collar crime
b) Folk devils
c) Occupational crime
d) Youth crime
e) Street crime
f) Corporate crime

Topic 9: What are the nature explanations of crime and deviance?

a) True
b) False
c) True
d) False
e) True
f) False

Topic 10: How do subcultures help to explain crime and deviance?

a) norms
b) criminals
c) break
d) area
e) three
f) nurture

Topic 11: How is social class linked to crime?

a) Material deprivation
b) Self-report study
c) Subculture
d) Cultural deprivation
e) Conviction rates
f) Victimisation

Topic 12: How is gender linked to crime?

a) more
b) 95
c) norms
d) less
e) evil
f) Men

Topic 13: How is ethnicity linked to crime?

a) Racism
b) Stereotype
c) Self-fulfilling prophecy
d) Ethnicity
e) Discrimination
f) Labelling

Topic 14: Is crime getting worse?

a) police
b) good
c) sensational
d) Wales
e) reported
f) recorded

7: Research methods

Topic 1: What is social research?

a) Secondary data
b) Data
c) Quantitative
d) Primary data
e) Qualitative
f) Pilot study

Topic 2: What are samples?

a) Random sample
b) Systematic sample
c) Target population
d) Opportunity sample
e) Sampling frame
f) Snowballing

Topic 3: What are questionnaires?

a) questionnaires
b) quick
c) response
d) returned
e) mail
f) repeated

Topic 4: What are the different types of interviews?

a) Methods
b) Structured interview
c) Interviewer bias
d) Unstructured interview
e) Respondent
f) Pilot study

Topic 5: What are the different types of observation?

a) Overt
b) Covert
c) Participant
d) change
e) affect
f) validity

Topic 6: How do sociologists choose a method?

a) primary (or research)
b) secondary
c) Quantitative
d) Qualitative
e) answers
f) answers (responses or choices also acceptable)

Topic 7: How do sociologists evaluate research?

a) Anonymity
b) Reliability
c) Confidentiality
d) Validity
e) Ethics
f) Psychological harm

8: Sociological theories

Topic 1: Marxism

a) Exploit – to use someone else for your own selfish purpose
b) Bourgeoisie – very wealthy people who own a great deal
c) Proletariat – poorer people and the working class
d) Raw materials – basic material from which a product is made
e) Ideology – a system of ideas and beliefs about how the world should be
f) Revolution – over-throwing a government
g) Communism – a belief that everybody should share equally in society
h) Alienation – a sense of not belonging to society

Topic 2: Functionalism

Marxism	Functionalism
Society is run for the benefit of the rich	Society is run for the benefit of everyone
Sees different groups in society as being in competition for the best things in life	Sees different groups in society as working together for the good of everyone
Social change is generally a good thing	Social change is usually dangerous for society
There are two separate groups in society, they are the rich and the poor	There are many groups in society but they all work together for the good of all of us
Is associated with the work of Karl Marx	Is associated with the work of Emile Durkheim and Talcott Parsons
Sees education as a way of controlling the minds of young people so they cannot think for themselves	Sees education as a way of passing on social values so children become good members of society

Topic 3: Feminism

a) False, men can be feminists too; however, some feminists are anti-male
b) True, they say men are often not allowed to express their emotional side
c) True, the reasons are many and varied
d) False, many people still believe that men and women are not equal and should fight for their rights
e) True, it is difficult to say that about everyone, but women are expected to do the triple shift
f) True, women are associated with cooking, cleaning, caring and checkouts
g) True, Google feminist to see some examples

Topic 4: Interactionism

a) theory
b) judge
c) others
d) prophecy
e) negative
f) influenced

Index